JEWS AND PALESTINIANS IN THE LATE OTTOMAN ERA, 1908–1914

Edinburgh Studies on the Ottoman Empire
Series Editor: Kent F. Schull

Published and forthcoming titles

edinburghuniversitypress.com/series/esoe

JEWS AND PALESTINIANS IN THE LATE OTTOMAN ERA, 1908–1914

CLAIMING THE HOMELAND

Louis A. Fishman

EDINBURGH
University Press

To the memory of my dear parents, Edward and Joyce,
who always supported me on my way and to the next generation,
my dear daughter, Alumah

Edinburgh University Press is one of the leading university presses in the UK.
We publish academic books and journals in our selected subject areas across the
humanities and social sciences, combining cutting-edge scholarship with high editorial
and production values to produce academic works of lasting importance. For more
information visit our website: edinburghuniversitypress.com

First published in hardback by Edinburgh University Press 2020

Edinburgh University Press Ltd
The Tun – Holyrood Road
12 (2f) Jackson's Entry
Edinburgh EH8 8PJ

Typeset in Jaghbuni by
Servis Filmsetting Ltd, Stockport, Cheshire

A CIP record for this book is available from the British Library

ISBN 978 1 4744 5399 8 (hardback)
ISBN 978 1 4744 5400 1 (paperback)
ISBN 978 1 4744 5401 8 (webready PDF)
ISBN 978 1 4744 5402 5 (epub)

Contents

Figures

Abbreviations

BEO	*Bâb-ı Âlî Evrak Odası*
BOA	Başbakanlık Osmanlı Arşivi (The Prime Ministry's Ottoman Archives)
CUP	Committee of Union and Progress
CZO	Central Zionist Archives, Jerusalem
DH.EUM	*Dahiliye Nezareti, Emniyet-i Umumiye Müdüriyeti Belgeleri (*Public Security Directorate, Interior Mnistry)
DH.EUM.4.Şb	*Dahiliye Nezareti Emniyet-i Umumiye Müdüriyeti Belgeleri* (Public Security Directorate, Fourth division, Interior Ministry)
DH.ID	*Dahiliye Nezareti İdare-i Umumiye* (Public Affairs, Interior Ministry)
DH.IUM	*Dahiliye Nezareti İdâre-i Umumiye Belgeleri* (General Administration, Interior Ministry)
DH.KMS	*Dahiliye Nezâreti Kalem-i Mahsus Müdüriyeti Belgeleri* (Private Secretariat, Interior Ministry)
DH.MKT	*Dahiliye Nezâreti Mektubî Kalemi* (Correspondence office, Interior Ministry)
DH.MUI	*Dahiliye Nezareti, Muhaberât-ı Umumiye İdaresi Belgeleri* (The General Communications Office, Interior Ministry)
DH.ŞFR	*Dahiliye Nezâreti Şifre Kalemi Belgeleri* (Cipher office, Interior Ministry)
DH.SYS	*Dahiliye Nezâreti Siyasî Kısım Belgeleri* (Political paper section, Interior Ministry)
DH.UMVM	*Dahiliye Nezareti Umûr-ı Mahalliye-i Vilayât Müdüriyeti Belgeleri* (Directorate for Local and Provincial, Interior Ministry)

MMZC	*Meclis-i Mebusan Zabıt Cerideleri* (Proceedings of the Ottoman Parliament)
MV	Meclis-i Vükela (Council of Ministers)
PRO	Public Record Office, British National Archives

Acknowledgements

I wrote this book between three cities: Istanbul, Tel Aviv and New York, over the last five years and a good part of it is based on a dissertation I finished at the University of Chicago, in 2007. Over the course of the last decade I was fortunate to live between the different cities, all of which made getting this book done a bit difficult. However, admittedly, in return, I was able to live some of the best days of my life, which were often spent late at night on side streets of Istanbul, listening to stories of different sorts of peoples (and sometimes telling my own story). During these years, I also broke out into journalism and reached new heights I never could imagine. It truly has been exciting. This time was needed and necessary to rethink how I was going to knock down the proudly built building that took the form of a dissertation, only to be rebuilt into the form of a book. It is my hope that this book will provide a compelling narrative that allows you, the readers, to look beyond what you might know and to rethink the history of late Ottoman Palestine.

I owe much of my knowledge to the outstanding scholars on Ottoman Palestine (and late Ottoman history in general). Their work, and that of others, has set the stage for robust debates about the history of the period, while their friendship has been rewarding. I am thankful to Emanuel Beška, Michelle Campos, Julia Phillips Cohen, Bedross Der Matossian, Abigail Jacobson, Vincent Lemire, Roberto Mazza, Devin Naar, Christine Philliou, Avi Rubin and Salim Tamari. They, and other new authors working on the late Ottoman era, all have turned the field into an exciting one to be a part of. Certainly, there is much more work to be done on Ottoman Palestine, and only by continuing to chisel away at the different national narratives will we come close to understanding it in all of its complexities.

I would like to extend my gratitude to those professors who have been so influential, starting from way back in BA studies at Haifa, when I had the honour to work with the late (and dear) Butrus Abu-Manneh, David Kushner, Ilan Pappe and Mahmoud Yazbak. At the University of Chicago, the late Menahem Brinker taught me so much I know about Israeli history and literature and Wadad Kadi's classes, even if not related to my topic, taught me more than I ever could have imagined. Special thanks goes the second reader of my dissertation, Hasan Kayali, whose class at the University of Chicago sent me back to the late Ottoman era. His support throughout the years has been more than generous and I truly appreciate it. This work would not have been possible without the mentorship of Rashid Khalidi, my dissertation advisor. His support has been unwavering and his ideas on Palestine and Palestinian nationalism have greatly influenced my own work.

I owe special thanks to Brooklyn College, which is part of the City University of New York. It has provided a home away from homes, a nice office with heat, and my department chairs, David Troyansky, Christopher Ebert, Gunja Sengupta, all have been so helpful. Within the department, I am lucky to have some real supportive colleagues, whose encouragement helped me get through this project. Thanks also to Bilal Ibrahim, my officemate, who has put up with my continued presence quite honourably. I am indebted to our administrators, Anne Ciarlo, Lorraine Greenfield and Arlene Neftleberg, for their devoted assistance. I am most grateful to the remarkable (and hardworking) students at Brooklyn College. Their drive and success are inspiring. I am particularly indebted to the students who participated in my colloquiums, their thoughts and papers have made me much wiser. Niv Konfino provided me with much assistance going through the Hebrew press, which was made possible through the Kurz Undergrad research assistant programme. Leonid Gozman's comments were very helpful towards the last days working on this manuscript. Most of all, working with Rabia Sirin has been a real joy and her help has been invaluable. I thank her greatly.

This book was also made possible due to a grant I received from PSC-CUNY and Brooklyn College's Tow Foundation. I also received the Whiting Fellowship from Brooklyn College, which allowed me to return to Istanbul and Jerusalem to complete my research. I extend my sincere thanks to the staff at the Başbakanlık archives and the Central Zionist Archives, located in these two cities.

Warm words of gratitude go out to Edinburgh University Press. Its editor Nicola Ramsey has ensured a helpful and transparent process, something that is not a given in today's world of publishing. The editorial board and the blind readers provided constructive criticism and feedback, and its acquisition editor, Kent Schull, helped me understand my own work better.

The following friends have helped me out in more than one way and their support is appreciated: Rıfat and Beti Bali, Giancarlo Casale, Sami Abou Haidar, Joseph Logan, Rakel Sezer, Yoav Shiber, Esther Solomon and Dror Zeevi. Hardy Griffin has read over parts of this work during the past few years, and I am thankful to him. There are so many more people whom I have not been able to thank, including close friends, not to mention the ones I know less but have spent a great amount of time with on social media, be it Twitter or Facebook.

Lastly, I thank my family, who has heard about this project for years, and can attest how often I was *absent* even when I was *present*, often caught between centuries. Of course, the hope and optimism come from Umut, who has made Brooklyn also a home. Lastly, to my daughter, Alumah – she is my inspiration.

Note on Translation and Transliteration

For transliterating the languages incorporated in this book, Ottoman and modern Turkish, Arabic and Hebrew, I utilise the following guidelines for citation. For Turkish and Arabic, I adopted the simplified version of the *International Journal of Middle Eastern Studies*, removing diacritical markings, except for the apostrophe to signify the usage of *'ayn* and *hamza*. For last names in Arabic, I use '-al' when presented as a full first and last name. However, when only using the last name, I remove the '-al', making 'al-Khalidi' simply 'Khalidi'. For Turkish proper names and places, I use the modern spelling, except when keeping the final voiced consonant that corresponds to the Ottoman spelling: 'Mehmed' instead of 'Mehmet'. For Hebrew, I utilise the system of the Library of Congress, with the diacritics removed. For place names, I will use the English name when possible, so, for example, rather than using the Turkish *Selanik*, or the Greek *Thessaloniki*, I use the English *Salonica*.

The following is a guide to pronouncing certain letters in modern Turkish and transliterated Ottoman Turkish:

- c = j, as in 'jump'
- ç = ch, as in 'cheese'
- ğ = gh, as in 'though'
- ı = short 'e', as in 'often' or long 'i' as in 'tea'
- j = zh, as in 'gendarme'
- ö = German oe, as in 'Goethe'
- ş = sh, as in 'short'
- ü = ew, as in 'ewe'

Introduction

[and] on the wrapper of the oranges . . . there is not one word in Turkish or in Arabic . . . if Hebrew and the Star of David are exhibited [on the orange wrappers] and propagated in this way, this forgotten language will be added to the already many languages which are used in the Ottoman lands and the addition of the Star of David will sooner or later be added to the struggle of the Cross and the Crescent.[1]

This is an official report from the Ottoman consul general in Budapest, who, in early 1914, sent his complaint on these controversial oranges and their wrappers to the minister of the interior in Istanbul. A customer had noticed the oranges in the main grocery in Budapest and brought them to the attention of the consul. What was most striking about these thick-peeled oranges – the pride of Palestine – was that they were sold in wrappers stamped with a Star of David, and with Hebrew and a bit of German printed on them. Even more concerning for the Ottoman consul was that the famous name, '*Filistin Portakalları*, "Palestine Oranges"' – he stressed the name by also writing it in English – had been replaced by the name of the 'Jewish colony "Petah Tikvah"'.[2]

Through the consul general's observations and recommendations to Istanbul, we learn how an Ottoman Turkish official was able to draw far-reaching conclusions over what many bureaucrats might have just passed off as completely mundane. Through this document, we are able to enter the thoughts, prejudices and feelings of this diplomat, just months before the world would go to war, and just years before the British promised the Jewish people a national home in Palestine – an event that none in Palestine, or the Ottoman Empire, could ever have predicted.

The consul general was outraged, and declared it a humiliation that Turkish and Arabic were not present on the wrapper, and that Hebrew – an extinct and abandoned language – had replaced them. From his description,

1

we see that he had little concrete information on the Zionist movement, but he was clear on the growing hegemony the Jewish community had vis-à-vis the Palestinians, or what he referred to as the 'indigenous population'. In fact, in this report the Palestinians do not have any agency, and it seems that it is up to the Ottoman Empire to investigate the matter to protect the interests of the Palestinians, since this bureaucrat also indicates his belief that it was not a Jewish-harvested orange, but actually that of the locals, who had been doing this type of work since 'time immemorial' as he put it, and that the oranges were actually purchased and repackaged by Jewish commission agents.

For the consul, the Hebrew set off an alarm since

> in Austria and Hungary there are two and half million Jews and in the neighbourhoods [known] for trade and industry they possess great and important areas and in Vienna and Pest, [yet] you will not come across any Hebrew outside of the word Kosher . . . which is on their butcher shops.

Furthermore, having Hebrew and the Star of David could hurt exports because of widespread anti-Semitism in Europe and America, although he does not put it in these terms. Rather, his greatest implied concern in the report is the proliferation of Jewish activity in Palestine, and how this might lead to new ethnic conflict.

At the end of his report, the consul recommended the Interior Ministry take steps against the Hebrew and religious symbols, and indeed a letter of warning was dispatched to the governor of Jerusalem since what was

> happening with the rest of the Tribe of the Children of Israel (*Kavm-i Beni Israil*) is not connected only to the Hebrew writing on the Jaffa oranges; unfortunately, it is well known that this [stamp] is becoming widespread on all the exports by Jews.

No less interesting, however, are the questions that the consul general does not ask, as well as his prejudices concerning both Jews and Arabs in Palestine. He most likely did not know that, just two years before, an Ottoman governor had visited the Jewish colony of Petah Tikvah, and showered the Ashkenazi colonists with praise. In fact, the governor at the time of the consul's report, Mecid Bey, was actually quite friendly with the Jewish community in Palestine. Perhaps from his position in Budapest, he also did not know that there was a new group of Zionist Ashkenazi Jews living in Petah Tikvah and the surrounding villages that had taken on Ottoman citizenship. Or, that some of these immigrants' children had just finished fighting in the Balkan Wars as proud Ottoman soldiers, and that within less than a year they would be recruited for the

Ottomans' eastern front fighting Russia, a country their parents had left only decades before.

At the same time, upon reading the report, the consul's lack of agency for the 'indigenous population' most likely would have angered Palestinians who had actively protested in the Ottoman capital against the growing Jewish hegemony in Palestine. Yet the consul was not the only Ottoman official to take away Palestinian agency, as Arabic newspapers writing about the Zionist threat were subjected to sanctions by the Ottoman authorities due to the potential risk of inciting conflict. No, the consul general most likely was not aware that by 1914 Palestinians were losing hope in the ability of the Ottoman government to address their concerns. Years earlier, one Palestinian had already described their protests as if they were 'screaming into a valley';[3] no matter how loud they protested, it simply went unnoticed by their fellow Ottoman citizens in Istanbul.

For over a century, the conflict in Israel/Palestine has persisted, with its Palestinian and Jewish populations entangled in a battle over a small strip of land that has historic and religious ties to both groups. While the conflict is often portrayed as an age-old religious one, in fact it is a modern one which dates back to the late 1800s, when the land was an integral part of the Ottoman Empire. During this time, it would have been impossible for the residents of Palestine to foresee that the first stirrings of tensions between the two communities would turn into one of the twentieth century's most persistent conflicts, with no end in sight at the current time. By the same token, it is impossible to understand the conflict in its totality without going back to the late Ottoman period, when it was first taking shape, as Palestinians and Jews began to transform into definitive political communities.

This book seeks to tell the story of how, following the 1908 Young Turk Revolution, Palestinians and Jews each began to transform into political communities, forming distinct local identities, and realising the need to take concrete steps to claim their homeland. For the Palestinians, this homeland was *Filastin* (Palestine), while for the Jews this was *Eretz Israel* (the Land of Israel). These local identities, which would eventually transform into modern national communities, did not envision 'the other' as comprising a part of its own *weltanschauung*, or, if you like, part of each one's potential social and political polity. Essentially, the two communities were divided, with the Palestinians coming to see themselves as a community independent of Syria, and the local Jewish community opting for separation from, and not integration with, the overall Palestinian population. By 1914, as World War I was about to shake up the region by bringing in new world powers, it was clear that a pattern had been set in place, where the minority Jewish community had become an independent actor, despite the growing protest of the Palestinian majority. Essentially, the two communities were placed on a collision course, paving the way for the violent reality that continues today.[4]

While the conflict was over the land, the act of *claiming the homeland* was mostly played out in its urban centres, in the press of Jaffa and Jerusalem, and with each side bringing its case to the Ottoman imperial capital of Istanbul, the Sublime Porte. Palestinians and Jews alike placed their hopes in Istanbul, where both groups also encountered disappointments. It was within this Ottoman system that the conflict transformed into a pattern of the Jewish minority in Palestine becoming a political hegemonic power, thereby leaving the Palestinians frustrated and in a state of despair – a pattern that defined the course of the conflict over the next century. This point needs to be reiterated since much of the research over the last few decades has focused on the dynamics of the settler-colonial paradigm,[5] when Jewish settlers set on a 'conquest of labour', and clashed with the Palestinian rural population, marking the first violent conflicts. While it would be wrong to disregard this paradigm as unimportant, we need to recognise that this was only a small part of a much greater picture, one that has been greatly neglected by past histories. What is also missing from this paradigm is that the colonial Jewish project developed within an Ottoman context, securing it legitimacy, and often praise, from the Ottoman administration in Palestine.

This book adopts an innovative approach by applying and combining multiple lenses to examine the Palestinian and the Jewish community in Palestine – an approach I argue sheds new light on the first years of the conflict. Further, this work rewrites the history of the area within the context of the late Ottoman period, without projecting onto it our views of later events. In my opinion, when writing histories of conflicts we often read history backwards, projecting the realities of today back in time, leaving us with a skewed picture of how conflicts are formed and how they emerge. For example, the history of this conflict is often written as if a Jewish state was the inevitable outcome of the Zionist movement's work, tracking it from the 1880s, and periodising it based on waves of mass migrations (*aliyot*) of European Jews, and linking it with political developments, such as the British promise of a Jewish homeland, highlighted in the 1917 Balfour Declaration. As for the history of Palestinians, most historians treat the period before World War I as if it was unimportant in understanding their eventual defeat in 1948, with some even preposterously claiming that there was no such thing as a Palestinian people,[6] and that their identity only emerged as a result of the European powers' eventual partitioning of Syria into three nation-states following World War I: Syria, Lebanon and Palestine.[7] What unites Palestinians and Jews during the years, and even months, before the war, is the fact that none could have predicted the eventual fall of the Ottoman Empire. Both, after all, had lived in an Ottoman world, one that had been in the midst of constant transformation for over a century. In fact it was the Ottoman world they lived in that united them as citizens yet divided them over the future of their shared homeland.

In the post-1908 Young Turk era, in 'Palestine as elsewhere throughout the empire [urban] Muslims, Christians, and Jews adopted the viewpoint that the Ottoman nation was composed of all the ethnic, religious, and linguistic elements of the empire bound together in civic, territorial, and contractual terms'.[8] However, before this story starts, it is necessary to go back to Istanbul a hundred years before. During the nineteenth century, the Ottoman state – *Devlet-i Osmaniyye* as it was known in Turkish – transformed from an empire made up of 'subjects', to a modern state of 'citizens'. This was the outcome of decades of reforms, known as the *Tanzimat*, and was marked by the issuing of the 1839 Imperial Rose Chamber Edict, which was read in the presence of European diplomats. Aimed at establishing a 'single legal system for all subjects' it was indicative of a shift in the official ideology of the state, reinvigorating the empire, while 'acquiring the international respectability required for membership in the European concert'.[9] The 1856 Reform Edict affirmed the previous one, and went a step further, essentially granting equality to the Empire's non-Muslims, doing away with the *cizye*, the non-Muslim poll tax. However, this was replaced by a *bedel* fee, which allowed non-Muslims to be released from military service, even if in the years ahead some Jews and Christians opted to serve.[10] Alongside these major reforms, the Millet system, which allowed each religious community to govern its own communal affairs, remained intact, as 'the official boundaries between religion and ethnicity became increasingly blurred'.[11]

The *Tanzimat* (reforms) were by no means only concerned with the status of non-Muslims, but amounted to a modernisation project that left its stamp on all forms of Ottoman life, introducing modern universities, newspapers, tax reforms and, in 1869, a citizenship law. The rapid changes also produced animosity and tension, with a dualism emerging. 'The ideal of an overarching Ottoman identity clashed with the increasing autonomy of religious communities within the empire; bureaucratic centralization conflicted with political fragmentation; the ideal of participation came up against the principle of top-down reform.'[12] The culmination of the

Tanzimat came in 1876, with the rise to power of Sultan Abdülhamid II. A favourite of the Young Ottomans – a group of progressive Muslims who supported a constitutional monarchy – Abdülhamid II opened the Ottoman Parliament, promulgating its constitution. Within a short period, however, progressives' hopes were dashed when in 1878 the sultan suspended the constitution and closed Parliament.

The Ottoman Parliament would remain closed for almost thirty years, ample time for an opposition to emerge – with many in exile in Europe – and to organise. Unlike the Young Ottomans, who worked to merge their Muslim identity with modernity, the Young Turks accepted non-Muslims within their ranks, creating a dynamic force against the authoritarianism of Abdülhamid II, who not only clamped down on the press and supported his regime through a network of spies, but also implemented a heavy-handed policy against Armenians, with massacres taking place throughout the Empire during 1894–6. The Young Turks' strength emerged from the ability to incorporate different groups under one umbrella, and, more importantly, to bring in the support of army officers in 1906, and, most importantly, their units.[13] As troops marched towards the capital of Istanbul in July 1908, Abdülhamid II was forced to reopen Parliament, elections were held and the Ottoman Empire, which was quickly losing its Balkan territories to the spread of nationalism, was given a new lease on life. Throughout the Empire, including in Palestine, the Young Turks' revolutionary slogan, *Liberty, Equality, Fraternity and Justice*, ushered in a new era of civic nationalism, where citizens, regardless of ethnicity or religion, embraced the notion of *Osmanlılık* (Ottomanism), which was 'a grassroots imperial citizenship project that promoted a unified socio-political identity of an Ottoman people struggling over the new rights and obligations of political membership'.[14]

As news of the Young Turk Revolution reached Palestine, a pro-revolution demonstration in the Palestinian coastal city of Jaffa was organised, with Jerusalem's hesitant governor, Ali Ekrem Bey, announcing the news publicly, sharing with the crowds the new reforms to be enacted. The next day, on 8 August, crowds took to the streets in Jerusalem, with Muslims, Christians and Jews all welcoming the reforms, much to the dismay of some of the Ottoman officials, who, even as they professed their support for the changes, were inherently connected to the former regime of Abdülhamid II.[15] *The Times* covered the 'enthusiastic rejoicing', describing how the streets of Jerusalem were decorated and the city lit up in the evening. During the daytime, the governor announced to the cheering crowds the news of the reinstating of the constitution:

A curious mixture of sheikhs, priests and rabbis denouncing the old regime, and Moslems, Christians, Jews, Samaritans, Turks and Armenians fraternised and then formed up in a procession, preceded by banners with emblems of liberty – the Jews by the Torah covered with gilt embroidery.[16]

Such incidents, however, were not unique to Palestine; in the Ottoman heartland territory of Anatolia, multi-religious/ethnic groups supporting the new spirit of the revolution were formed, such as the Society of Patriots (*Vatanperverler Cemiyeti*), which was made up of Muslims, Greeks, Armenians and Catholics.[17]

This new communal spirit was replicated within the halls of the Ottoman Parliament a few months later – a realisation of the Young Turks' tenet that Parliament should create a space for the different religious and ethnic communities within the Empire.[18] According to Hasan Kayali, 'balloting took place in a festive atmosphere and became the occasion for celebrating the principles that the elections symbolized: liberty, equality, and justice'.[19] When it opened, Parliament was home to 288 deputies, and included 26 Greeks, 14 Armenians and 4 Jews, plus a large number of Arab deputies, in addition to a smaller group of Albanians, and a slim majority of Turks.[20] Some of these parliamentarians played an important role in the events described in this book, such as the Jewish MP Nissim Mazliah, representing Izmir, and the Palestinian Ruhi al-Khalidi, representing Jerusalem. In fact, the Jews of Jerusalem, Sephardic or Ashkenazi, often placed their hopes much more in Mazliah than in Khalidi.

Less than a year later, after Sultan Abdülhamid II tried unsuccessfully to regain control from the Young Turks and was deposed – events known as the 31 March Incident – a similar solidarity between the different religions in Palestine surfaced again. Once news reached Jerusalem that the CUP government had been overthrown, a British official noted that excitement took over the city, stating 'public opinion was unanimous . . . a meeting was convened which was attended by the Mutasarrif and the principal officials, civilian and military, and a large number of the inhabitants without distinction of creed'.[21] Weeks later, following the accession of the new sultan, Mehmed V, banquets were held with notables from Jerusalem coming to Jaffa, and then the notables of Jaffa reciprocating by visiting Jerusalem, and visiting Bethlehem and army barracks as well. Interestingly, the British official present noted that the multi-religious delegations 'were quite orderly, and aroused much interest, if not very much enthusiasm among the inhabitants of this city'.[22]

The question of how much these revolutionary spirits spread to other sectors of Palestinian society has not been properly addressed; however, it would appear that it did not extend much further than the urban elite taking part in the celebrations. At the same time, one British official in Palestine noted that there were 'some attempts being made throughout the remoter parts of the district by Emissaries of the Committee of Union and Progress to disseminate among the fellahin ideas of equality and constitutionalism. But much time must elapse before these bear fruit'.[23] A reoccurring theme throughout this work is the question of how widespread the feeling of unity was between the different ethnic and religious groups.

In Jerusalem's walled city, there had already been somewhat of a blending together of the different religious and ethnic communities, which went beyond political gatherings. Michelle Campos brings this to light in her book *Ottoman Brothers: Muslims, Christians, and Jews in Early Twentieth-Century Palestine* by noting the personal memoirs that demonstrated

> deep ties between Old City Muslims, Christians, and Jewish families and neighbours across religious lines – sharing a courtyard, visiting each other on religious holidays, engaging in a business partnerships . . . Muslim girls learned Judeo-Spanish from their Sephardi Jewish neighbours; Christian and Jewish musicians performed at Muslim weddings and holidays.[24]

Indeed, her book is ground-breaking and one of the first works that highlighted intercommunal relations during the late Ottoman era. Abigail Jacobson explains that within the Old City a special relationship emerged where many Jews rented living space from Muslims, often living in the same compound. Further, they also met each other in public baths (*hamams*) and coffee houses.[25] This work looks beyond communal relations, and rethinks these scholars' findings concerning the extent of relations between Sephardic Jews and Palestinians, as well as argues that even as they lived side by side and celebrated the Young Turk Revolution together, the two communities had two very distinctly different worldviews concerning Palestine's future.

In Jerusalem, relationships were also formed between Jewish and Arab intellectuals, such as two important people from the period, the Jewish Eliezer Ben-Yehuda and the Ottoman Palestinian Muslim parliamentarian Ruhi al-Khalidi, who met 'to understand each other and the various groups of which they were leaders'.[26] The coming together of these two intellectuals must have been quite unique given that during a joint meeting held between Jews and Muslims following the breakout of World War I, a local Sephardic Jew, Avraham Elmaliah, stated it 'was the first time that the two peoples gathered to discuss their relationship', and that for 'tens of years they (the Jewish community) have been living in Eretz Israel without realizing that there is another people living with them'.[27]

Edhem Eldem, another scholar of the era who focuses on Ottoman Istanbul, argues, however, against understanding mixing between different communities as something widespread in Ottoman cities, and as an experience that the bulk of the population never experienced. Eldem states:

> Indeed, the quaint and endearing image of Greeks, Armenians, Muslims, and Jews sharing space, business, and entertainment tends to mask the very real fact that the overwhelming majority of the population, across the board, was in fact held at bay from this protected and restrictive environment.[28]

Nevertheless, by the late nineteenth century, in Jerusalem, as in other Ottoman cities, new urban arenas opened up space to the different communities. In Jerusalem, Jaffa Gate (Figure I.1), and the newer Jaffa road, 'served as a lively commercial and social centre, in which one could find many stores, banks, coffee shops, and a large public garden'.[29]

Figure I.1 Jaffa Gate, Jerusalem, late Ottoman period. Jacob Wahrman Collection, National Library of Israel, <http://beta.nli.org.il/he/archives/NNL01_Wahrman002716403/NLI_Photo#$FL7833040_>

The Ottoman historian Bedross Der Matossian also criticises applying this sense of mixing to the political sphere, despite certain moments following the 1908 revolution: '[R]omanticising the period and arguing that the different ethno-religious groups within the empire tried to see themselves as part of an Ottoman nation under the label "civic nationalism" is rather misleading'; moreover, 'constitutionalism failed to create a new understanding of Ottoman citizenship, grant equal right to all citizens, bring under one roof in a legislative assembly, and finally resuscitate Ottomanism from the ashes of the Hamidian regime'.[30] Adding to this, I argue that the revolution's abolishment of the Millet system and the introduction of the new multi-ethnic Parliament introduced a period of 'renegotiating the Millet system' with each community drawing new boundaries and reaching new understandings of what these changes really meant in practical terms, something that will be explored in Chapter 1. In short, the reality, whether on the streets of Istanbul, Salonica or Jerusalem, can be described as one of intercommunal relations (and even this seemingly minimal), which should not be mistaken for multi-culturalism.[31] Further, while it would be difficult to argue that a 'civic-Ottomanism' did not exist, clearly the communities remained divided, whether in the provinces or the urban areas, with each non-Muslim community separately voicing their grievances vis-à-vis the Muslim political elite of Istanbul.

Even if the conflict in Palestine was developing into a conflict of competing political communities, this sense of religious identification remained an important factor. This held particularly true in Palestine where, following the revolution, Palestinians and Jews juxtaposed each other's claims vis-à-vis the other's as they vied for support in Istanbul. In Palestine it was not different groups of non-Muslims in competition, but essentially Jews versus Muslims. In essence, following the Young Turk Revolution, the previous preferential status of Palestinian Muslims was replaced with equality before the law, giving them equal status with the Jews. This in effect was at the cost of Muslims relinquishing power, which on the flip side led to closer ties between the Muslim and Christian communities, a bond that had already begun to be forged in the late nineteenth century with the rise of Arab nationalism.

Most recently, historian Jonathan Gribetz has focused on understanding the roles religion and race played in the unfolding conflict. He argues that 'the [Jews, Muslim and Christian] intellectuals [in Palestine] . . . often thought of one another and interpreted one another's actions in terms of two central categories: religion and race [and not in terms of nationalist groups]'. He continues, 'the historical actors, that is, tended to view their neighbours as members of particular religions – as Jews, Christians, or

Muslims – or of genealogically, "scientifically" defined races ("Semitic" or otherwise).'[32] This dynamic cannot be underestimated with Jews and Palestinians during this period constantly navigating between understandings of religion, nationalism, race and ethnicity.

Despite the differences of opinions concerning relations between the different populations, Abigail Jacobson reiterates in the introduction of her book *From Empire to Empire: Jerusalem between Ottoman and British Rule* that Jerusalem needs to be treated as a 'mixed city', and the importance of her work lies in

> integrating Jews and Arabs into one historical analysis . . . [which] recognizes and investigates the differences between and within these two groups and their experiences, and examines the forces and dynamics that influenced them and the dilemmas they faced at this time of transition.[33]

This sentence perhaps sums up best the work of a group of new historians working on Ottoman Palestine, who, together, offer refreshing new interpretations of Jerusalem during the late Ottoman years.

Palestinians

A major shortcoming in the literature on the Palestinian–Israeli conflict during the late Ottoman period (and other ensuing periods) is the lack of attention dedicated to understanding the make-up of each people and their formation into a distinct identity. The Palestinians, who in 1914 made up at least 85 per cent of the total population, are often seen only in relation to the much smaller Jewish community and in terms of the developing conflict between the two peoples, and are therefore to a great extent 'invisible'.[34] Such an approach ignores historical and sociological aspects of the Palestinian people, including the process of the formation of a unique Palestinian identity. In other words, the Palestinians, who were the majority, only become a focal point in the historical narrative when they are observed through the lens of the Jewish minority. In this sense, the historiography of Palestinians can be compared to how Native Americans have been depicted vis-à-vis the British colonial settlers. In his ground-breaking work on the history of Native Americans, Daniel K. Richter points out that by shifting the focus away from the European settlers and towards the Native Americans, we receive quite a different historical understanding of them. He states, 'Throughout the period before the United States declared its independence, the vast majority of eastern North America was neither English nor French nor Spanish territory. It was, clearly, Indian country . . .' He goes on to explain, if we shift our perspective to try to view the past in a way that faces east from Indian country, history takes on a very different appearance. Native Americans appear in the foreground, and Europeans enter from distant shores. North America becomes the 'old world' and Western Europe the 'new,' Cahokia (present day St. Louis) becomes the centre and Plymouth Rock the periphery.[35]

This approach, when applied to Palestine, allows us to understand the need to rethink how the history of the Palestinian–Israeli conflict is written. In other words, rather than starting from the perspective of the Jewish minority, it is essential to look at the Palestinians as an independent factor, who possess a rich history in Palestine.

Ending the exclusion of Palestinians from Palestinian history was championed by Beshara Doumani, who made a call to 'write the Palestinians into history', arguing that 'the major lacuna in the historiography of Palestine during the late Ottoman period is the absence of a live portrait of the Palestinian people'.[36] This task is daunting due to the fact that for years it has been claimed that the emergence of a Palestinian identity was a post-World War I phenomenon and only a reaction to Zionism.[37] The scholar Rashid Khalidi admits that

> the assertion that Palestinian nationalism developed in response to the challenge of Zionism embodies a kernel of a much older truth: this modern (Palestinian) nationalism was rooted in long-standing attitudes of concern for the city of Jerusalem and for Palestine as a sacred entity which were a response to perceived external threats. The incursions of the European powers and the Zionist movement in the late nineteenth century were only the most recent examples of this threat.[38]

In other words, it would be impossible to deny the role that Zionism and British colonialism played in the creation of a Palestinian identity, but, of course, there were other factors at work, some completely removed from the period and contexts of the Palestinians' reaction to these later developments.

The fact that Palestinians are often portrayed by some historians of Arab nationalism as indiscernible from the greater Syrian Arab population has created barriers for writing about the emergence of a separate Palestinian identity. In these cases, Palestine is treated as an integral part of *Bilad al-Sham*, or Syria, known as Southern Syria (*Suriya al-Janubiyya*).[39] In fact, the paradigm of Palestine composing a political geographical entity within Syria was put forth by George Antonius, in his classic account of Arab nationalism, *The Arab Awakening*.[40] According to Antonius, since Roman times Palestine has been the 'southern part' of Syria, which had been 'truncated' from Syria by the British and French following the Allied Occupation.[41] Despite this notion being adopted by many scholars, pre-World War I documents reveal that Palestinians referred to the geographical region they were living in as *Filastin*, and some had already begun to define themselves as 'Palestinians'.[42] In other words, the notion of Palestine comprising a political or geographical entity known as 'Southern Syria' has become embedded in collective memory as a result of the founding of King Faisal's Syrian Kingdom (1918–20), and the Palestinians taking part in the project that resulted in the break-up of the Empire following the British and French occupation of the Middle East after the war.[43] Connecting the post-World War I era with the period of late Ottoman rule, Haim Gerber sums up the core dilemma well: 'The British may have established Palestine as a state, but they did not, indeed could not, establish Palestinian nationalism.'[44]

A simple review of the Palestinian press in the late Ottoman Empire also demonstrates how Palestinians had a clear understanding that Palestine was separate from Syria, beyond the obvious fact that one of the main newspapers was named *Filastin*, which in itself is quite telling, something which has been reiterated by scholars of Palestine, such as Rashid Khalidi and Haim Gerber. Of course, both scholars use this as a launching point to discuss the topic more in detail.

From my own review of the newspaper *Filastin*, I think what is most striking and has not received the due attention it deserves is the fact that within the newspaper it is clear on every sheet that for the reader, or for whom it was being read to, there was never a question that the land they were living in was Palestine. This can be spotted even in random adver- tisements: for example, in this advertisement for Tuborg Beer (Figure I.2), it directs people interested in wholesale purchases to contact Yusuf Aleyna, the distributor for 'Palestine and Syria'. Besides the fact that this advertisement poses interesting social questions that are beyond the scope of this book, it clearly portrays Palestine and Syria as separate entities. Lastly, we find one more interesting source that helps us understand that for Arabs, in addition to 'the Holy Land', the land was simply referred to as Palestine. We see this in the heading of a letter by Jerusalem's Chief Rabbi (Figure I.3), where the Hebrew *Eretz HaKodesh* (the Holy Land) is translated in Arabic as '*Filastin*'. This is a rare case where we see a direct translation from Hebrew to Arabic and helps us understand that Jews also were clear that their '*HaAretz*' was the same land as the Palestinians' '*Filastin*'. During the years, the fact that it was called *Filastin* was not a matter of controversy for Jews as well, but rather it was a simple fact. It was only years later that the term was politicised with some Israelis – and other international historians and political pundits – trying to erase the

بيرا تيبورغ

المبيع السنوي ٨٧٠٠٠٠٠٠ زجاجة

إذا كنت تريد مشروبا
مرطبًا ذا طعم لذيذ
فعليك ببيرا تيبورغ
احسن انواع البيرا
المعروفة فهي خالية
من حامض
السليسليك والمواد
المضرة . فاذا لم
تجد هذه الماركة
عند بقالك فاطلبها
من محل الخواجا
يوسف الينا الوكيل العمومي لفلسطين وسوريا

Figure I.2 Tuborg Beer advertisement, *Filastin*, Historical Jewish Press website –
www.Jpress.org.il – founded by the National Library and Tel Aviv University (see:
<http://web.nli.org.il/sites/JPress/English/about/Pages/tems-of-use.aspx>)

term *Filastin* from existence. Importantly, claiming that Palestinians did
not perceive Palestine as comprising an entity called Southern Syria does
not discount the fact that Palestinians shared common concerns and traits
with Syrian Arabs during the late Ottoman era, and together they embraced
the cultural Arab movement and the advancement of their mutual political
rights within the Ottoman Empire.

In order to understand the emergence of regional identities that predated

Figure I.3 Letterhead of the Chief Rabbi of Jersualem. Clip of document from Central Zionist Archives; Gad Frumkin papers, A199/61

the division of the modern Middle East into nation-states, it is helpful to look at Carol Hakim's work on the contours of what she calls 'Lebanism', which emerged during the late Ottoman years. According to Hakim: 'the focus of scholars and historians on Arab nationalism has generally over-looked other national and communal representations, allegiances, and identities'. She goes on to explain that 'Lebanism' was a local political identity which existed within the greater context of Syria.[45] Nevertheless, she stresses that like the other emerging terms such as Ottomanism, Arabism, Syrianism, Lebanism was denoting 'the development of national ideals and representations among the local populations of the Empire, which displayed some elements of modern nationalism but had not developed into articulate and coherent nationalist ideologies or movements'.[46] Lastly, and more important for our work, Lebanism did not stand in contradiction to Ottomanism and Syrianism, but provided an additional option to denote 'distinct projects to address the particular problems of their own province'.[47]

This book applies a similar approach to Palestine, where it can be argued that even if it was far from being a full-blown nationalism, Palestinians certainly possessed a great deal of what can be described as a local patriot-ism in the years before World War I, which, following the war, would transform into a clear case of Palestinian nationalism; as will be discussed further in the book, of course, the post-World War I nationalism was greatly shaped due to the political outcomes of the war, and was not at all an inevitable outcome.

So how can we describe this local Palestinian sense of identity during the years leading up to World War I? In this work, I am introducing the term *Palestinianism*, which is aimed at denoting the essence of what it meant to be a Palestinian before the rise of nation-state nationalism, when in the late Ottoman era a modern notion of patriotism to Palestine began to be expressed among the local Arab population.[48] This 'self-understanding' of one's belonging to a Palestinian collective identity merged together with other units of 'identification', such as being an Ottoman citizen, an Arab and a Muslim or a Christian (not necessarily in that order); and, on a more local level, allegiance to one's city or extended family.[49] If we look beyond the identity debate – whether Palestinians possessed during the late Ottoman era a strong sense of being Palestinian – the term *Palestinianism* moves us towards a new way of describing how the Palestinians came together as a unit, encompassing a feeling of 'connectedness' and 'commonality', which led them to join together to take action, to defend, preserve and place claim over their perceived homeland, without having national aspirations towards establishing an independent state.[50] Certainly, this notion of *Palestinianism* provides a way to incorporate the multiplicity of meanings of what it meant to be a Palestinian in an age when the land was radically being transformed by Ottoman centralisation, Jewish migration to Palestine, peasant displacement, the threat of European imperialism and Arab migration from Palestine. These events not only reshaped existing hierarchies but also transformed existing loyalties and created new ones. The Palestinian society during the late Ottoman era was such that understandings of homeland resonated on different levels and that the interconnectedness between traditional urban notables, a new educated elite, village leaders and peasants allowed the sense of *Palestinianism* to emerge not as a project of educating peasants by a nationalist elite, but rather being based on an interchange of ideas among these different groups, with each groups (made up of individuals) being influenced by the other.

Lastly, it is important to highlight that the sense of being Palestinian was present among both Muslims and Christians, who, in the years before World War I, began to jointly incorporate in their language such words as 'Palestinians' (*Filastiniyyun*), and other words, such as *al-Sha'b al-Filastini* (the Palestinian people), *Ahali Filastin* (people of Palestine), *Ibna' Filastin* (sons of Palestine) and *Rijal Filastin* (men of Palestine), began to become more common.[51] Importantly, it was Christians and Muslims in Jaffa, Haifa and Jerusalem who joined together in the local Palestinian press to educate their readership about the plight of the peasant, separating Palestine's urban community from its counterparts in cities such as Damascus and Beirut. While Palestine's urban elite certainly had strong ties with Syria, their sense of *Palestinianism* separated them from their brethren there, though this did not contradict the fact that both Syrians and Palestinians belonged to the Arab people of the Empire as Ottoman citizens, who often were joined under a mutual struggle to enhance their role as Arab citizens of the state.

Palestine's Jewish Community

As with Palestinians, defining Palestine's Jewish community during the late Ottoman era is a difficult task given its ethnic and linguistic divides. First, the community was divided along Ashkenazi–Sephardic lines, with the Ashkenazim tracing their origins back to Eastern Europe and the Sephardim tracing their roots back to Spain, whose expulsion of the Jews in 1492 sent many to cities in the Ottoman Empire, such as Salonica (Thessaloniki),[52] Edirne, Istanbul and Izmir, and to those in the Ottoman Arab heartlands, such as Damascus, Beirut and Jerusalem. However, it is important to remember that within each of these two main categories, there were numerous subgroups. In fact, the late nineteenth-century Yishuv[53] was made up of immigrants from different parts of Eastern Europe, the Arab lands, the Balkans and North Africa, some of them speaking Yiddish and Russian, while others spoke Ladino and Arabic. Furthermore, there were other groups that did not trace their roots back to Ashkenazim or Sephardim at all, such as the Persian-speaking Jews of Bukhara, and the Arabic-speaking Jews of Iraq and Yemen, just to name a few. In addition, there were the Jewish families who could trace their roots back for generations in Palestine.

While the multiplicity of Palestine's Jewish community often divided them, during the period following the Young Turk Revolution, this hodge-podge of groups began to unite under the banner of adopting the Hebrew language as the lingua franca, or at least the dominant language of the Yishuv, which was conducive to creating a new sense of unity, not only vis-à-vis the Palestinians, but also in terms of their relations with their Jewish brethren elsewhere. Most remarkably, those adopting Hebrew often remained distant from the Zionist Organization, founded by Theodor Herzl in 1897, when it convened its first annual conference aiming to establish an independent Jewish state in Palestine. For Herzl, immigration to Palestine would only be possible following an international power promising the Jews a homeland in Palestine, or in such far-off places as Argentina. The immigrants arriving in Palestine did not necessarily see independence as a means to their aims. Rather, living in the Holy Land, speaking Hebrew and strengthening the modern Yishuv was what motivated their immigration.

In fact, following the Young Turk Revolution, in Istanbul as in Palestine and other areas of the Ottoman Empire, a local type of Zionism took hold, which would greatly transform how Jews in the Empire (Ottoman citizen and non-citizen alike) would perceive Zionism. Julia Phillips-Cohen explains that

> proponents of the Movement judged their interest in the renaissance of Jewish culture and the Hebrew language to be in line both with the national aspirations of other Ottoman *millets* and with the promise of the new constitutional regime more generally . . . [And] they were careful to articulate a vision in which Palestine would become a national centre and place of refuge for persecuted Jews without becoming a separate state . . .[54]

True, even if some of Istanbul's small Jewish elite adopted anti-Zionist stances, such as the influential editor of the Sephardic newspaper *El Tiempo*, David Fresco, and the Chief Rabbi Haim Nahum, they were losing the youth of the community. According to Sarah Abrevaya Stein, '[David] Fresco's anti-Zionist tracts (in *El-Tiempo*) were blind to the originality and flexibility of Ottoman Zionism', which would slowly start to persuade a new following among the different Jewish communities.[55] One of these young members of the community was Nissim Mazliah, who supported Zionism as a cultural movement. Following the Young Turk Revolution, he was elected as MP as a member of the ruling Committee of Union and Progress and prided himself on promoting both Turkish and Hebrew studies among Turkey's Jews.[56] For him, the aim of Zionism was not to promote an independent Jewish state in Palestine, but rather have the land serve as a modern 'spiritual national centre'. He also deeply believed in the revival of Hebrew as a national tongue of Jews, stressing that in Jewish kindergartens throughout the Empire 'Hebrew should be the language of instruction and speech', while 'in the middle schools, which are supported by the government, Turkish should be the dominant language'.[57] These differing views in Istanbul demonstrate how true Abigail Jacobson's statement is that 'Zionism was not a monolithic ideology, but played out in different ways by various actors', and, importantly, I will add that this often varied from one region to another.[58] Its monolithic treatment in most of the historiography has created a false binary of Zionist versus anti-Zionist, blurring the nuances, and limiting our ability to understand the pre-World War I Jewish community in Palestine and the Ottoman Empire.

In Palestine, the cultural revival of Hebrew had already started to take hold as a new generation of children of Ashkenazi immigrants and local Sephardim were raised speaking Hebrew, and, following the Young Turk Revolution, this connected their future with the survival of the Ottoman state. They even went so far as to join the ranks of the Ottoman military as patriotic Zionists. For these youngsters – born and bred on a synthesis

of local Zionist ideology and Ottoman patriotism – there was no contradiction between supporting the Ottoman state and settling the Land
of Israel through a slow but steady migration. The process was in sync
with changes occurring among the Greeks and Armenians of the Empire,
where a national revival of language and culture were integrated with the
newly emerging civic-Ottomanism. This led to a sort of trade-off where
these ethnic religious groups encouraged an Ottoman patriotic agenda in
exchange for linguistic and national rights, which ended up leading to the
beginnings of separatism. In the words of one Ottoman Armenian MP,
Vartkes Bey,

> freedom of languages more than anything else will [show] the people of the
> Empire that the Ottoman flag is the best shelter for their national freedom, and
> this feeling will unite everyone together and will link everyone with the great-
> est patriotism to the Ottoman homeland, and will enlighten everyone together
> to love the flag and always be able to defend it.[59]

For Jews in Palestine, in contrast to Ottoman Jews in other areas of the
Empire, the new found love of Hebrew was much more than an apprecia-
tion of the language; rather, it was a key component in their transformation
into a unique political group – regardless of whether they were Zionists or
not – paving the way for Israeli nationalism decades later.

Fascinatingly, similar to the way in which the Palestinians have been
written out of the history of Palestine, the official Israeli state narrative has
written out – or glossed over – the multiplicity of Jewish communities in
Palestine and the role they played – or did not play – in the construction of
a Jewish collective identity during the late Ottoman period. This official
Israeli narrative places an emphasis on the Zionist labour movement and
the contribution of its leaders towards a Jewish state, the same ones who
would eventually construct the Israeli national narrative that shaped the
way many current-day Israelis understand their history. This narrative
is based on the idea of a historical inevitability in the Zionist dream to
establish a modern Jewish homeland in Palestine beginning in Europe in
the early part of the nineteenth century, when the 'forerunners of Zionism'
emerged; this notion informs the first wave of Jewish modern immigration,
known as the First Aliyah (1881–1903), the rise of political Zionism under
Theodor Herzl and continues with the Second Aliyah (1904–14). It then
jumps to the issuing of the 1917 Balfour Declaration, when Britain promised the Jews a homeland. From there, it moves to the British Mandate
period, or what is also known as the 'State in the Making', to World War
II, the Holocaust and the founding of the Jewish state in 1948. This book
breaks this smooth narrative by painting a much more complex picture of

how by 1914 the Jewish community in Palestine was well on the way to transforming from multifaceted Jewish groups into a collective national one based on a new overarching 'Hebrew' identity that allowed each group to retain its own unique traits – even as the groups that made up this collective national identity never envisioned an independent Jewish state as a viable option. It should not go ignored that most histories of the Palestinian–Israeli conflict, and at times Palestinian history itself, have been written according, or, as a reaction, to the official Israeli narrative, which has also been detrimental to understanding Ottoman Palestine in all of its complexities.

This book veers away from the trend of referring to the Jewish community of Palestine as 'Palestinian Jews'.[60] Even if this definition serves the practical purpose of defining them in terms of geography, during the late Ottoman era the Jewish residents did not define themselves as *Palestinians*, nor did the Palestinian population define them in this way. In fact, there was no single way in which they defined themselves, despite the tendency to move towards more nationalist self-definitions by replacing 'Jews' with more moderate definitions, such as *Eretzisraeliyim* (Eretz Israelis), or the more radical *Ivriim* (Hebrews). In sum, the Jews during the years before World War I, regardless of origin, never saw themselves as comprising a part of Palestinian Arab society, even if they forged connections and shared commonalities within urban politics. Therefore, when referring to the Jewish community as a collective, the most appropriate umbrella term would be the one in use at the time, the Yishuv. Throughout this book, what becomes apparent is the extent to which Jews in Palestine, and throughout the Ottoman Empire, were redefining themselves, as new understandings of nationalism and language took hold and transformed their own sense of belonging in Palestine, and in the Ottoman Empire at large.

It is within these complexities of emerging nationalisms, ethnicities and identities that the first years of the Palestinian–Jewish conflict took shape. The changes in Palestine's political landscape following the Young Turk period transformed both Palestinians and Jews from communities characterised by their multiplicity into two coalesced semi-unified groups, each vying for political hegemony. This book sets out to explain that process, defining how the conflict would progress in the coming years to be eventually characterised by its rampant violence. And, although the post-Young Turk Revolution period was not characterised by violence, as we see during the British Mandate and ensuing years, it certainly paved the way for the conflict that has now gone on for over a century.

Contextualising the Palestinian and Jewish Communities

Defining the Palestinians and Jews during the late Ottoman era in terms of nationalism is problematic and needs to be examined in detail. First and foremost, it is of the utmost importance when reading this book to keep in mind that during the period under discussion, neither Palestinians nor Jews envisioned an independent state in Palestine, or, for that fact, imagined a land free of the other. This claim might on the surface seem absurd, especially when speaking of a Jewish nationalist movement, Zionism, whose stated aim was precisely an independent Jewish state in Palestine. However, following the Young Turk Revolution, Zionist officials also in Europe slowly came to the conclusion that this goal was an impossible feat, and they needed to revise their thinking, eventually reaching the conclusion to support the growth of the Jewish Yishuv and secure immigration, working within the Ottoman system. This was a radical change from Herzlian Zionism that was staunchly opposed to immigration to Palestine without a charter that secured international or Ottoman recognition of a Jewish political entity in Palestine.

For Palestinians, the claim that they did not envision an independent state can be easily argued; in fact, such a claim would be absurd, since Palestinian nation-state nationalism only came about in the post-World War I era, and, even then, such as that under the 1918 Arab Kingdom of Faisal, they opted to be a part of the Syrian Kingdom. However, this is a good place to clarify a point that has already been briefly addressed, which is that for Palestinians, the concept of Palestine was not new, and even during the pre-nation-state period the geographical conceptualisation of Palestine was one that should not be seen as anything less than simple fact. Thus, while it is true that the Palestinians could not have imagined an independent state, the steps they took in defending their land were uniquely *Palestinian* – a layer of truth missing from most historical narratives.

During the 1908–14 period, beyond the fact that both communities could not foresee the fall of the Ottoman Empire and were working within an Ottoman system, another development that historically took place in tandem was the transformation into tangible political communities. For Palestinians, the transformation into a political community did not undermine their ethnic ties with Syrians or cast doubt on their loyalty to the Ottoman state. For Jews in Palestine, their transformation revolved around the adoption of a Hebrew language and culture, which, at least at this stage, did not undermine their ties with their Jewish brethren outside of Palestine. Importantly, the goal of this book is not to define these political communities as emblems of 'proto-nationalism', or to document them as one 'stage' in the development of each group's nationalism. Rather, its aim is to understand the dynamics of how each group during this period started to 'imagine' themselves as political communities, or how they transformed into what Benedict Anderson coined as 'imagined political communities'.

Anderson's claim that 'Nation, nationality, nationalism – all have proved notoriously difficult to define, let alone to analyse'[61] certainly applies to Jews and Palestinians in Ottoman Palestine. This holds especially true since had history turned out differently, perhaps neither of them would have transformed into a national people, and both very well could have remained local political communities united on issues of language, a local patriotism and a sense of belonging to the land. However, in histories we do not deal with 'what-ifs', and we know that following World War I, the two peoples became locked in a national conflict; therefore it is essential to understand that already in the late Ottoman era, both groups were basically acting politically independent of each other, and, at times, against each other.

The political separation between the two communities, however, was much more conceptual, rather than in the actual physical surroundings, where in rural and urban arenas Jews and Palestinians often lived and interacted together.[62] In this work, it becomes apparent that Ottoman politics actually facilitated this separation, with intercommunity politics also playing a role. At this juncture, it is useful to observe the formation of two different communities within one theoretical lens of Anderson's *Imagined Communities*, specifically focusing on the role of 'print-capitalism', where the spread of the local Hebrew and Arabic press 'made it possible for rapidly growing numbers of people to think about themselves, and to relate themselves to others, in profoundly new ways'.[63]

The press mushroomed throughout the Ottoman Empire after Abdülhamid II was forced by the Young Turks to restore the constitution and to reopen Parliament; of note, prior to this, the rule of Abdülhamid II was synonymous with press censorship and the silencing of any opposition. In Istanbul, and throughout the Empire following the Young Turk Revolution, print-capitalism – the profit-making mode of sharing information – quickly became the space where the new ideas of homeland, language, Ottoman patriotism and many other notions were tested, revised and manufactured.[64] During this period, a total of four Arabic newspapers were published in Palestine: *al-Quds* and *al-Nafir* in Jerusalem, *Filastin* in Jaffa and *al-Karmil* in Haifa, all of which catered to the Palestinian population, that is, both Muslims and Christians. On the other hand, the Hebrew press was geared towards Jerusalem's different Jewish communities: the mostly Sephardic *HaHerut*, and the Ashkenazi *HaTzvi*, the religious Ashkenazi *Moriah* and the more ideological (and limited to the small Labour movement) *HaAhdut* and *HaPoel HaTzair*.

For all the recent work on shared societies in Palestine, what is perhaps most obvious in looking at the press is that there was not one newspaper in Palestine that was directed towards both communities. True, some Jews read Arabic, and it is well documented that Sephardic and Ashkenazi Arabic speakers followed the Arab press closely to keep tabs on its anti-Zionist rhetoric; however, clearly none of the Arabic press was geared to the Jewish population; the same held true for the Hebrew press, and even if some Palestinians could read Hebrew, they were never part of the intended audience. The one exception perhaps was, for a brief period, the Jewish-run newspaper *Sawt al-'Uthmaniyya* (The Voice of Ottomanism); however, this paper was mostly used as a means of propaganda by a group of Arabic-speaking Sephardic Jews who wanted to show the Palestinians that the Zionist movement was not aimed at harming them. It was never aimed at a Jewish readership.

In the pages of the Arabic press, Palestinians vented their anger about the lack of Ottoman interest in the rise of Zionism; it was the place they spoke of the future of industry in the country and the development of sea ports; it was where its Greek Orthodox readers could rebel against their church leaders, and Muslim clerics could dream of making Palestine a centre for education throughout the Islamic and Arab lands. For Jews, the Hebrew press was the place they could imagine a Hebrew-speaking land, where they could argue over what it meant to be a modern Jew in the ancient homeland; where they could declare themselves proud Ottoman citizens and call for others to join in; and where they could speak of their relations with Palestinians. All these newspapers also reported regularly about news from Istanbul, Syria and Lebanon; however, the understandings of these events were often portrayed quite differently within the Arabic and Hebrew press. In sum, for all in Palestine, the proliferation of the local press opened up doors to an imagined world, one that perhaps did not necessarily fit realities on the ground but offered new realms of understanding, created divisions and also proved to be a place where all could dream of contesting futures.

Sources and Breakdown of this Book

Claiming the Homeland joins a number of recent books published on post-1908 Ottoman Palestine that challenge an outdated literature on Palestine during the late Ottoman period. In contrast to most of the recent literature, which has been briefly discussed above, this book relies heavily on government documents found in Istanbul's Prime Ministry's Ottoman Archives, which provide a rich source of material that gives the current book a unique perspective. Using the Ottoman archives expands our knowledge of the first years of the conflict by focusing on how it played out within an Ottoman political framework, with Jews and Palestinians looking beyond Palestine towards Istanbul to make claims on Palestine.

Delving into the Ottoman archives, one becomes aware of how much of Palestine's history remains undiscovered, buried under multiple nationalist narratives, be it Jewish, Arab or Palestinian. This book demonstrates how important it is for the historian to look beyond the headlines of the Palestinian–Israeli conflict, and to put together a story from what on the surface might often appear to be completely unrelated circumstances described in archival documents, such as the story above about oranges being stamped with a Star of David, a British archaeological dig in Jerusalem and reports of the building of an Arab university in Jerusalem. However, once the documents are scrutinised and analysed, a historical past emerges that presents us with a narrative of how the two communities became distinct political communities during the late Ottoman era and also reflects how each community was unable to imagine that within a decade of the 1908 Young Turk Revolution, Palestine would no longer be a part of the Ottoman world. For anyone within the borders of the Empire, this indeed was something truly unimaginable.

While the Ottoman government documents on Palestine present us with a deluge of new information, they cannot be read without the Hebrew and Arabic press as supplementary sources, both of which often colour in a much more vivid picture of events described in the documents. In fact, those unfamiliar with the period might be surprised to see what a vibrant press Palestine had during the last years of the Ottoman Empire and the breadth of information available to today's scholar. In fact, with so much information at our fingertips, the archival work often serves as a compass to pinpoint relevant historical material in the newspapers. For example, if I had not explored the Ottoman archive's dossier on a British archaeological dig, it seems likely I would never had taken notice of the headlines in Palestine and the international press of what I have coined the 1911 Haram al-Sharif incident.

In addition to the local papers, newspapers in Istanbul, New York and London also provide important sources to understanding Ottoman Palestine. Today, with so many newspapers coming online, the historian of Ottoman Palestine has endless stories waiting for them. Lastly, documents related to this topic in London's Public Record Office also make up an important piece in the much greater puzzle of Ottoman Palestine. Also, this book incorporates a limited amount of material from the Zionist archives; however, they also were essential to the narrative, especially that of the last two chapters. Importantly, many of these sources have also been documented in the large amount of extant scholarly work on Zionism. Moreover, this work incorporates private letters and personal journals. The very fact that many of these different sources overlap, presenting contrasting and complementing narratives, bears testament to the fact that even as the two peoples were carving out and imagining separate worlds, they were very much connected to each other, whether in Jerusalem, or in the Ottoman capital of Istanbul.

This book comprises five chapters. The first chapter provides an overview of the history of the Land of Palestine from the late eighteenth century up to the main period under discussion, the 1908 Young Turk Revolution. This will be integrated with the presentation of the historic ties of Palestinians and Jews to the Land, and draws out the borders of Palestine in an era when Palestine was not demarcated by modern borders, but nonetheless was an entity within the minds of its residents and the Ottomans who ruled over it. It also focuses on the question of why the Jews and Palestinians both welcomed the Young Turk Revolution, as well as looking at Palestinian opposition to Zionism in the late 1900s. It then moves on, introducing what I define as the 'renegotiation of the Millet system',[65] explaining how the two communities grew separately as a result of the Young Turk Revolution. In future scholarly endeavours, this section could also serve as a reference point for the study of other communities within the Ottoman Empire.

Chapter 2 embarks on a study of how, following the 1908 Young Turk Revolution, Palestinians began to unite as a people and to take steps to claim the homeland. With Palestinians perceiving Palestine as being under direct threat from Zionism and British colonialism, a collective struggle began to emerge, with Palestinians drawing up petitions and voicing their worries in the Arabic press, through the newspapers *al-Karmil* and *Filastin*. It was during these years that a sense of 'Palestinianism' developed – a local identity that separated the Palestinians from Syria and incorporated both Muslim and Christian Arabs living in Palestine – and urban Palestinians began to define themselves as 'Palestinians', as well as reaching out to create new ties with Palestine's Arab peasant population.

The 1911 Haram al-Sharif incident is the topic of Chapter 3. When a British archaeological team set out on a treasure hunt in the Haram al-Sharif compound, Palestinians united against the Ottoman administration, who was blamed for its collaboration with the British team. In the wake of this scandal, Palestinians, seeing themselves as the protectors of the Islamic holy sites of Palestine, set out to strengthen their hold of the city, which included opening an Islamic university which would serve the greater Middle East. This incident provides us with a case study of how Palestinians did not merely unite over their opposition to Zionism but also in their apprehension of British imperialism, all the while growing weary of the Ottoman administrators.

In the last two chapters, the book takes a turn towards the Jewish community in Palestine. Chapter 4 focuses on how previous divisions between the Jewish community in Palestine – Ashkenazi vs Sephardic, religious vs secular or Zionist vs anti-Zionist – began to blur as these groups adopted Hebrew as their main mode of communication. This coincided with their attempts to redefine the Jewish connection with Palestine, *Eretz Israel*, in light of the fact that a new type of cultural Zionism emerged which interlocked with Ottomanism, the civic nationalism that dominated in the Empire after the Young Turk Revolution. However, where past research looks at how this ideology drew Jews closer to their Palestinian neighbours, this study argues that it actually hindered relations between the two communities. The chapter then moves on to take a glimpse at how Ottomanism led to Sephardic and Ashkenazi Jews joining the Ottoman army out of a new radical understanding of what the Empire had to offer them, and what they had to offer the Ottoman Empire.

Chapter 5 takes the reader to Istanbul, where Jews and Palestinians took their grievances and laid 'claim on their homeland'. For Jews, this was done by coming to Istanbul, learning Turkish and forging ties with the local Ottoman Jewish community. While Zionists in Istanbul, including David Ben-Gurion, later to become Israel's first prime minister, were not able to convince large numbers to support the Zionist cause, they found support among some Jewish parliamentarians. In fact, it was in the Ottoman Parliament that Jerusalem's Arab Members of Parliament lobbied against the growing Jewish dominance in Palestine. However, Zionism found sympathy not only among Jewish parliamentarians, but also Armenian ones, who defended the right of the Jews to settle in Palestine. This chapter explains how within the new Ottoman system of equality, the Jewish community in Palestine moved forward with plans for autonomy as Palestinians became frustrated with the Ottoman state's inability to accept their fears that the Jewish community would one day succeed in taking control of their homeland.

The Conclusion recaps the main arguments of the book and highlights how this book's findings change our understanding of the overall conflict, as well as stressing the need to revise the existing Palestinian and Israeli national narratives. In this section, we also see that at least within Palestine both peoples did not envision the eventual fall of the Ottoman Empire. Further, the implication of these new findings is that later histories on the Palestinian–Israeli conflict need to be revised, as most of these histories see the conflict taking root following the 1917 Balfour Declaration, and in the subsequent British occupation and mandate periods. This should lead to a reconsideration of how we understand the separate histories of both Jews and Palestinians and how they transformed their identities during the late Ottoman era.

Notes

1. DH.ID 1332.Ra.23 108–2/14; 19 February 1914.
2. DH.ID 1332.Ra.23 108–2/14; 19 February 1914.
3. *Filastin*, 10 September 1913. This expression was one used quite commonly in the newspaper *Filastin*; in one article, it was used to speak of general frustrations of Arab population with the Ottoman state, leading to a trial and a brief closure of the newspaper.
4. This reality was noted previously by Gershon Shafir, who stated in his monumental work that the 'late Ottoman period' should be considered the 'pre-mandate period'; see Shafir, *Land, Labor and the Origins of the Israeli-Palestinian Conflict*, p. 22.
5. Shafir, *Land, Labor and the Origins of the Israeli-Palestinian Conflict*.
6. For a discussion of this see Khalidi, *Palestinian Identity*, p. 92.
7. Roberto Mazza makes an important argument why it is necessary to rethink the periodisation of Jerusalem's history, looking at the transformation from the late Ottoman era to the British Mandate. See Mazza, 'Missing Voices in Rediscovering Late Ottoman and Early Jerusalem', *Jerusalem Quarterly*, pp. 61–71.
8. Campos, *Ottoman Brothers*, p. 5; Hanioğlu, *A Brief History of the Late Ottoman Empire*, pp. 76–7.
9. Hanioğlu, *A Brief History of the Late Ottoman Empire*, pp. 76–7.
10. For more on early recruitment of Ottoman Jews, see Cohen, *Becoming Ottomans*.
11. Hanioğlu, *A Brief History of the Late Ottoman Empire*, p. 75.
12. Ibid., pp. 104–5.
13. Ibid., 146–9.
14. Campos, *Ottoman Brothers*, p. 3.
15. Ibid., pp. 27–9.
16. *The Times*, 11 August 1908.
17. Kılıçdağı, 'The Bourgeois Transformation and Ottomanism among Anatolian Armenians after the 1908 Revolution', p. 68.

18. Kayali, 'Elections and the Electoral Process in the Ottoman Empire', *IJMES*, pp. 265–86.
19. Ibid., p. 272.
20. Shaw and Shaw, *History of the Ottoman Empire and Modern Turkey*, p. 278.
21. PRO FO 795/2321, p. 144.
22. Ibid., p. 164.
23. Ibid., 12 July 1909, pp. 232–3.
24. Campos, *Ottoman Brothers*, p. 18. One of the memoirs often quoted is that of Wasif Jawhariyyeh, which exhibits the close social ties some Jews and Arabs incorporated into their everyday lives. See Tamari, 'Jerusalem's Ottoman Modernity', *Jerusalem Quarterly*, pp. 5–27.
25. Jacobson, *From Empire to Empire*, p. 86.
26. Gribetz, *Defining Neighbors*, p. 39.
27. Jacobson, *From Empire to Empire*, p. 33.
28. Eldem, 'Istanbul as a Cosmopolitan City', in *A Companion to Diaspora and Transnationalism*, pp. 212–30.
29. Jacobson, *From Empire to Empire*, p. 56.
30. Der Matossian, *Shattered Dreams of Revolution*, pp. 2–3. In another article, Eldem explains the extent of mixing between the different religious groups among the professional class of Istanbul. See Eldem, '(A Quest for) the Bourgeoisie of Istanbul', in *Urban Governance Under the Ottomans*, pp. 159–86.
31. A similar case of appropriating one's current understanding of intercommunal relations onto the past can be found in Mark R. Cohen's analysis of al-Andalus, who claims that portrayals of the Islamic Middle Age has been misrepresented and that the 'interfaith utopia was to a certain extent a myth'. See Cohen, 'The "Golden Age" of Jewish-Muslim Relations', in *A History of Jewish-Muslim Relations*, p. 28.
32. Gribetz, *Defining Neighbors*, pp. 2–3.
33. Jacobson, *From Empire to Empire*, p. 2.
34. Mazza, *Jerusalem*, p. 11.
35. Richter, *Facing East from Indian Country*, pp. 2–8.
36. Doumani, 'Rediscovering Ottoman Palestine', *Journal of Palestine Studies*, p. 6.
37. Khalidi, *Palestinian Identity*; Porath, *The Emergence of the Palestinian-Arab National Movement, 1918–1929*.
38. Khalidi, *Palestinian Identity*, p. 30.
39. Muslih, *The Origins of Palestinian Nationalism*, p. 11. Muslih claims that Palestine was also referred to as *Suriya al-Janubiyya*. I have not found one such reference in all the primary sources.
40. Antonius, *The Arab Awakening*, p. 1.
41. Antonius, 'Syria and the French Mandate', *Royal Institute of Internal Affairs*, pp. 523–39.

42. In fact, throughout all of my archival research, I have rarely encountered Palestinians referring to Palestine as comprising a part of geographical Syria, or *Bilad al-Sham*. See Gerber, 'Zionism, Orientalism, and the Palestinians', *Journal of Palestine Studies*, pp. 23–41.

43. Khalidi, *Palestinian Identity*; Porath, *The Emergence of the Palestinian-Arab National Movement, 1918–1929*, p. 164. In regards to the debate over whether or not the Palestinians should support the Syrian Arab Kingdom, see Muslih, 'The Rise of Local Nationalism in the Arab East', in *The Origins of Arab Nationalism*.

44. Gerber, *Remembering and Imagining Palestine*.

45. Hakim, *Origins of the Lebanese National Idea*, pp. 2–3.

46. Ibid., p. 7.

47. Ibid., p. 8.

48. The term *Palestinianism* I first coined during a lecture I gave at Haifa University in 2008, entitled: '"Palestinianism": Defining Palestinian Identity during the Young Turk Period'. Then I noted that in Hebrew (*falastiniyut*), Arabic (*filastiniyya*) and Turkish (*filistinlilik*) one can convey such a notion (even if remaining vague) of the essence of being Palestinians in one word, and from that I opted to develop the term *Palestinianism*. Only later did I come across Hakim's term, *Lebanism*, just making the term even more relevant.

49. Khalidi, *Palestinian Identity*, p. 19.

50. Brubaker and Cooper, 'Beyond "Identity"', *Theory and Society*, pp. 1–47.

51. *Filastin*, 10 September 1913, p. 3. In this article, the above-mentioned terms are used interchangeably. In one article in *The Times* the Arabs of Palestine are also referred to as 'Palestinian Arabs', in a letter to the editor, which was written by an English Zionist, Herbert Bentwich. *The Times*, 7 October 1912.

52. During the period under discussion, Salonica was a major cultural centre of the Ottoman Empire, up until the Balkan Wars when it became part of Greece (with the majority of citizens living there using the Turkish pronunciation and not the Greek). Therefore, I will use the Turkish name of the city and not the Greek *Thessaloniki*, or the English *Salonica*.

53. The Hebrew word used to refer to the Jewish settlement in the Holy Land, and in the post-Zionist era, would later denote the modern political Jewish community in Palestine before statehood.

54. Cohen, *Becoming Ottomans*, p. 104 (italics in original).

55. Stein, 'The Permeable Boundaries of Ottoman Jewry', in *Boundaries and Belonging*, p. 18.

56. *HaOlam*, 3 March 1909, pp. 13–14.

57. Ibid.

58. Jacobson, *From Empire to Empire*, p. 83.

59. *HaTzvi, 01* March 1911, p. 1.

60. Shapira, *Land and Power*.

61. Anderson, *Imagined Communities*, p. 3.

62. See Lemire and Dalachanis (eds), *Ordinary Jerusalem 1840–1940*, for an assortment of articles on this question.
63. Anderson, *Imagined Communities*, p. 36. According to Rashid Khalidi, 'in Palestine in particular, what Anderson describes as "print capitalism" thereby helped shape a broad community of interest, and imagined community that came to describe itself as Palestinian . . .'; Khalidi, *Palestinian Identity*, p. 88.
64. As historians today, we are slowly in fact coming in touch with the extent of the press revolution in Palestine as online editions and access to thousands of pages of Palestine's history become available to us with the click of a mouse. To say it is overwhelming is an understatement and certainly proves new challenges to the next generation of historians.
65. I first coined this term in a paper I presented at the eighth Workshop for Armenian-Turkish Scholarship (WATS), which took place in Amsterdam in 2011. I would like to extend my thanks to Fikret Adanir, Ronald Grigor Suny and Fatma Muge Gocek, who as discussants of my paper provided me with important feedback.

1

Setting the Stage before Conflict

I am sure that with time they [Jews] can and will be successful in establishing their own state in Palestine.

Exiled Sultan Abdülhamid II, 1911[1]

This statement is attributed to the former sultan, Abdülhamid II, who during his exile in 1911 presupposes the inevitability of the founding of the Jewish state in Palestine. It further strengthens the Zionist historical narrative, which presents the formation of the later Jewish state as if it were an inevitable outcome of the Zionist project. However, the situation on the ground in pre-World War I Palestine was much more complex and none of the parties involved – the Ottomans, the Jewish community in Palestine and the Palestinians – could have predicted that in such a short period of time, Britain would occupy Palestine and issue the Balfour Declaration, stating that it favoured 'the establishment in Palestine of a national home for the Jewish people', which would eventually lead to Jewish political hegemony in Palestine, and the eventual establishment of a Jewish state in Palestine in 1948. For example, in one 1911 document, the Ottoman governor of Nablus stated that Palestine would be under Ottoman rule for hundreds of years to come.[2] All the while, Jews were teaching the Ottoman language in their schools, with some dreaming of being in the Ottoman Parliament – the same parliament in which Palestinian MPs were voting daily on issues concerning the Ottoman political world.

Palestine, or the Land of Israel, has a history spanning more than 2,000 years, during which it has been home to Jewish kingdoms, been a part of the Roman, Byzantine and various Islamic empires, been subject to the Crusades and the period of Mamluk rule and finally became part of the Ottoman Empire in 1516–17, following the successful military campaign of the Ottoman Sultan Selim I. The Ottoman state would rule over

Palestine for approximately 400 hundred years, until Great Britain occupied it during 1917–18. So the changing nature of the Palestinian–Israeli conflict, which embodies both nationalistic and religious characteristics, is also a struggle over the historical interpretations of Palestine's past, with each group using aspects of their current existence to justify their interpretations of the past. While there is no single starting date for the subject of the current work, a brief survey of each group's historical understanding of the past needs to be placed into context.

For Jews, historically speaking, the roots of the Land of Israel go back to the region of Canaan, which in the twelfth century BC became a province ruled by ancient Egypt. During this period, we see the first record of a *Hebrew* people, as well as the arrival of the Philistines, from which the term Palestine is derived – 'Philistines' evolved from Assyrian, Greek and Latin; in Arabic this term transformed into *Filastin*. In the Kingdom of Israel and Judah, during the reign of King David (1040–970 BC), Jerusalem became the capital, with his son, Solomon (970–31 BC), making it the site of the First Temple. Despite this, the geographical borders of *Eretz Israel*, the Land of Israel, did not always fit the borders of this first kingdom, transforming over time as is evident in different Jewish texts throughout history, which describe the borders sometimes expanding up into modern Iraq, Syria and Turkey. What is clear, however, is that by 300 BC, the larger understanding of the land was compacted into the area from Beer Sheba in the south to the northern river of the Dan, and from the Jordan River in the east to the Mediterranean Sea in the west – an area which can be perceived as the nucleus of the Israelite Land.[3]

Following the fall of the Second Temple, in 70 AD, and the failed Bar Kokhba revolt in 136 AD, Palestine fell under Roman control, at which point it was renamed the 'Syria Palaestina' province, which was divided into three zones: Palaestina Prima, Secunda and Tertia. Despite the fact that Jews no longer ruled over the Land, it remained a central part of Jewish ceremonies and prayer, and the concept of Jerusalem as a holy city and *Eretz Israel* as the Holy Land never faded. In fact, it was only with the rise of modern nationalism that the Jewish national movement, Zionism, would succeed in radically reshaping the Jewish peoples' ties to the Land through a sense of modern nationalistic ownership.

For Palestinians, while some fervent nationalists might trace their roots back to pre-Roman times, there is no doubt that, similar to other Arab national movements, the rise of Islam, and its spreading to the different regions of the Middle East, offers an excellent beginning point for this story (and one that has been incorporated by Christian Arabs as well). The Islamic conquest of Syria and Palestine took place during the years 636–8, under the reign of the second caliph, Umar b. al-Khattab, and opened the way for contiguous Muslim control in Palestine for almost thirteen centuries, save for the years of the Crusades. During Muslim rule, the subsequent empires – the Umayyads, Fatimids, Ayyubids, Mamluks and Ottomans – gave special significance to Jerusalem as a city holy to Islam. Jerusalem came to occupy an important place in Islamic praise literature, *Fada'il al-Quds*, named after the city Muslims refer to as al-Quds (the Holy), or Bayt al-Maqdis (House of the Holy). *Fada'il al-Quds* literature draws a picture of historical Palestine in the mind of the reader that extends beyond Jerusalem, describing holy sites all the way from Safad in the north to Gaza in the south, covering an area quite similar to the Jewish understanding of the Holy Land.[4]

After the Caliph Umar set the precedent for prayer on the Temple Mount, the Umayyads set the stage for the preservation of this holy tradition, building the Dome of the Rock, and the al-Aqsa Mosque; the former, a shrine housing the rock on which Abraham was going to sacrifice Isaac, and the latter the place the Prophet Muhammad ascended to heaven (known in Arabic as the *Mi'raj*). Just as important, Jerusalem was the first 'qibla', or prayer direction, before Mecca became the direction of prayer. The compound area that Jews recognise as the Temple Mount is known by Muslims as the *Haram al-Sharif*, the Noble Sanctuary. Administratively, the Umayyads chose to divide the Holy Land into two military districts: the southern region was known as Jund Filastin, with Lydda as its capital, the northern as Jund Urdun, with Tiberias as its administrative capital. It was not until the conquest of the Crusaders and the establishment of the Kingdom of Jerusalem (1099–1187) that Palestine was once again united into one geographical district. Of particular import for the current study is how the Crusader onslaught and the later victory of Saladin in Jerusalem would become a vivid part of history for the Palestinians, who compared the influx of Europeans and Jewish immigration in the early part of the twentieth century to the Crusades.

Following the Crusades, the land was subject to a constant pull between powers in the north and south, this time falling under the Egyptian Ayyubid and Mamluk empires. However, with the conquest of the Levant by the Ottomans in the sixteenth century, Palestine became an integral part of the Ottoman Empire in 1516, with Sultan Selim visiting Jerusalem a year later, once again highlighting to its inhabitants its religious significance. The next sultan, Suleiman the Magnificent, fortified the city in 1535 by building the walls which still exist today.

Linguistically, Arabs referred to Palestine by its Arabic name, *Filastin*; for the Ottomans, the Turkish *Filistin* or *Arz-ı Filistin* (the Land of

Palestine); and, lastly, for the Jews, the Hebrew *Eretz Israel* (the Land of Israel). In addition, all three of these groups used the term 'Holy Land', in their corresponding languages. For the residents of Palestine, regardless of whether they were Palestinian or Jewish, the status as a disputed land throughout history must have strongly affected their collective memory. However, despite being portrayed as solely a twentieth-century phenomenon, turmoil in Palestine was present much earlier. From the late eighteenth century up through the mid-nineteenth century, conflict was an inseparable part of the land. In fact, this period was central in setting the stage for the Palestinian–Jewish conflict, with discourses of nationalism and colonialism steadily becoming lived realities.

Ottoman historians see the rule of Selim III (1789–1808) as the turning point in the Empire, when Istanbul began to demand that its provincial officials reign in control, paving the way for a century of government centralisation. While most Ottoman historians focus their attention on the rebellious Derebeys of the Balkans, who challenged the rule of Istanbul, and eventually would play a role in deposing Selim III, Palestine also presented a challenge to Ottoman authority, with the rise of a local leader, Dahir al-Umar, who, through alliances with the Egyptian Mamluk and Russian empires, spread his control from a northern base in the Galilee city of Acre as far as Beersheba in the south.

Umar is one of the rare cases where a local leader indigenous to Palestine would actually rule the land. His stature also caught the attention of Europeans, with Umar's life documented in an eighteenth-century travelogue, entitled *Travels through Syria and Egypt*.[5] In other words, with the ascendance of Umar, Palestine regained its importance on the map for Europeans, who took note that the Holy Land might one day break free from the Ottoman Empire. However, after decades of Umar challenging their rule, the Ottomans succeeded in taking back Acre in 1775, and Ahmed Jezzar Pasha, who had recently been appointed governor of Sidon (and at times Damascus), chose the city as his administrative centre. While Jezzar is most famous for defeating Napoleon Bonaparte's troops in 1799 as they made their way from Egypt up the coast of Palestine deeper into Ottoman lands, he is equally remembered for his cruelty toward the local population, which suited his name, Jezzar, the 'butcher'. Unlike Umar, Jezzar was not indigenous; rather, he was a Bosnian Mamluk, who rose through the ranks, and even as he remained greatly autonomous from the Ottoman court, his loyalty to the Sublime Porte was never compromised.

Similar to Umar, Jezzar Pasha also profited from the monopolisation of cotton, grain and olive oil, and from trade with European markets, which provided the needed sources to finance his administration as a regional power.[6] Both Umar and Jezzar Pasha[7] provide examples of how a single location in Palestine during much of the eighteenth century, and the early part of the nineteenth century, served as a base to rule most of the rest of Palestine and parts of Syria and Lebanon. Further, beyond his trade with Europe, Umar strengthened ties with the Russian Empire to concentrate power against the Ottomans; on the other hand, Jezzar protected Palestine from Napoleon and the first major European invasion since the time of the Crusades.

What is compelling is that during both of their ruling periods, Palestine (and parts of Syria and Lebanon) was at the centre of international conflicts: Umar (with the support of Russian troops) repelled the Ottomans, while Jezzar Pasha fended off the French. Yet even after these conflicts, the instability in Palestine and Syria was far from over. In 1831, just a little over three decades after the French invasion, Egyptian forces, led by Ibrahim Pasha (the son of Mehmed Ali, the rebellious Ottoman governor) invaded Palestine, making their way up the Levantine coast and reaching deep into Anatolia. Sultan Mahmud II sent in troops (having to rely on Russian troops to prevent the potential fall of Istanbul), leading to an international agreement – the 1833 Convention of Kutahya – which entitled Mehmed Ali to govern over Syria and Palestine, in addition to his governorship of Egypt. The Egyptian occupation of Palestine set in motion major changes; domestically, Muslims were angered that a head-tax was imposed on them, which bore a striking resemblance to the *cizye* tax, an Islamic poll tax placed on the Jews and Christians of the Empire.[8] In addition, even as the existing social structure of Palestine was challenged during the time of both Umar and Jezzar Pasha, Egyptian reforms went even further, shaking up relations between the Muslim and non-Muslim populations. Ibrahim Pasha gave preference to Christians and Jews, quite probably to impress Britain and France, while at the same time utilising a simple 'divide and conquer' mentality, allowing these minorities to renovate churches and synagogues, and creating a general sense of security for them, even in cities such as Nablus, which had up to that time been known as a dangerous place for non-Muslims and foreigners.

The greater significance of Egyptian rule, however, was that it 'enabled the West to gain a foothold in Palestine from which it was not henceforth to be dislodged'.[9] It was during these years that European countries and the United States opened up diplomatic missions in Jerusalem, which marked the beginning of extensive missionary-school networks.[10] In fact, the proliferation of a European presence was the topic of an 1857 British consul report, which focused on the growing presence of Russians, Prussians, Austrians, French and even, for the first time, an American consul. While most of the Europeans' work was within the realm of creating ties with Palestine's local Christian communities and the proliferating missionaries, the British report also remarked on the steady increase of Russian Jews;[11] importantly this was about twenty-five years before what is considered the first modern wave of Jewish Russian migration in the 1881 First Aliyah. In addition, according to the British consul, it was not only Polish and German Jews who were 'buying land and building houses in all directions', but also Germans who were establishing prosperous settlements, and French people, who were expanding a network of Roman Catholic schools, hospitals and orphanages.[12] Of these groups, the German settlers can be seen as a prelude to the Zionist settlement in Palestine. In 1868, a group of German Christians, known as the 'Templars', embarked on settlement in Palestine, forming communities in Haifa, Jaffa and Jerusalem. In an 1891 British consulate report, the consul of Beirut, H. Trotter, supplied an account of this community's achievement in Haifa, stating that 'the most striking object at Haifa is the German Colony . . . which consists of about sixty houses and 400 inhabitants', and that 'one might imagine oneself to be in the heart of Germany'.[13] The Templars' returning to the Land of Israel in order to prepare it for the Second Coming of the Messiah serves as an example of the revived European interest in the region and a useful comparison for Jewish communities returning to Palestine as a means to prepare for the Coming of the Messiah. Lastly, for Jewish newcomers settling outside of Jerusalem, the Templars provided a settlement system to emulate.

These new immigrants to Palestine, however, were not met with an empty land, nor, as has often been described in Zionist history, a land suffering from 'centuries of Turkish indifference and misgovernment', and a 'neglected backwater of the Ottoman realm'.[14] Many of the Western accounts of Jerusalem, for example, depicted the city as a 'dreadful place misruled by the "terrible Turks"'.[15] However, during the last few decades a plethora of research has emerged that depicts a much different Palestine; one that possessed a local industry, economy and urban growth. This held true not only for Jerusalem, but also for Nablus, and new cities such as Jaffa and Haifa, and smaller budding cities such as Gaza and Tulkarm.[16] Palestine's countryside provided important agricultural imports to Europe, such as grain, and other cash crops like sesame seeds, olive oil, tobacco and cotton. In addition, in the latter part of the nineteenth century citrus cultivation was introduced, which produced the Jaffa orange.[17] One Palestinian city that only appears in passing in the current book but is important to show Palestine as making up a part of the global economy was Nablus. During the eighteenth and well into the nineteenth century, it was the centre for Palestine's trade and manufacturing, connecting the northern regions of the Galilee with the southern regions down to Hebron, and home to self-sustaining villages.[18] Beshara Doumani argues that the

> qualitative leap in trade with Europe between 1856 and 1882 ... could only have taken place given an already commercialized agricultural sector, a monetized economy, an integrated peasantry, and a group of investors willing to sink large amounts of capital into the production of cash crops.[19]

Even if Nablus during the Ottoman period provides a prime example of a vibrant land interconnected through tradition, trade and culture, Palestine was never a demarcated zone or a separate administrative district. Following the rule of the Egyptian Ibrahim Pasha, Palestine was once again divided into three administrative districts, known in Turkish as *sanjaks*. These three districts, Jerusalem, Nablus and Acre, were attached to the greater administrative district *Vilayet-i Şam*, Damascus, which was administratively connected to Istanbul. In 1872, Jerusalem was detached from Damascus, and was turned into an independent district, *mutasarrıflık*, which was headed by a governor, a mutasarrıf, who was appointed by Istanbul (Figure 1.1).[20] Under its jurisdiction were the cities of Jaffa, Gaza, Ramlah, Beer Sheba and at times Nazareth. Even if the Jerusalem district in Ottoman documents was not interchangeable with the geographical *Filistin* in official government documents, during the period of Abdülhamid II, it was often referred to as such, also appearing interchangeably on Ottoman maps.[21] For the British consul serving in Jerusalem, the district of Jerusalem was at times interchangeable with Palestine as well.[22]

In 1888, *Vilayet-i Şam* was reorganised, with Nablus and Acre becoming part of the *Vilayet-i Beyrut* (district of Beirut; Figure 1.2). Concerning the division of Palestine into separated districts, Jonathan Gribetz astutely points out that

> to acknowledge the lack of political boundaries around a land called Palestine is not to imply that such boundaries, however imprecise and flexible, did not exist in people's minds. Moreover, noting the absence of official borders should not be taken to suggest that an 'imagined' territory is any less significant historically than one that was politically, legally, or sovereignly bound.[23]

Modern Jewish Migration and Reviving the Homeland

During the nineteenth century, as we saw above, European Christians and Jews showed renewed signs of interest in Palestine; however, different from such examples as the Templars, some Jewish communities in Europe

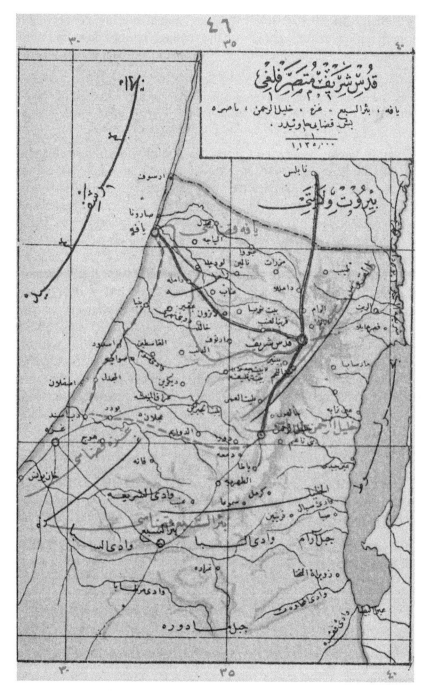

Figure 1.1 The mutasarrifate of Jerusalem; source: Memalik-i Osmaniye cep atlası/*The Pocket Atlas of the Ottoman Lands*, Author/Yazar: Tüccarzade İbrahim Hilmi, 1905/6

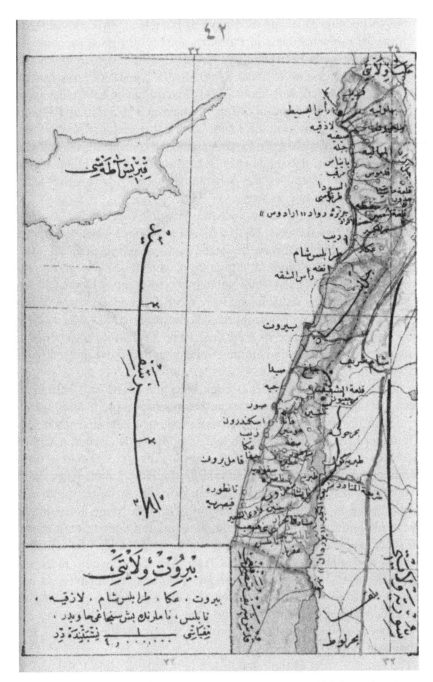

Figure 1.2 The district of Beirut, Vilayet-i Beirut; source: Memalik-i Osmaniye cep atlası/*The Pocket Atlas of the Ottoman Lands*, Author/Yazar: Tüccarzade İbrahim Hilmi, 1905/6

started to imagine Palestine as a modern homeland, strikingly different from the Jewish inhabitants in Palestine already. By most accounts, the Jewish population of Palestine was small during the early part of the nineteenth century, made up of about 7,000 people.[24] In 1836, Jerusalem had the largest population, with about 2,200 Sephardim and 650 Ashkenazim, with other Jews spread out in different cities such as Safad and Tiberias in the north, and Hebron in the south. During this period, new centres of Jewish populations also began to sprout up in the coastal cities of Jaffa and Haifa. It seems clear that the Jews of Palestine were divided ethnically and linguistically, not just along the Ashkenazi–Sephardic divide, but within each of these two groups as well.

Unique to the Ashkenazim was the fact that they tended to divide according to religious sects, often with their religious leaders remaining in Europe. The Sephardim on the other hand, despite their multitude of origins and different periods of immigration, were united into one community under a locally elected Chief Rabbi in a system set up by the Ottoman authorities. While the Ashkenazim were more dependent on the *Halukah*, the system in which money from their home communities was collected to support their existence in Palestine, some Sephardim also relied on resources sent from Istanbul allotted to help support those in need within the community.[25]

Just as Ibrahim Pasha's rule over Palestine (1831–40) shifted the social balance between the different religious groups, it also sparked the idea in Jewish communities across Europe that Palestine could serve as a modern Jewish homeland. In fact, Zvi Hirsch Kalischer, a rabbi in East Prussia, came up with this plan, claiming that Jews should return to Palestine and carry out the 'redemption of the Holy Land'. After failing to convince the Rothschild family to help kick start the initiative, in 1838 he succeeded in capturing the attention of Moses Montefiore, another Jewish philanthropist. In place of the mass migration of Jews, however, Kalischer proposed a more subtle plan to prepare the land by setting up agricultural settlements. Just a year later, Montefiore would meet with Egyptian leader Mehmed Ali, who agreed on an initial plan to set up a Joint Stock Bank to fund this project.[26] Although the Egyptian occupation ended just a year later and the plan was never realised, the idea of a modern Jewish homeland continued to capture the minds of Jews throughout Europe.

The renegotiation of the relationship between the Holy Land and the future of the European Jewish people also occurred among secular Jews. In his book *Rome and Jerusalem*, Moshe Hess, a socialist who had at times (for better or worse) close ties with Karl Marx, was influenced by the writings of Kalischer, despite his abandonment of religious life.[27] Influenced by his observations of European nationalism, and especially the rise of Italian nationalism on the 'ruins of Christian Rome', Hess asserted that the Jews were the 'last great national problem', and declared that the future of the Jews would be in Palestine. However, this home would be a socialist one, where Jews would be redeemed through labour, and would bring an end to their existence as a 'phantom people'.[28] While Hess's words made no major waves in Europe, his thoughts would later fill the writings of major Zionist thinkers, such as Leon Pinsker and Ber Borochov.

The Zionist movement, however, only gained momentum in the 1880s when the Jewish communities in Russia were increasingly subjected to a wave of state-promoted anti-Semitic actions. Such pogroms greatly shaped the future of Zionism. According to the foremost scholar on Zionist history, Anita Shapira,

> The Zionist movement was born out of a deep disappointment: the dream of the nineteenth century that progress was destined to carry the world forward toward an enlightened future in which the distortions, legal perversions, and discrimination of past eras would appear like a passing nightmare, revealed itself to be nothing but a figment of the imagination by the close of that century. Modern anti-Semitism erupted onto the scene during the 1880s in Central Europe.[29]

This disappointment in Russia was twofold, given the fact that

> hopes were dashed that the reforms of Alexander II in respect to Jewish life . . . would serve as a basis of reference for additional reforms in the future. [And] . . . in their stead, in 1881, came a series of vicious pogroms that raged through scores of cities and towns in Southern Russia.[30]

While Russian pogroms were not new, this spate was particularly severe, inducing mass migration of Jews to the United States, with a small trickle heading for Palestine. Thus, while most Western European Jews were relinquishing ties with their kinsmen in order to forge new ones with the greater population through the adoption of citizenship, Jews in Russia forged a new modern understanding of their own community, with some turning towards Jewish nationalism, others towards socialism, or yet others who were working to integrate into Russian society despite its seemingly stringent walls of separation. In fact, it is within these new confines that Jews also began showing new interest in Hebrew, which challenged Yiddish culture, just as more Jews were also adopting Russian as their lingua franca. Within decades Hebrew would become the dominant language of the Jewish Yishuv in Palestine.

41

In 1881, in what would become known as the First Aliyah marking the beginning of the New Yishuv, Jews mostly from the Russian Empire began to migrate to Ottoman Palestine as an alternative to the mass migration underway to the United States.[31] The new-versus-old dichotomy would dictate the Zionist narrative and later the Israeli state narrative, with the First Aliyah (1881–1903) seen as the start of the Zionist project in Palestine, ushering in five more major *aliyot*, leading to the establishment of the state of Israel. Recently, Anita Shapira has reassessed to what extent the Jews arriving post-1881 marked a major shift over those Jews who already inhabited the Land, stating that 'the old Yishuv had undergone slow processes of change and [these] included elements seeking modernization in employment and housing', and she documents the well-accepted fact that Jews had begun to expand beyond the walls of Jerusalem, and be transformed into modern-day farmers.[32] She goes on to clarify that

> not every member of the First Aliyah was worthy of the name New Yishuv, if that phrase was supposed to signal commitment to the Zionist idea. Many new immigrants were much like their old Yishuv predecessors; they hastened to Jerusalem in hopes of getting *halukah*[33]

or funds that were collected by Jews in the Diaspora to support Jewish life in the Land of Israel. At the same time, during the First Aliyah, as well as the Second Aliyah (1904–14), modern Jewish farming settlements became increasingly visible, and, before World War I, Jewish immigrants had already established forty farming colonies, which formed three main blocks concentrated in southern, central and northern Palestine.[34]

The First Aliyah also predated the foundations of political Zionism, which was started by Theodor Herzl in 1897, following the first Zionist Organization's international meeting in Basel, Switzerland. As a result, during the period before World War I, two main strands of Zionism emerged: the practical Zionists, who chose to settle in Palestine in the absence of an international charter, and the political Zionists, who were united by Theodor Herzl in believing that a Jewish state could only be reached through diplomatic means. Thus, while the political Zionists supported the Yishuv, they often did so hesitantly, fearing reprisal from the Ottoman administration. This would significantly change during the Second Aliyah, when the Zionist Organization based in Berlin would take a much more active role in financially supporting some aspects of the Yishuv by appointing an official representative.

The Ottoman administrative divisions that divided Palestine into separate zones did not erase the Arab or Jewish inhabitants' memory of a geographical Palestine that stretched from the Mediterranean in the west to the Jordan River valley in the east and from the southern Negev desert as far north as the Litani River, areas reaching into the modern state of Lebanon.[35] It was in this territory, whether in the north, coastal regions or areas surrounding Jerusalem, that the two groups, Palestinians and Jews, first started formulating their claims to a homeland and began to transform into national communities. In fact, the Palestinians took note of the First Aliyah and the potential threat this posed to their own existence. This held true not only for Palestinians, but also an Ottoman government that realised the complications that came with a modern immigration of Jews to Palestine. However, the main reasons for Ottoman refusal to allow the free flow of Jews to Palestine had little to do with the Palestinians, a trend that would continue even up to the years just before World War I. In his monumental book, *The Arabs and Zionism before World War I*, Neville Mandel cites two main reasons for the Ottomans' initial rejections of early Jewish migration. While there was much speculation over Ottoman motivations for the immediate attempt to block migration, Mandel credits it to the Porte's fear of importing a new national group into the Empire and the reluctance to allow a large group of European Jews into the Empire, in which they could benefit from the extraterritorial rights allotted to them through the capitulations.[36]

Between 1880 and 1914, the Ottoman government placed numerous restrictions on Jewish immigration and blocked all proposals for transferring Jews as a collective. Today, Abdülhamid II (1876–1909) is remembered for his staunch opposition to Zionism, and he had not been in power even five years when, already in 1880, a proposal to transfer Jews to Palestine was shot down. This proposal is barely mentioned within official Zionist history, but serves as an important precedent since it paved the way for three decades of official opposition to Zionist immigration. In 1879, a well-known British millennialist, Dr Oliphant, encountered first-hand a Jewish community in Romania that had suffered anti-Semitic attacks, leading him to take part in an early Hovevei Zion meeting in Jassy (the Hovevei Zion were a variety of organisations started in response to the pogroms in Russia that promoted Jewish immigration to Palestine). Motivated to save the Jews from despair and destitution, the British Christian went on to Istanbul, and then to Palestine, to search for a possible territory in Palestine that could be carved out for Jewish settlement, in the end settling on Belka, a land on the east bank of the Jordan River, attached to the jurisdiction of Nablus. Oliphant's proposal of a mass transfer of Jews into Palestine would be facilitated by the formation of an Ottoman company, which would provide the state with a thriving economy. However, in May 1880, these plans were halted by Ottoman opposition which outlined the dangers they posed to the state, because these plans created 'a state within a state', and also cited the unrest they would bring to the region's Bedouin tribal make-up.[37] What is striking in this case is how similar this early plan is to the later plan of the Zionist leader Theodor Herzl, who like Oliphant secured meetings with high officials in Istanbul (it is unclear if Oliphant, like Herzl, was able to meet Abdülhamid II).[38] In the Ottoman archive, one can find the letters that Herzl dispatched to the Sublime Porte, where he proposed setting up an Ottoman company that would finance the Yishuv and at the same time pay off a huge amount of Ottoman debt.[39] Both proposals, however, were unable to convince the sultan, who was known for his suspicion 'of all foreign proposals', of the benefits Jewish migration would bring to the Empire.[40]

Within one year of Oliphant's proposal, in November 1881, as Jewish immigrants began trickling into Palestine, the Ottoman authorities issued a statement concerning immigration to Palestine, which was directed to an unnamed representative (presumably in Istanbul), on the part of 'British and German philanthropists, who are endeavoring to promote migration of Jews to Turkey'. The memo, which was also dispatched by the Porte to St Petersburg, Berlin and Bucharest, stated that 'Jews would be allowed to enter and establish themselves in separate communities in all parts of the Empire, except Palestine, but would be subject, without any exception or reservation' to Ottoman law and citizenship.[41] Interestingly enough, as discussed in Chapter 5, some Russian immigrants took up the Ottoman offer to migrate to other regions within the Empire, and, during the reign of Sultan Abdülhamid II, Jewish farming communities were established by Ashkenazi immigrants in Anatolia and in the vicinity of Istanbul. These settlements must have looked much like the First Aliyah's settlements in Palestine, which transformed into settler-colonial projects. By 1904, thirty Jewish colonies had been established in Palestine, with over 5,000 settlers. Most of them quickly ran into economic hardship, and started to drain the Hovevei Zion, then coming under the patronage of the Baron Edmond de Rothschild, which for him was no less of an economic burden. Much to the dismay of many of the colonists, economics trumped ideology, and what was meant to be a renewal in Jewish farming life, turned into a settler-colonial project similar to Algeria, where Palestinians were a major part of the workforce. However, in applying the settler-colonial paradigm, one complication emerges: many of the colonists adopted Ottoman citizenship, some of their children were born and raised as Ottoman citizens and one day these children would be fighting as Ottoman soldiers in the country's wars. Moreover, the colonies were often praised as successful models to emulate by the Ottoman administration in Palestine, both in the period before and after the Young Turk Revolution.[42]

Palestinian opposition to Jewish migration reaches back to the 1880s when urban notables began to protest the influx of Jews coming with the First Aliyah. In fact, had it not been for the local population's opposition, it is unlikely the Ottoman government would have maintained such a stringent official policy towards the new immigrants. Admittedly, 'the reconstruction of the opinions, positions, and actions of anti-Zionist Arabs in the period before the Young Turk revolution is a difficult task', due to the 'shreds and fragments' that remain from a multitude of sources, including a highly censored and low-circulation press.[43] In 1891, we receive a glimpse of this opposition when, just a decade after Palestine had seen the First Aliyah, the Muslim population of Jerusalem grew impatient with the government's lack of ability to stop the flow of Jews. In this case, Jerusalem's mufti and some notables dispatched a petition to the Sublime Porte, which had been done behind the backs of the Ottoman-appointed Turkish officials, including the governor. According to *The Jewish Chronicle*'s correspondent who was in Jerusalem:

> The petition represented to His Majesty [the sultan] the enormous increase of foreign Jews; the increase of immovable property in possession of these strangers who are not willing to become Turkish subjects, and thus increase influence of the foreign Powers in Palestine, mostly that of the greatest foe of Islam – Russia; the poverty of the Mohammedan inhabitants of Jerusalem, who having sold at a very high price their lands near Jerusalem, squandered it away and remain without any means of living, the expensiveness of living having trebled since the foreigners came here; the equilibrium of the different populations in Jerusalem, the Jews being two-thirds of the entire population in Jerusalem, which is a great danger in itself . . .[44]

Responding to the question of the correspondent, the governor said this had nothing to do with prejudice against Jews, and that all that was asked of them was to adopt Ottoman citizenship, stressing that except for Palestine, they could settle in all other areas of the Empire. Despite this ban, however, he noted that 200 Jews had arrived on a visit and were allowed in due to the Turkish consular stamp in their passports. Nevertheless, the bans were somewhat successful since parallel to this it had been reported that Russian Jews, and Jews from the Greek island of Corfu (who were fleeing attacks on their community), were denied entry into Palestine and that they had made their way to Alexandria, Egypt, where the local Jewish community there was receiving them and taking care of the new refugees. Still, as was discussed above, every Ottoman clamp-down on Jewish immigration was followed by a loosening up on the ban, something that Palestinians recognised, with more settlements being established and more Jews moving to the urban centres.

While we do not have the name of the mufti in the above-mentioned petition, it must have been made in reference to Muhammad Tahir al-Husayni, who served as Jerusalem's mufti (and at times serving as a qadi as well) from 1865 until his death in 1908. Historian Emanuel Beška considers him to be perhaps the first known person of influence to take a stand against modern Zionist immigration and land purchases. Active since the early 1880s, he finally succeeded in chairing a local committee at the turn of the century set up by the Ottoman authorities to investigate land transfers, and he managed to delay some sales for several years.[45]

Another prominent voice against the Zionist Organization's plans to settle Palestine was the MP from Jerusalem, Yusuf Diya' al-Khalidi (the uncle of Ruhi al-Khalidi), who in 1899 penned a letter to Theodor Herzl via the Chief Rabbi of France, Zadoc Kahn. In this, in reference to Palestine, he posed the question 'by what right do the Jews demand it for themselves?'. He went on to say that only by the force of cannons would they be able to conquer it, and pleaded, 'For the sake of God, leave Palestine in peace.'[46] However, Khalidi could take refuge in the fact that Herzl, unlike the Jews influenced by the Russian and Romanian members of Hovevei Zion, was staunchly opposed to immigration to Palestine as long as it was not legitimised by an international charter, which would not happen as long as Sultan Abdülhamid II was in power; not to mention the fact that the Zionists were preoccupied with Britain's 1903 Uganda proposal, the 1904 early death of Herzl and the Zionist vote in 1905, which ended any hopes of a Jewish homeland in Uganda. Coupled with this, in the first years of the twentieth century, there also was a lull in the number of new immigrants reaching Palestine. All of these factors merging together must have provided some optimism for Palestinians and been somewhat of a sigh of relief. Nevertheless, in 1904, with the advent of the Second Aliyah, Jews started once again to pour into the country dashing their hopes that migration to Palestine would continue to see a decline in Jewish immigrants.

Despite a clear policy opposing Jewish immigration – which was backed up by numerous government correspondences and enquiries back and forth between Istanbul, Jerusalem and Beirut forbidding foreign Jews from settling and buying land in Palestine, both in the period of Sultan Abdülhamid II, and during the Young Turk period, 1908–14 – the Ottoman administrative directives remained nothing more than a stumbling block in the way of Jewish immigration. Firstly, Jewish migrants often received the support of European powers whose citizens were allowed unhindered travel in the Empire; particularly to Jerusalem, as a place of pilgrimage. Thus, the capitulations allowed foreign embassies to intervene on behalf of the right of their citizens to enter Palestine, often leaving the Ottoman state's prohibition against Jewish immigration and settlement null and void.[47] And, it was not only Jews who were coming to Palestine; since the mid-1800s Russian pilgrims had started to make their way to Palestine, making attempts to stop foreigners from remaining all the more complicated. For example, in 1910, it was reported that 33,000 Christian pilgrims reached Palestine, many of them Russian and Greek.[48] By the late nineteenth century, tourism had also increased.[49] Further hindering attempts to stop Zionist expansion and Jewish immigration was the fact that Palestine was not one geographical administrative unit, which often hampered steps taken to limit migration.[50] It is noteworthy that in 1892, one group of Jews was not so lucky. According to an Ottoman archival source, a group of 200 Iranian Jews were sent back to Iran, and 300 more were prevented from reaching Palestine, which indicates that as they were not coming from a European country, they had little leverage vis-à-vis the local Ottoman administration.[51]

For most of the period under discussion, the red-slip system was in force. This allowed Jewish pilgrims to enter Palestine on condition that they relinquish their passports at the port of entry and enter on a temporary document (which was red in colour and thus designated the 'red-slip'). This 1901 decree was cancelled in 1913 by the government, which recognised that the policy had completely failed to prevent Jewish immigration. On 17 September 1913, Ottoman government ministers reviewed the question of Jewish immigration and decided to cancel the system due to its ineffectiveness, especially since it had led to a high level of corruption among Ottoman bureaucrats.[52] The meeting's report also highlighted that Jewish immigration was illegal, whether from other parts of Ottoman lands or from foreign lands; yet the report did not offer any other immediate solutions to the problem of Jewish immigration.[53]

According to the British consul in Jerusalem, it was cancelled 'on the ostensible grounds that this system had given rise to abuses and failed in its object of limiting Jewish immigration'. The consul further noted that a local commission was to be formed to decide more effective measures to prevent Jews from remaining; however, he was sceptical if this would happen due to the 'Jewish influence in high places'.[54] Less than four months later, the Ottoman Interior Ministry once again requested a clarification, complaining that 'in the land of Palestine, they [the foreign Jews] are buying lands and receiving the title deed', as if there were no law forbidding them from doing so.[55]

In 1908, the governor of Palestine, Ali Ekrem Bey, reported that the Jews 'pursue the red notes with great zeal and they view it as a crutch which ensures their safety . . .' and that 'whatever the interest, expertise, or good intentions of the police they cannot overcome the existing obstacles and follow each and every one of the hundreds and thousands of Jews entering Jerusalem with a red note . . .'[56] In the same dispatch, Ali Ekrem made clear that without direct intervention from Istanbul, it was unlikely that even a mutasarrıf like him, who was adamant on stopping the incoming flow of Jews, could succeed. In his words:

> Yes, some of the Jews enter Jerusalem and do not leave. Yes, some officials in the port take money. These things have been taking place since the time of Rauf Pasha. Jewish immigration has decreased at times, but has never dropped to zero. I admit this. But as I have reported officially, too, the fault does not lie with the Mutasarrif of Jerusalem, or the mutasarriflik of Jerusalem, but rather with the adoption of a decision which from the outset has been impossible to implement. This is the decision at the core of which is the prohibition on entry into Jerusalem and acquisition of property of Jews. How could this be implemented when it is clear that it contravened the Conventions [that is, the capitulations].[57]

In May 1914, just months before the war broke out, the Interior Ministry warned both Beirut and Jerusalem that the Foreign Ministry had notified their offices that a large group of Jews from *Rumeli* (Ottoman European territories) were coming to Palestine holding foreign passports with a hidden political agenda, and had ordered that only those holding Ottoman citizenship or Ottoman passports should be allowed entry. This document highlights the fact that Jews were arriving from within the Ottoman lands and not just from abroad using Palestine's port cities; the immigrants were arriving first in other Ottoman territories, and then proceeding on to Palestine, creating an 'internal migration'. While we do not have a direct answer to the enquiry, Istanbul also was investigating if Jews from Salonica were coming to Palestine.[58]

In the pre- and post-revolution period, the Ottoman authorities were bound to the capitulations, forcing them to respect foreign passport holders' entry into Ottoman territories, which hampered their efforts.[59] Therefore, even after it had been decreed yet again that Jews could not enter in early 1914, upon being refused a visa from the Ottoman consulate in Odessa, 150 Jews continued their journey to Palestine, completely disregarding the Ottoman refusal. From the records, it seems that the Jews entered the port in Jaffa, and only afterwards were the port officials notified. However, apparently such officials were quite lenient since the Interior Ministry's question was simply, 'did the Russians entering Palestine have passports or not, since they did not receive a visa from Odessa?' By this we learn that some Jewish immigrants were able to enter Palestine even without a passport,[60] which, according to a similar report, was a 'result of bureaucrats taking bribes'.[61] At the same time, during this period, numerous mixed messages were dispatched from Istanbul's different ministries concerning the question of immigration, leading to confusion among local Ottoman officials,[62] which in turn allowed more Jews to enter. In July, it was reported in *Moriah* that Ottoman officials had blocked Jews from disembarking from their boat in Jaffa and after it made its way to the port of Haifa, they were also unable disembark. Unlike in the past, the Russian consulate was not able to help at first. However, the Russian official returned shortly after wearing his 'official uniform' and boarded the ship, and despite the Ottoman officials' initial refusal, they finally appeased the Russian official, 'showing respect' for his authority.[63]

These new attempts at stopping Jewish migrants from entering must have been related to a report dispatched in May by an Ottoman emissary who came to investigate Zionist expansion. Reporting back to the Internal Security office, the official warned Istanbul that Zionism was a real threat and to take the Jewish attempts at seizing Palestine as a homeland seriously, noting that local Ottoman officials in Palestine were unconcerned.[64]

In short, Jews successfully found ways to enter; in cases where Jews were blocked from entering by Palestine's ports, they entered by land, whether en route from Istanbul, or entering through British-occupied Egypt; in cases where Ottoman policy was enforced, Jewish migrants were able to bribe Ottoman officials; and, in cases where land purchases were blocked in Jerusalem, Zionist purchases moved to the north, which was in a different administrative district where at times it was easier to overcome the restrictions.[65] One British source states that bribing Ottoman officials was widespread.[66] Lastly, in the upcoming chapters it will become evident that following the Young Turk Revolution, some Ottoman governors in Jerusalem, along with officials in Istanbul, actually seemed not to have objected to the Jewish migration, and instead viewed some of the changes that came with the new immigrants positively. For them, the new immigrants were agents of modernisation and would help transform the land into a source of prosperity.

The inability of the Ottoman administration to stop migration can be seen in the sheer numbers of Jews arriving. During the First Aliyah, about 25,000 Jews entered Palestine, along with another 30,000 during the Second Aliyah. Even if the Jews were still the clear minority, their population was on an upward trajectory.[67] Population statistics for Ottoman Palestine are a point of contention, which has been documented by Justin McCarthy in his book *The Population of Palestine*.[68] According to McCarthy, for the most accurate statistics on Palestine, one should rely on the Ottoman statistics (with minimal corrections), which places the Ottoman Jewish population at 39,000 Jews,[69] with an additional 18,000 non-citizen Jews,[70] making the Jewish population at the eve of World War I approximately 57,000. However, current to the period under discussion, Arthur Ruppin, the Zionist representative in Palestine, estimated that in 1913 the Jewish population made up 14.3 per cent of the total population, or 86,000.[71] More recently, other scholars have cast some doubt on McCarthy's findings, adding new complexities to the study of Jewish immigration to Palestine. For example, Kemal Karpat explains that Jewish immigration was much more complicated than what has been usually attributed to this phenomenon.[72] In his article 'Jewish Population Movements in the Ottoman Empire, 1862–1914' Karpat asserts that the Jewish population saw a sharp increase in Palestine, from 10,000 in 1839 to about 100,000 on the eve of World War I, and that from 1860 onwards the Jews were the majority in Jerusalem:

> The reasons for this big growth should be sought in the dynamics of Ottoman demography, as much as in European immigration. Obviously, the demographic history of Palestine, which has been the chief preoccupation of most Israeli demographers and other scholars, cannot be understood if detached from the history of population movements in the Ottoman Empire as a whole. The scholar who ignores the general Ottoman matrix in which the contemporary history of the Middle East was drawn can fall into grave errors.[73]

What is interesting is that Karpat assesses the Jewish community as 100,000, a figure that was often claimed by both Palestinians and Jews who lived during the period under discussion.[74]

For the Palestinian population, McCarthy almost entirely accepts the official Ottoman statistics, estimating that there were 602,377 Muslims, and 81,012 Christians, together totalling 683,389 people; making the overall population of Palestine in 1914 approximately 740,000.[75] However, even after McCarthy's exhaustive study, we see that many unanswered questions remain, especially in terms of the problems of taking Ottoman statistics at face value, with only minor adjustments being applied, and by not taking Muslim and Christian emigration into account. This shortcoming will be addressed in this work, along with the fact that the Palestinians in numerous documents propose that the Jewish population was higher than all of the above statistics. Nevertheless, McCarthy clearly demonstrates that during the period of 1878–1914 there is no truth to the claim that Zionists' colonies induced a mass migration of Muslims coming to

Palestine for economic opportunities, stating 'the province that experienced the greatest Jewish population growth (by .035 annually), Jerusalem Sanjak, was the province with the lowest rate of growth of Muslim population'. He then moves on to demonstrate that in other regions of Palestine, where Jews were less predominant, there was actually an increase in the Muslim population.[76] Karpat's findings that in some regions Muslim populations grew independent of Jewish migration is important in debunking a myth which has persisted among Zionist historiography, whereby before modern Jewish migration to Palestine in the late 1880s, Palestine was a barren land and only after the Jewish migration did Arabs from other regions come to Palestine for employment.

In addition to the points addressed above, in order to understand the dynamics between the Jewish and Palestinian populations, it will be necessary to challenge previously reported migration patterns and population statistics. These issues are important since the Palestinians' perceptions of the threat posed by Zionism can only be understood within the context of not only the migration of Jews to Palestine, which in itself was substantial, but also in the exodus of Palestinians that was taking place, both in terms of internal and external migration. This factor was seen to be of crucial importance by the Palestinians during the period, and was accordingly discussed in numerous Ottoman documents and newspaper articles. In terms of internal migration, one substantial fact unearthed by this work is the creation of a landless peasant class predating the British Mandate period, which not only posed obvious challenges in identifying those peasants who were actually living on the land, but also weakened the hegemony of the local village leaders, the *mukhtars*. In terms of external migration, while the emigration of urban Palestinians and Syrians to the Americas has been well documented as mostly a Christian phenomenon, we see in this book that it was also a common occurrence among Muslims, and was not only an urban phenomenon. Lastly, this book will highlight that Palestinians had a much higher rate of infant mortality, a fact that was recognised by the Jewish community, and was another reality jeopardising Palestinian hegemony in the land.

The Young Turk Revolution: A New Era in Palestine?

It would be a mistake to see the Young Turk era as marking a major shift in the Ottoman government's official policy towards Jewish migration and Zionism. Actually, despite the radical changes ushered in by the 1908 Young Turk Revolution, on the issue of Palestine, one could argue that the Committee of Union and Progress never really parted from the policy of the *ancien regime* of Abdülhamid II; Jewish immigration remained illegal, and despite the land sales discussed in this work, there was not a huge overall increase in Jewish ownership over the land, or rural settlement during the 1908–14 period. One could even argue that the new political cadre in Istanbul faced similar problems to the former regime, in that they were completely unequipped to halt the Jewish migration. So, if Zionists, whether in Jerusalem, Istanbul or Berlin, were unable to reach a deal with the new regime, then why can we still interpret the 1908 revolution as a major turning point for the Yishuv? Further, how can we explain the sharp divisions that emerged between Jews and Arabs within such a short period of time, who in the summer of 1908 had celebrated the revolution together as Ottoman brothers?

As elsewhere in the Empire, in Palestine, the Jewish community, including those within the community who held growing national aspirations, quickly saw new opportunity following the Young Turk Revolution. One of the first concrete changes came in the replacement of the Ottoman governor, Ali Ekrem Bey. Under his almost two years of rule, there was a marked deterioration in relations between the Jewish community in Palestine and the Ottoman administrators. During the governor's tenure, there was a clamp-down on land sales to Jews, and his staunch opposition to Jewish immigration had already been reported to Istanbul.[77] Just months before the revolution, the Jewish community had experienced a particular violent incident that became etched into the minds of the Yishuv. In March of 1908, Asaf Bey, the Ottoman Kaimakam – the local administrator of Jaffa who was a subordinate of Ali Ekrem – fell out with the Jewish community in Palestine at large. The Jaffa affair occurred on the day before Purim, when a fight broke out between Jews and Muslims in Jaffa. Following news that one of the Muslims received serious injuries, Jews fled to a locally owned Jewish hotel, followed by Ottoman police, who arrived together with Russian guards, *kavas*, from the consulate (under the system of the capitulations, the Ottoman security forces needed to be accompanied by Russian ones due to the fact that the hotel was owned by a Russian citizen). In the end, five Jews were arrested. Had it ended like this, it is most likely that this incident would have been forgotten. However, a gathering at a hotel where a festive celebration for Purim was being held aroused the attention of the police. At first the hotel was only paid a visit by the police, with no arrests taking place. But shortly after that, the hotel was raided, and thirteen Jews, all apparently innocent bystanders, were seriously injured, some even by bullets shot off by police, with local Muslims joining in on the raid.[78]

For the Jewish community, the events of that evening raised fears that a pogrom had taken place in Jaffa, reminiscent of the violent attacks many had previously suffered in Russia. According to one Jewish bystander, 'sorry to inform you that the tactics of the Russian Government have been copied by their representatives in this country, who, in combination with the Turkish authorities at Jaffa, were responsible for an event unprecedented here since the Jewish Wars'.[79] He went on to state that the

> Trouble began with the arrival of the Kaimakam, who is an enemy of the Jews, some eighteen months ago. During this period not a week has passed without a Jew being wronged in one way or another. This state of affairs reached its climax on Purim eve . . .

and that the 'whole Jewish community [is] in a state of panic', with some asking, 'Can such things happen in Jaffa, where the Muslims and Jews live together on such friendly terms?'[80]

The affair ended with the swift removal of the Kaimakam, who was summoned to Istanbul with Sultan Abdülhamid II issuing a statement to the Jews 'conveying his greetings to the Jewish community and expressing his sympathies for the unfortunate event'.[81] Ali Ekrem was forced to make public statements condemning Asaf Bey in attempt to show that he was not an anti-Semite and, in order to mend ties with the community, he added a Jew to the Administrative Council of Jerusalem.[82]

The Jaffa affair serves as a good example of how a certain event connected the multiplicity of groups within the Jewish community, despite their array of religious, political and social allegiances. Such an incident should not be seen as necessarily a source of unity, since often violent outbursts between Jews and Arabs in the Yishuv could also spark a blame game between different factions, with both the Ashkenazim and Sephardim at times placing blame on the colonists, or other groups, from among them. The Yishuv during the late Ottoman period was often fraught with internal conflict: not just between Zionists and anti-Zionists, but also Sephardic–Sephardic and Ashkenazi–Ashkenazi, and of course Sephardic and Ashkenazi clashes. Younger members of the multifaceted community, however, had already begun to become more similar, and former divisions were now lessening as new horizons opened up possibilities in the imagination of the youth. These changes, however, not only brought them closer to their own co-religionists, but also to other ethnic and national groups present in the urban arena, not just in Jerusalem, but also in Istanbul, the once far-off capital that had become more accessible.

For the Palestinians, this anecdote shows us that in Jaffa, tensions were running high between Jews and Arabs, and must have been present in Jerusalem as well. As we saw in the Introduction, and will see below, that certainly was not always the case. However, before we discuss Jewish–Arab relations in Palestine during the days of the Young Turk Revolution in more detail, it will be necessary to first place Palestinian local patriotism within the growing trend of Arabism, or, if you like, early Arab nationalism. In order to understand the development of Arabism and its importance to what was happening in Palestine, it will be necessary to briefly look back to the previously discussed mid-nineteenth-century *Tanzimat* reforms, where, unlike in the Balkans, in 'Arab provinces, the political and economic dislocations that centralization and Western economic penetration caused did not have immediate nationalist or separatist implications, but actually led to the integration of the [Arab] provinces into the central administration'.[83] However, even if notables were able to reach high positions in the administration, they often encountered a 'glass ceiling', with Muslim Turks filling the highest positions in Istanbul. This point was made by Rahim Badran, a Syrian Arab and a member of the newly opened 1876 Parliament, who asked: 'Has anyone from Syria attained in the last six hundred years the office of the grand vizier, *Şeyhülislam*, or minister of finance?'[84]

Certainly, the Syrian Arabs, including Palestinians, had legitimate grievances. One of the Arabs, who was integrated yet at times estranged, was Yusuf Diya' al-Khalidi, who came up earlier. Born in Jerusalem in 1842, the heyday of the *Tanzimat*, Khalidi could be described as the model Ottoman Arab citizen who embraced modernity, transcending temporal and geographical borders. Khalidi was the only one of eight children who opted for a Western education, which was in addition to a traditional Islamic one. He eventually reached Istanbul and studied at the Imperial Medical School and the esteemed Robert College, making important ties, via his brother Yasin, who was familiar with the top echelon of the Istanbul political elite. At the young age of 23 he returned to Jerusalem, where he established the first modern Ottoman middle school (*rüşdiye*) in 1868, which, to his dismay, was handed over to a Turkish teacher from Istanbul. Soon thereafter he become mayor of the city, a position he held for five years, and later in his life he also was mayor for two more brief periods. Following his five-year term as mayor, he returned to Istanbul to work in the translation bureau, and then served briefly as an Ottoman consul in a Russian Black Sea port city. Next, he travelled throughout Eastern Europe, going to Odessa, Kiev, Moscow and St Petersburg. For a short period, he also taught Arabic and Turkish at the Imperial Royal Academy in Vienna. His career took a twist when Abdülhamid II promulgated the constitution, and Khalidi was elected an MP, and in Parliament he was known as a staunch constitutionalist, which eventually led to his demise, as Abdülhamid II clamped down on freedoms, suspending the constitution, and closing down Parliament. Khalidi was one of the ten parliamentarians forced to leave Istanbul (five of them Arab), due to his liberal stance. Before returning to Palestine, he served a brief exile in Vienna, and his last years were spent as Kaimakam of Jaffa, where he would meet the first waves of Jewish newcomers, and later fill other minor provincial posts. He died in 1906.[85]

Khalidi, like other Arabs, was aware of a latent discrimination – and at times mistrust – on the part of Turkish officials for their Arab counterparts. While the parliamentary group remained loyal Ottoman citizens, even if at times disgruntled, groups which showed an interest in Arabic and Arab heritage were being formed, some even calling for separation from the Empire.[86] Such activity, even if not widespread, could be found also in the later Young Turk era.[87] However, later scholars have pointed out that early historians of Arab nationalism inflated the role these groups played in the formation of Arab national movements, very much in the way early Zionist history created a historical narrative that highlights the inevitability of this nationalism. Later historians, such as Albert Hourani,[88] reassessed the situation, leading to a plethora of research showing that overall the great majority of Arabs within the Empire remained loyal Ottoman citizens. Hourani, through his work on the 'politics of the notables', explained how the notables of Arab cities served as intermediaries between the Ottoman administration and their societies at large, which led to their integration into the political system. In the case of Jerusalem, the main notables were from three main families (among other smaller ones): Husaynis, Nashashibis and Khalidis, all who in the mid-to-late nineteenth century based their wealth greatly on land ownership.[89] Central to the Ottoman political system, control was divided between different families, thereby not giving one too much power over the other, while guaranteeing the loyalty of all. It should be noted, however, that the manipulation of the different families in the urban arena also lessened the chances for the social and political mobility needed for imperial politics in Istanbul. Thus, in this sense we should see Yusuf Diya' al-Khalidi, who was at once a local leader and an imperial statesman, as the exception to the rule.

Following Hourani's work, C. Ernest Dawn revised George Antonius's account of Arab nationalism, and pointed out that political Arabism developed much later than previously indicated and that most Arabs remained loyal Ottoman citizens up until World War I.[90] Following this, new research highlighted the phenomenon of multiple and overlapping identities; in other words, for many Arabs, Arabism and Ottomanism did not necessarily stand juxtaposed to each other, rather the identities worked in unison.[91] More recently, in his work on Syria following World War I, James Gelvin argued for a more comprehensive understanding of nationalism in the Arab Middle East, one that moved beyond 'a singular and undifferentiated Arab nationalism and Arab National movement', mostly dominant among the Arab elites and intellectuals, towards 'alternative constructions of nation and nationalism', examining what was happening among popular politics.[92] This notion will resonate well in the current work, with expressions of *Palestinianism* emerging from a coalescing of voices from multiple levels of the society, and certainly not found only among elite and educated groups.

Furthermore, and central in understanding Muslim and Christian unity in Palestine (and in Syria in general), it is important to insert here that Arabism went against the trend of other ethnic nationalisms within the Ottoman Empire (and for that matter most of the nationalism emerging in the Russian and Austro-Hungarian empires), where ethnicity was inherently connected to religion. For example, the rise of Turkish nationalism in the late Ottoman era was ethnic-religious in nature, where the ethnic *Turk* was inherently Muslim; similar to how Armenians and Greeks of the Empire belonged to their own churches. Not surprisingly, the formation of Jewish nationalism emerging in Palestine and other Ottoman lands was heavily influenced by these types of exclusive south-eastern and Eastern European nationalisms.

Due to alliances made between the exiled Young Turks and Arab citizens during Abdülhamid II's sole rule,[93] it must have been no surprise to Jerusalem's governor, Ali Ekrem Bey, that many Syrians and Palestinians met the Young Turk Revolution with jubilation. First and foremost, for Arabs 'it seemed then that the new freedoms would indeed allow the Arab population a greater say in administering their provinces, as well as more active participation in the affairs of the state in general'.[94] In fact, in Jerusalem tensions ran high between the governor and Jerusalem's Arab notables, similar to his strained relationship to the Jewish community. Ali Ekrem Bey, in one personal and one official letter, expressed his fear that the Ottoman administration in Palestine would face some sort of resistance from Jerusalem's influential families, and that these problems would not be confined to Palestine, but would also affect Syria.[95] In upcoming chapters, we will see also how Jerusalem's notables indeed did challenge the administration and how this led to the removal of a later governor, Azmi Bey. Further, Chapters 4 and 5 examine how some Ottoman administrators looked positively on Jewish immigration as a way to offset geographically large regions populated almost totally by Arabs, which they perceived as posing a threat to Turkish hegemony.[96]

The declaring of the revolution in Jerusalem was a sight to see. The coming together of the different religions and peoples led to commentary not only within Jerusalem, but in Istanbul and in the newspapers of London and New York. For both Arabs – Christians and Muslims – and Jews – from the multitude of communities – it appeared a new era had emerged. However, the question that remains is if there was a chance for unity, and, how, within six years, such antagonism would come to exist between the two communities.

Renegotiating the Millet System

Over the last decade, the study of the Ottoman Empire following the Young Turk Revolution has taken great strides. The first set of scholars discussed briefly in the Introduction show the euphoric reaction that the urban arenas of the Ottoman lands encountered following the reinstating of the Ottoman constitution, with Jews, Christians and Muslims joining together to celebrate. However, following this, I also described how a new group of scholars are offering a critical response to this literature, arguing for a more nuanced portrait which questions the extent of intercommunal relations. This book falls into the second category in that it challenges a nostalgic depiction of the relations between the different communities in Palestine. Importantly, however, it does not discredit the fact that there *were* relations but rather uses the work of the latter group of scholars as a launching point to reach new conclusions and provide a clearer historical picture of Palestine's last years under Ottoman rule.[97]

This work argues that the *hürriyet* (freedom) and *müsavat* (equality) the Young Turk Revolution promised was never intended to implement a 'horizontal' type of equality between the members of the Empire's different religious and ethnic communities, but rather set up an equal playing field for these ethnic and religious communities.[98] Essentially, this was what I call 'renegotiating the Millet system', which strengthened the notion of a 'civic family of nations', actually fortifying the differences between the different groups, rather than bringing them closer.[99] For the different ethnic (and religious) groups, Ottomanism was exactly that, 'a framework for promoting their identities, languages, and ethno-religious privileges, as well as an empire based on administrative decentralization'.[100] Furthermore, within this new sense of 'civic-Ottomanism', there remained a hierarchy, with the non-Muslim communities having to convince the secular Muslim political elite that their wishes were not detrimental to the Empire. Simply put, the Committee of Union and Progress set up a new reality, transferring the power from the Muslim bureaucracy of the sultan towards a new progressive – much more secular – Muslim political elite, where each community would have to separately renegotiate their demands vis-à-vis this new bureaucratic *metropole*.

It is within this model that the Jewish community in Palestine in the post-1908 revolution functioned: while their participation in multi-religious celebrations and political rallies was an act of a mutual civic-Ottomanism, it was also an act of separation, giving their voice legitimacy and a political space which was lacking under the former regime. Ironically, for them, the act of separation could only be achieved through integration; by becoming full citizens, active within the political realm, they would ensure a new freedom to build and strengthen their own community. It needs to be highlighted here that the dynamics the Jewish community were undergoing in Istanbul were quite different. In the capital of Istanbul, Jews, like Greeks and Armenians, developed a duality, where they 'simultaneously belonged to the broader, more general Ottoman political arena and the narrower, more particular arena' of their own community.[101] However, in Palestine, a local Zionism, fused together with a new community of Sephardic and Ashkenazi groups embracing the Hebrew language, created a new type of cultural nationalism that was not a separatist movement, but one that expanded the prior religious Millet system into one fostering a national identity.

For Palestinians, this had another angle to it, which is crucial to understand. On the one hand, the convergence of Christians and Muslims, socially and politically, which was central to Arabism, continued its course in Palestine. Here Christians did not vie for parliamentary power (although some, like Khalil Sakakini, ran unsuccessfully), allowing the traditional Muslim notables to fill the positions. Their role in the press – *Filastin, al-Karmil, al-Quds* were all run by Christians – during the post-revolution era played a central part in spreading a sense of *Palestinianism* within the public sphere. The Christian–Muslim alliance, both as Arabs and in defending Palestine from the Zionist threat, was championed by this press.[102] By 1914, Christians and Muslims had become one camp on the issue of Zionism and it should be no surprise that, immediately following World War I, the two joined forces with the formation of the Muslim–Christian associations, known for their staunch anti-British and anti-Zionist front.[103]

The Muslim notables, who, during the nineteenth century, became integrated into the Ottoman state, continued their role representing their constituencies, albeit through elections. In this sense, to a great extent the *politics of the notables* continued within the new democratic system, meaning a formalised local leadership would continue to represent the interests of their people. However, the problem was that the new Turkish

Muslim bureaucracy that introduced these democratic institutions did not implement a mechanism where the representatives could actually influence policy change. During the period 1908–14, Palestinian MPs butted heads with Istanbul, with no leeway being made to accommodate the needs and wishes of their constituencies.[104] This is despite the Jerusalem MPs being part of the governing party throughout the Second Constitutional Period, unlike the situation of most Syrians.

Now, what needs to be addressed is how this new political system contributed to the emergence of a local Palestinian political community. For this, an important perspective is offered by Feroz Ahmad, who argues that a new political geography emerged as the result of the divisions of the Empire into electoral districts, stating: 'People unwittingly adopted new local identities and began to see themselves in terms of the newly designated electoral districts.' He continues, 'this was particularly true of the elites of these districts, who were elected by the primary voters and then, as secondary voters elected the deputies from among themselves . . .' and he adds that during the 'three electoral campaigns campaigns – 1908, 1912, 1914 – the sense of localism was strengthened among both the elites and the general public'.[105] Supporting this claim, in this current work it becomes clear that the 1908 revolution created a transition point, where, in the Ottoman Parliament, the Palestinian Jerusalem MPs would become recognised as the 'first-round' defenders of Palestine, and other Arabs, in this case Syrians, 'second-round' defenders. In other words, the very fact that the Jerusalem MPs were Palestinian gave them a source of legitimacy that other Arabs did not have. Adding to this, a new sense of a local political community was also being formed due to the Jerusalem MPs realising the special responsibility they possessed in protecting the homeland.

Within this formula, it is crucial to understand that the voices defending Palestine from among the educated and urban elite merged together with voices of peasants, small landowners and *mukhtars*, the village leaders, who were petitioning the Ottoman state and suffering most at the hands of huge tracts of land being sold to Zionists by their absentee landlords (and also from among Palestinian notables).

As we see, the Young Turk Revolution actually caused a division between Jews and Palestinians. The Jewish community gravitated towards Istanbul, and, within a very short time, they placed their hopes of representation in the Jewish MPs in Parliament, in addition to the Chief Rabbi, Haim Nahum, who, even if not a Zionist, felt a responsibility to represent all Jews, including Zionists, among the many other different communities. For Palestinians, they now united under their leadership in Parliament and the ties between Muslims and Christians within the land were strengthened. Ironically, the Young Turk Revolution offered all equality; however, the system that was put in place created new and at times sharp divisions. This of course was not only true in Palestine but would soon become a common denominator among different ethnic and religious groups living throughout the Empire.

It is within this context that the Palestinian and Jewish communities will be addressed in the following chapters. Certainly, following the 1908 revolution, it was not inevitable that these two communities would have ended up on a track of conflict, lasting over a century. And, certainly, the exiled sultan, Abdülhamid II, had no crystal ball to foresee that one day the Jews would succeed in achieving their goal of transforming Palestine into a Jewish state. Nevertheless, the changes ushered in with the 1908 Young Turk Revolution strengthened the divisions between the two communities. It was during this period that both Jews and Palestinians set out to *claim the homeland*.

Notes

1. Atıf Hüseyin Bey, *Hatıralar*, Turkish Historical Association Library y-225, handbook no. 8, p. 17, quoted in Öke, 'The Ottoman Empire, Zionism, and the Question of Palestine (1880–1908)', *IJMES*, pp. 329–41.
2. DH.ID 1329.Ca.15, 34/18; 14 May 1911, 3/1–2.
3. Krämer, *A History of Palestine*, p. 9.
4. Khalidi, *Palestinian Identity*, p. 29.
5. Volney, *Travels through Syria and Egypt, in the years 1783, 1784, and 1785*. To access, see Google book edition: <https://books.google.com/books?id=G1NFAAAAYAAJ> (last accessed 23 May 2019).
6. Krämer, *A History of Palestine*, p. 62.
7. For more on Umar and Jezzar Pasha, see Yazbak, *Haifa in the Late Ottoman Period, 1864–1914*, pp. 13–20.
8. Even if in essence this was a discriminatory tax, Jews and Christians were relieved from military service; further, Ottoman society was built on hierarchies, and there was never a sense of equality among the Muslim community as well. This would change, however, in the late nineteenth century and beginning of the twentieth century, when the *Tanzimat* reforms and the 1908 Young Turk Revolution put an emphasis on equality among all Ottoman citizens.
9. Shepherd, *The Zealous Intruders*, p. 73.
10. Krämer, *A History of Palestine*, p. 66.
11. J. Finn to Earl of Clarendon, 'Remarks on Political Conditions during the Year 1857'; FO 78/1383–no.1; in Eliav (ed.), *Britain and the Holy Land 1838–1914*, p. 190.

12. Eliav (ed.), *Britain and the Holy Land*, p. 246.
13. H. Trotter to E. Fane, 'Report on Haifa and Jewish Colonization', in *Britain and the Holy Land*, p. 260.
14. Sachar, *A History of Israel*, p. 23.
15. Mazza, *Jerusalem*, p. 11.
16. For examples of books focusing on Palestine's urban areas, see the above-mentioned work on Jerusalem by Roberto Mazza, and the more recent work by Farid al-Salam on Tulkarm and Mahmoud Yazbak's book on Haifa. Doumani, *Rediscovering Palestine*; al-Salim, *Palestine and the Decline of the Ottoman Empire*; Yazbak, *Haifa in the Late Ottoman Period*.
17. Krämer, *A History of Palestine*, p. 91.
18. Doumani, *Rediscovering Palestine*, p. 8.
19. Ibid., p. 10.
20. Mazza, *Jerusalem*, p. 21; Kushner, 'The Ottoman Governors of Palestine, 1864–1914', *Middle Eastern Studies*, p. 275.
21. Büssow, *Hamidian Palestine*, pp. 5, 45, 47 and 57.
22. When reporting on the Jerusalem Governor's trip to Constantinople, the consul stated the following 'I have the honour to report that Subhi Bey, the Governor of Palestine, proceeded to Palestine . . .'; PRO FO 795/3231, 12 July 1909, p. 231.
23. Gribetz, *Defining Neighbors*, pp. 17–18.
24. Sicker, *Reshaping Palestine*, p. 4.
25. Ibid., pp. 7–11.
26. Ibid., p. 16.
27. Sachar, *A History of Israel*, pp. 10–11.
28. Ibid., p. 11.
29. Shapira, *Land and Power*, pp. 3–4.
30. Ibid.
31. Shapira, *Israel*, p. 30.
32. Ibid., p. 3.
33. Ibid., p. 30.
34. See map of Jewish colonies in Shafir, *Land, Labor and the Origins of the Israeli-Palestinian Conflict*, p. xxvi.
35. Krämer, *A History of Palestine*, p. 3.
36. Mandel, *The Arabs and Zionism before World War I*, pp. 2–4.
37. Y. A. Res, 5/58, 9 May 1880, p. 233 (Ottoman Archival Book).
38. Öke, 'The Ottoman Empire, Zionism, and the Question of Palestine (1880–1908)'.
39. BOA.YPRK.BŞK 80/55.
40. *The Jewish Chronicle*, 11 June 1880, p. 4.
41. Ibid., 18 November 1881. Without a doubt, as Mandel notes, this one sentence forged the guidelines for Jewish immigration to the Ottoman lands, and its stance on Palestine for the decades to come.

42. Gelvin, *The Modern Middle East*, p. 91; Shafir, *Land, Labor and the Origins of the Israeli-Palestinian Conflict*, pp. 1–21.
43. Beška, 'Responses of Prominent Arabs towards Zionist Aspirations and Colonization Prior to 1908', *Asian and African Studies*, p. 22.
44. *The Jewish Chronicle*, 28 August 1891, p. 12.
45. Beška, 'Responses of Prominent Arabs towards Zionist Aspirations and Colonization Prior to 1908', pp. 24–5.
46. Khalidi, *Palestinian Identity*, 75.
47. Shafir, *Land, Labor and the Origins of the Israeli-Palestinian Conflict*, pp. 26–7.
48. Mazza, *Jerusalem*, 78.
49. Ibid.
50. MV 1327.C.2, 129/4; 21 June 1909.
51. DH.MKT 1911/115, 14 January 1892, p. 265 (Ottoman Archival Book).
52. MV 1331.L.15, 180/32; 17 September 1913.
53. Ibid.
54. PRO FO 195/2452/1254, 27 October 1913, p. 330.
55. MV 1332.S.27, 184/67; 24 January 1914.
56. Kushner, *To be Governor of Jerusalem*, 193.
57. Ibid.
58. DH.KMS 1332.C.27, 18/41, p. 3.
59. DH.ŞFR 1332.C.27, 41/63; 23 May 1914.
60. DH.KMS 1332.C.27, 18/41; 23 May 1914; and DH.ŞFR 1332.C.27, 41/59; 27 May 1914.
61. DH.ŞFR 1332.B.20, 42/4; 14 June 1914. While not using the word 'bribe', the meaning is clear from language used accusing the bureaucrats of 'su-i istimal istifade (taking advantage)'.
62. Mandel, *The Arabs and Zionism before World War I*, p. 13.
63. *Moriah*, 17 July 1914, p. 2.
64. Unfortunately, in my archival research, I did not come across this document. See Kaiser, 'The Ottoman Government and Zionist Movement during the First Months of World War I', in *Syria in World War I*, p. 107.
65. Mandel, *The Arabs and Zionism before World War I*, p. 21.
66. PRO FO 195/2377, 104B.
67. Sachar, *A History of Israel*, p. 72.
68. McCarthy, *The Population of Palestine*.
69. Ibid., p. 23. According to Ruhi al-Khalidi, in his 1911 speech to the Ottoman Parliament, he estimated that there were 100,000 Jews in the district of Jerusalem. See: Parliament report, p. 557.
70. McCarthy, *The Population of Palestine*, p. 23.
71. Ruppin, *The Jews of To-Day*, p. 284.
72. Karpat, 'Jewish Population Movements in the Ottoman Empire, 1862–1914', in *The Jews of the Ottoman Empire*.
73. Ibid., p. 41.

74. This is also a number that was suggested in a news report coming from Palestine in 1912. *The Times*, 28 September 1912.
75. McCarthy, *The Population of Palestine*, p. 10.
76. Ibid., p. 16.
77. Mandel, *The Arabs and Zionism before World War I*, p. 26.
78. Ibid., p. 27.
79. *The Jewish Chronicle*, 3 April 1908.
80. Ibid. For a look at a previous scuffle that led to a Jewish death and its aftermath, see Halperin, 'A Murder in the Grove', *Journal of Social History*, pp. 427–215.
81. *The Jewish Chronicle*, 10 April 1908.
82. Mandel, *The Arabs and Zionism before World War I*, p. 28.
83. Kayali, *Arabs and Young Turks*, pp. 18–19.
84. Ibid., p. 29.
85. Khalidi, *Palestinian Identity*, pp. 71–3.
86. Kushner, *To be Governor of Jerusalem*, p. 136.
87. Mazza, *Jerusalem*, p. 33.
88. Hourani, 'Ottoman Reform and the Politics of Notables', in *Beginnings of Modernization in the Middle East*.
89. Mazza, *Jerusalem*, p. 32. Mazza comments on the fact that there were also Christian and Jewish notables.
90. Dawn, *From Ottomanism to Arabism*.
91. Cleveland, *The Making of an Arab Nationalist*; Cleveland, *Islam against the West*.
92. Gelvin, *Divided Loyalties*, p. 287. In his recent work on Egypt, Ziad Fahmy investigates 'the agency of ordinary Egyptians in constructing and negotiating national identity', in an attempt to also move away from historiograpd hy that focuses on elite politics in the development of Egyptian territorial nationalism. See Fahmy, *Ordinary Egyptians*, p. xi.
93. Kayali, *Arabs and Young Turks*, see chapter 3.
94. Kushner, *To be Governor of Jerusalem*, p. 137.
95. Kushner, 'Moshel Hayyiti be-Yerushalayim: Ha'ir ve haMa'ahoz be'einav shel Ali Ekrem Bey [A Governor in Jerusalem: the City and District according to Ali Ekrem Bey]', Ali Ekrem Bey's letters translated to Hebrew.
96. While I have only been able to document a few such cases, this phenomenon deserves greater attention in future research.
97. A major turning point in the historiography of Palestine can be attributed to Zachary Lockman's highlighting the problematic nature of writing on Palestine, in which he defined the need to move past the 'dual-society' paradigm. In this work, even if I examine each community to a great extent separately, I have worked to show that the communal identities are not 'natural and pre-given', and that each group's claiming the homeland happened within an Ottoman system, which contributed to the dichotomy of the

two communities working vis-à-vis one another; see Lockman, *Comrades and Enemies*, p. 3.

98. Der Matossian argues that the supreme ideal of the revolution was a 'political system in which individuals would participate as citizens of the empire rather than as members of disparate ethnic blocs'. However, he goes on to explain that this was an unsuccessful goal. See Der Matossian, *Shattered Dreams of Revolution*, p. 7.

99. Wallach, 'Rethinking the Yishuv', *Journal of Modern Jewish Studies*, p. 288.

100. Der Matossian, *Shattered Dreams of Revolution*, p. 7.

101. Nobuyoshi, 'Patriarchal Crisis of 1910 and Constitutional Logic', *Journal of Modern Greek Studies*, p. 19.

102. I did not include al-Nafir, also Christian ran, and supported by Zionists. Gribetz, *Defining Neighbors*, p. 192.

103. Mazza, *Jerusalem*, p. 69.

104. Ottoman Palestinian history will hopefully in the future branch off into this realm of works beyond the conflict, looking towards other issues that interested, worried and preoccupied Palestinians during this period.

105. Ahmad, *The Young Turks*, p. 113.

2

The Emergence of a Collective Palestinian Identity

Oh Palestine! You have slept for so long
Oh Palestine! Your glory is withering away
Oh my people, if we only knew our reality
We would weep [and mourn] over the [loss of the] land . . .
Oh my homeland! You have fallen into the hands of the enemy.
You have been plundered and are under the injustice of those who hate.
My land! Save my homeland!
My heart, spirit, and soul . . .

This is an excerpt from an Arabic poem published in July 1914 in two Palestinian newspapers, first in Haifa's *al-Karmil*, and then reprinted in the Jaffa-based *Filastin*.[1] The poem captures an early look at a collective Palestinian identity, prevalent among both Christians and Muslims, during the last years of the Ottoman period. Notably, the poem expresses a sense of despair, serving as a marked example of how even before World War I some Palestinians understood that their homeland was in danger of being lost to the small Jewish community of Palestine. The poem serves to shatter the myth that a Palestinian identity only emerged later during the years of the British Mandate, and registers the fact that a local patriotism among its Arab residents was prevalent and specifically directed towards Palestine, and not Syria as some have argued in earlier scholarship. This document, when placed within the context of other newspaper articles and Ottoman petitions sent to Istanbul by the Palestinians, shows us how a pattern of fear, that they were in danger of losing their homeland, was real and widespread. In other words, this poem should not be seen as an exception, but rather representative of attitudes in the period.

Following the poem's publication in Arabic, a Hebrew translation of it was featured in *Moriah*, one of Jerusalem's Jewish newspapers, in a section dedicated to 'Headlines from the Arabic press'.[2] The fact that the

poem was featured in the Hebrew press also provides us with an opportunity to see how some Jews, depicted here as the 'aggressors', perceived
Palestinian opposition to Jewish migration. Commenting on the poem,
the Jewish author states that the newspapers '*al-Karmil* and *Filastin* are
the most anti-Semitic press in Syria; and, in order to increase the hate
among the local population towards us, our enemies (the editors of these
papers) have also started to publish anti-Jewish poems'.[3] What is even
more striking is that *Moriah* was not aligned with the Zionist movement,
but was rather identified with the Hasidic movement. Nevertheless, as we
see in other cases as well, the Palestinians' depiction of their Jewish neighbours was placed in the context of anti-Semitism, and not anti-Zionism.
In fact, during the years before World War I, Jews in Palestine, regardless if Ashkenazi or Sephardi, often perceived the Palestinian opposition to the Jewish community as motivated by anti-Semitism, and not
out of Palestinian fears of growing Jewish dominance. Moreover, with
Palestinians raising objections to the continued Jewish migration, it needs
to be highlighted that even before the breakout of World War I, the Jewish
community in Palestine – whether anti-Zionist or Zionist, Sephardic or
Ashkenazi, Ottoman citizen or immigrant – realised that their presence
there was now being challenged.

Although there is no mention of the Ottoman administrators in the poem,
this in no way indicates that their presence was absent from the debate.
Palestinian editors were well aware that such language was pushing the
limits of what the authorities were willing to tolerate. Just months before
this, *Filastin* was briefly shut down by the Ottoman government (for a
third time) for publishing an article that contained 'anti-Jewish' content.[4]
In fact, it seems that the government only became aware of the incident
after the Ottoman state's Chief Rabbi in Istanbul, Rabbi Haim Nahum,
complained about its hateful language to a government minister. This
we learn from a story that appeared in Istanbul's major Judeo-Spanish
newspaper *El Tiempo*, also known for its staunch anti-Zionist stance,
and subsequently reported in *Moriah*. It is important to state that even
though Nahum was not a Zionist, he perceived the articles as hateful,
and, as the representative of all Jews in the Ottoman lands, including the
Jewish community in Palestine, he took steps to block the newspapers'
free expression. This case was not an isolated one since as far back as
1910 the Chief Rabbi had intervened on behalf of the Jewish community
in Palestine in Istanbul, claiming that the Palestinian newspaper *al-Karmil*
was founded to 'spread discord and sow dissension between the Jews and
other Ottomans'.[5]

Also important here is the fact that the absence of Ottoman authority in the poem reflects that the Palestinians saw themselves as alone in their struggle, with the Ottoman state unable, or at times even unwilling, to place a halt on Jewish immigration and land sales. This of course was not a foregone conclusion. However, as more lands were purchased by the Zionist movement and Jews continued to make their way to their spiritual homeland – and for some now a national one – this was the general trend. This fact cannot be underestimated and would greatly contribute to different Palestinian groups uniting in this struggle. Further, even if the Palestinians at times received solidarity and support from their Arab cohorts in Syria and Lebanon, in practical terms this had little influence on Ottoman policy.

A daunting task for scholars of Palestine is writing the Palestinians into their own history, with its majority of peasants and townspeople missing from historical narratives.[6] Without a 'live portrait of a Palestinian people',[7] it has been a long journey to understanding the roots of a Palestinian identity, which for years had been claimed as a post-World War I phenomenon and only a reaction to Zionism.[8] In the next two chapters, it will become apparent that attaching a political identity to Palestine's Arab population's mutual sense of belonging to the land is not a divergence from the historical reality, but rather a necessary step at historicising *Palestinianism* in the late Ottoman era. Further, while this identity was far from composing a full-blown nationalism, it certainly serves as a marker in time, when patriotism and perceptions of a home-land did not need political borders to define a people's existence and collective struggle.

One question that has been at the centre of Palestinian history is, when did the Palestinians begin to think of themselves as 'Palestinians'?[9] During the Ottoman Second Constitutional Period, 1908–14, I argue, a unique local Palestinian sense of being emerged, and even before the First World War, we see that the Arabs of Palestine had begun to form into a unified people. However, it is crucial to understand that this new collective loyalty, similar to the emergence of other local identities in the Ottoman state's Arab regions, was not a separatist nationalism that aspired towards statehood, but one that induced an awareness among Palestine's Arab community that they were locked in a similar fate and only by joining forces would they be able to secure their special interests.[10] Further, this new sense of *Palestinianism*, as previously explained, coexisted with their religious (Islam and Christianity), ethnic (Arab) and national (Ottoman) identities.

Surveying Ottoman documents and the local Palestinian press dem-onstrate that essentially a local patriotism did not merely emerge as a reaction to the Zionist movement, but also in reaction to the encroachment of British imperialism and the influx of Western culture, as well as the Ottoman state's inability to protect holy sites, and the mass corruption prevalent among local administrators; all of which counter the claim that Palestinian identity was merely a reaction to the Zionist movement.[11] Adding to this, Palestinians started to realise during this period that the land they inhabited was contested and that Jewish immigration and the growing presence of Europeans stood as a challenge to their existence. This fear was exacerbated by the simultaneous flow of Palestinian emigrants out of Palestine, which was directly related to the continuing land disputes between the two communities. In fact, it was all of these dynamics merging together that must have motivated them to begin to define themselves during this period as *Palestinians*, and to adopt the modern term, *al-Sha'b al-Filastini* (the Palestinian people),[12] and, in 1914, even as *al-Umma al-Filistiniyya* (the Palestinian Nation).[13]

Land Disputes and Peasants

Where Zionism did not pose an immediate threat to the urban centres of Palestine, the reality was different for peasants who were gradually becoming landless. To begin with, most of the land the peasants lived and worked on was not owned by them but rather by notables, or *effendis*, often absentee landlords from Beirut, who, following the 1858 Ottoman land reforms, registered the lands in their names, exploiting peasant fears that by registering the land in their own names they would be targeted with conscription and taxes.[14]

With the steady flow of Jewish immigration beginning in 1881, the value of land rapidly increased, and, much to the peasants' dismay, the *effendis* began to sell huge tracts to the Zionists, or to other absentee landlords who it was feared were working on behalf of the Zionist movement. These land sales often lead to clashes between peasants and the Jewish newcomers, and sometimes even led to the peasants' evictions.[15]

During the period after the 1908 revolution, the eviction of peasants and the growing clashes between Palestinian peasants and Jewish settlers was one of the main factors that made Zionism central to Arab political discourse before World War I.[16] While Arab newspapers in Palestine and Syria reported on the peasant plight and the lands being lost to Zionist control, Palestinian local leaders also created new bonds with the peasant class through petitions written to local Ottoman administrators, or directly to the central government in Istanbul.

The joining together of the notables with the peasant class should be seen as a crucial factor in the creation of a Palestinian identity that would cross social and religious boundaries. In fact, the peasants' role in the creation of a national identity is universal, as we see in the case of Russian nationalism and other types of European nationalist movements. Also, among the Jewish national movement as it falls within the scope of this research, we see that the Labour Zionists worked towards the creation of a new Jew who would be tied to the land and agriculture to fill this gap in nationalist cultural mythology.

Much closer to Palestine, the Egyptian national movement transformed into a nationalist struggle when the urban elite recognised the need to incorporate the peasant cause, a development that was marked by the Dinshaway incidents of 1906.[17] Taking place in British-occupied Egypt, the incidents were characterised by clashes that broke out between villagers and British officers, who were pigeon-shooting in the village of Dinshaway. In a series of events that began with a barn being set on fire by a stray bullet, a wife of a villager was injured, a British officer was killed and an innocent bystander, a *fallah*, who was actually helping the injured officer, was beaten to death by British troops. Subsequently, the village was collectively punished with four villagers executed and twenty-one sentenced to prison or flogging. This injustice struck the attention of the Egyptian public, especially that of the anti-British politicians and journalists, turning it into a watershed moment with the *effendiya*, the country's elite, forging an imaginative linkage with the country's peasants, in what scholar Zachary Lockman argues transformed the peasants for the first time into 'Egyptians', with nationalist intellectuals now imagining the nation as including also 'the peasants and the urban lower class'.[18]

Unlike that of Egypt, the place of the peasants within the historiography of the Palestinian–Israeli conflict only emerges in the post-World War I era. In fact, in his ground-breaking 1970s book on the roots of the Arab–Israeli conflict, Neville Mandel points out that

> the *fellahin* formed the majority of the population of Palestine. But they were inert, socially and politically, and by the end of the nineteenth century their sheikhs had lost most, if not all, their political power. Thus, while their reactions to the Jewish colonies set up in their midst are interesting, they are not central.

Unfortunately, even though this book was written in the 1970s, many of the new works that look at late Ottoman Palestine focus on Jewish–Arab relations within the urban sphere and do not calculate within their narratives the Palestinian peasantry (the majority of the population).[19]

The disregarding of the importance of the peasants overlooks how, like in Egypt, the educated and urban Arab elite in Palestine became highly conscious of the peasants' plight, adopting it as a cause and making it central in forming a cross-the-board struggle whereby land disputes were turned into national issues, and not merely sidelined as vague questions about why the new Jewish farmers were unable to reach understandings with their Arab neighbours. In one commentary discussing the role of the newspaper *Filastin*, a contributor to the paper highlighted that this newspaper was the 'only paper defending the rights of the peasant';[20] however, as we will see, other newspapers, like Jerusalem's *al-Quds*, with time also started to raise the plight of the peasant. Nevertheless, for the newspaper *Filastin*, educating the masses was a defined mission. For example, the editors made sure that a copy of each edition was sent out to the *mukhtar* of every village that had a population of 100 people or more, with a great number of the villages located within a close proximity to the Jewish colonies located near Jaffa. The dispatching of the newspapers was done in order to show the peasant 'what is happening in the country, and to teach him his rights, in order to prevent those who do not fear God and his prophets from dominating him and stealing his goods'.[21] The fact that these papers were being read aloud in public spaces, such as cafes or during village events, allowed peasants, villagers and urban folk alike to become aware that tensions with the Jewish community were not merely isolated ones, but a growing phenomenon throughout Palestine. It was also key to creating bonds between different parts of the society, with peasants and villagers forming new ties with urban populations, importantly, not only Muslim but also Christian; local understandings of Palestine were now being merged with a terminology of intellectuals, forging new understandings and bonds of *Palestinianism*.

The power of the spoken word in the age when newspapers were read out aloud in public venues is summarised well by Egyptian historian Ziad Fahmy, who argues that 'active public readings and the inevitable conversations and discussions such readings were bound to trigger contrast rather vividly with the more cerebral, silent, and entirely visual type of reading described by Benedict Anderson in *Imagined Communities*'.[22] In fact, there were many venues for those who did not read (or did not have access to newspapers) to receive information, with news being relayed at mosques, on local pilgrimages and through rumours. Moreover, newspapers were often read in marketplaces and discussed among friends. Certainly, with some imagination on our part, it is not hard to understand how important the role of the press was in helping connect the dots between the different communities, allotting them the ability to *imagine* themselves as a community connected by a common fate.

The purchasing of lands, which led to the eviction of peasants and clashes with the new Jewish farmers, affected different regions of Palestine and caused a wave of unrest in 1910–11 in Palestine's northern region, along the Jordan River valley, and in the lands south of Jaffa on the road to Gaza city. In all these cases, the interaction between the different strata of Palestinian society to block the Zionist land purchases created this bond between the uneducated and educated, peasants and village leaders, and the rural leadership and the urban one. In essence, the emerging dynamic was one of common nationwide struggle. Emanuel Beška, a scholar focusing on this period, explains that 'the relatively short period at the turn of the year 1910–1911 was of profound importance for the development of political opposition to Zionism in Palestine and its neighboring Arab regions'.[23]

The most well documented of these cases of political opposition was the Fula land sale in the Jezreel Valley, which was known by the Palestinians by its Arabic name, Marj ibn 'Amir. It comprised an area of about ten square kilometres and included the region's most fertile soil.[24] The sale by Elias Sursuq, an absentee landlord who resided in Beirut, to the Jewish National Fund (JNF) – a Zionist organisation founded in 1901 that aimed to purchase lands in Palestine for Jewish settlement – was seen as a major Zionist success. Once the title deed of 10,000 dunams was handed over to the JNF in February 1911, Arabs were evicted and tensions ran high. Just three months later, the situation deteriorated when a Jewish guardsman of the new settlement of Merhavia killed an Arab.[25]

While headlines about this event eventually brought the Ottoman administration into an open battle of words with Arab politicians, almost two years before the incident, in May 1910, the local village *mukhtar* petitioned the Ottoman state, calling for their assistance to stop this injustice. This petition, which counters Mandel's previously mentioned derogatory description of the non-central nature of Palestinian peasants' interactions with Jewish settlers, was made in a telegram to Istanbul in May 1910 and serves as perhaps one of the first rural voices we receive, in which the *mukhtar*, 'Abd al-'Isa, expressed his deep sorrow over the land sale:

> Elias Sursuq, who owns our village lands, has sold our lands to the Zionist Society, stomping upon our Ottoman nobility. From time immemorial, we have accepted Ottoman rule . . . we refuse to submit to the rule of a group of foreigners . . . Our children and families, which numbers more than a thousand, will need assistance to live and we [no longer] have property and land. We will remain homeless and our children and families will become slaves; we asked for your help that we do not become slaves to Jews.[26]

The unfiltered voice of the *mukhtar* demonstrates that while Jews and Arabs often worked together, even sometimes living in the same neighbourhood, for rural Arabs, the meaning of Ottoman nobility and a hegemonic Muslim status was well imbedded within their worldview. Despite the strong – and discriminatory – words, negating the ideas of the Young Turk Revolution, the Ottoman Ministry of Interior took 'Abd al-'Isa's words with the utmost seriousness, and within three days of receiving the telegram contacted Beirut's governor to enquire about his complaint. However, from the brief response ordering an investigation, it seems the Ottoman authorities were completely unprepared for the wave of opposition they would receive and the sheer amount of attention the event gathered. What would follow would be a collection of tens of documents – spanning almost two years – on the land sale, reflecting the bureaucratic quagmire the Palestinians faced. The case was made even more difficult due to the fact that Fula was attached to Akka, with correspondences and telegrams being sent back and forth from Beirut, Istanbul and Jerusalem, between different ministries and local administrations. In fact, the purchase of Fula lands seems to have been facilitated by the fact that just months before the sale, the district of Nazareth was returned to the jurisdiction of Beirut, after it had been detached three years earlier and placed under that of Jerusalem. The British consul in Jerusalem explained in a report that it being under Jerusalem's administration was inconvenient, since

> Nazareth can only be reached from Jerusalem via Nablous or via Haiffa, both of which belong to the vilayet of Beirout. One reason for uniting it with Jerusalem perhaps – perhaps the only one – was to facilitate the journey of pilgrims, who would not be required to procure tezkeres (permission documents) [these documents granted people permission to move from one district to another] . . .[27]

The Ottoman governor of Jerusalem, Subhi, claimed that due to Nazareth's distance, it was difficult to administer from Jerusalem and that it should be returned to Akka's administration, with the necessary process taking place in Istanbul to return it to its former status.[28] However, the point needs to be made that if it had remained under Jerusalem's jurisdiction it is hard to imagine that such a huge land sale would have been approved by its governor.

Leading the protest was Nazareth's Kaimakam (shortly thereafter becoming an MP representing Syria), Shukri al-Asali, a Damascene and graduate of Istanbul's prestigious university, the *Mekteb-i Mülkiye*. He did his utmost to prevent the sale of land, making headway in the local Arab press in Syria and Palestine by writing numerous articles under the pen name Saladin.[29] He made a plea for the Ottoman government to purchase the land from the Lebanese Sursuq, or to sell it to those farming it in instalments. Asali went so far as to use his administrative position to stop the title deed being handed over to the Zionists, only to have the governor of Beirut, Nurettin Bey, use his higher position to force him to comply. Once again this was delayed when he appealed to the military headquarters in Akka to stop the sale; at last, the Ministry of Interior interfered declaring the sale legal as the purchaser was an Ottoman citizen. Upon claims that the new owner was a disloyal citizen he answered that his brother was even in the Ottoman army.[30] According to Khalidi,

> the al-Fula incident became a cause célèbre . . . with dozens of articles appearing in newspapers in Damascus, Beirut, Haifa, and elsewhere over a year . . . [and that] it was the spectacle of Arab peasants resisting expulsion from their homes and lands to make room for foreign colonists which gave this incident its potent impact for most Arab audiences.[31]

Despite the wide coverage, and Asali's new position as the Member of Parliament representing the district of Damascus, the fact that he was an opposition member greatly limited his ability to make progress against Zionist settlement (as will be discussed in Chapter 4). Nevertheless, the Ottoman administration did not sit quietly and argued that their move was justified, with Beirut's governor addressing Asali in Beirut's press. Nurettin Bey was adamant that he would not address Asali's accusations, but thought it was only right to put the record straight:

> every one that is educated in the laws of liberty and freedom, knows that the first obligation of an enlightened government is to ensure the rights of its people, and every man can do what he pleases, as long as it does not break the law.

Clearly he was alluding to the fact that the person purchasing the land was an Ottoman citizen, and within the new system of freedoms it would have been inconceivable to block the sale of land.

Even if Nurettin Bey brushed it aside, the Ottoman administration embarked on investigations into the claims of Asali, who was working hard to find a loop-hole in order to cancel the land sale; one such was that to claim the land was a matter of state security since Fula was in close proximity to the Hijaz Railway lines, and the fact that it was also home to the fortress of Saladin, and held other historical archaeological importance.[32]

Closer to home it was also during this period that the Arab press in Palestine started to speak up in the name of the peasant. One article appeared in the moderate, pro-government *al-Quds*, appearing on the front page, one that was usually reserved for events in Istanbul or international news; and, even if the article did not mimic Asali's raucous tone (who seemed motivated not only by the injustice done to the peasants but also by his sheer hate of the government), the article serves as an example of how urban Palestinians began to adopt the peasant cause. In his article, 'Rufaqa bil-Fallah', the author, Anton Shukri Lorens, starts by saying,

> this is our land, known for its fertileness and its quality crops and our country is without a doubt the centre of good agriculture and Palestine especially – with it already being said in the Old Testament that it is the land of milk and honey.

The author then goes on to describe the strength of the peasant, saying that 'this *fellah* of ours is already known for his solid structure, the strength of his forearms, and continues to work the length of the day, and his body endures exhaustion and tiredness'. Later, he continues and expands on the notion that no attention is being paid to what is happening in the land, while foreigners understand its potential. Towards the end, the author quickly comes to his point:

> the land is our land, and the fellah is our brother, so why do we not help him in his work? And, why is the government placing pressure on him, and not on the foreign colonists of our land? The fellah is the source of our prosperity in this land . . . [the fellah] is our provider of food and nourishment . . .[33]

While this story of the Fula sale has been discussed in previous works, the similar case of Baysan proves an important comparison, as here also a huge tract of land was set to be sold to Zionists despite the overwhelming opposition of the local population. However, unlike Fula, Baysan was one of numerous privately held lands, *çiftliks*, owned by the former sultan, Abdülhamid II, which were to be sold by the Young Turk government to generate income for the state. In total, the ousted sultan owned 56 million dunams located in the Arab provinces of the Ottoman lands, of which 115 tracts covering some 832,333 metric dunams were in Palestine.[34] One source quoted the Baysan *çiftlik* of comprising 390,000 dunams,[35] or almost half of the former sultan's estate in Palestine.

During the years 1909–14, similar to other regions of the Empire, the planned sale of the Baysan *çiftlik* turned into a major point of contention between the Palestinians and the Ottoman state, which was exacerbated by the fact that it was feared that Zionists were out to purchase the lands through intermediaries, such as Najib Asfar from Beirut. While this was adamantly denied by the Ottoman authorities, and recorded as such in the historical research, it seems clear that this very well could have been the case with the Jewish press closely following the sale of the *çiftlik*s to the potential buyer, Asfar.

The first news of lands being auctioned off in Palestine came just months after Abdülhamid II had abdicated in the summer of 1909, and was announced in the Hebrew newspaper *HaTzvi*, which highlighted the impressive amounts of *çiftliks* to be sold at prices much cheaper than the market value.[36] Over a year later, the issue was once again brought up in a Hebrew newspaper in Warsaw, which mentioned that the Ottoman government had not changed their stance on forbidding Zionists from purchasing the land in the Jordan Valley (Baysan) and that there was a danger that it would be sold to Christians in Beirut acting as intermediaries for the Zionists.[37]

The fear of sales had also reached a peak as a result of the above Fula incident and the case of land sales to Sursuq was now compared to that of Asfar. In fact, Asali turned to the press to vent his anger, using the pen name Saladin to publish numerous articles in the Syrian *al-Muqtabas*, and reprinted in Haifa's *al-Karmil*. In one of the articles in *al-Muqtabas*, Saladin appeals to the Ottoman generals to confront Zionism:

> I beg you ... to hurry up and repel the Zionist threat from Palestine, whose soil soaked with the blood of the Prophet's companions and with the blood of the armies and for which retrieval I have sacrificed [the lives] of my brothers, my people, my commanders.[38]

As if this was not enough, he also published in Istanbul's *al-Hadara*.[39] The Hebrew *HaHerut* followed these highly provocative calls against Zionism as well, translating them into Hebrew. In the *al-Hadara* article, Asali highlighted the role Asfar was to play in purchasing lands for the Jewish settlement company, which was in the 'hands of foreign powers', and that 'most [people] did not have a clue about the purchasing and sales of Palestinian lands'.[40] The author went on to criticise Abdülhamid II, whose administration poorly managed the Empire's land, and even accused the sultan of actually stealing lands for his own benefit. According to Asali, the major outcome of this was the suffering of the peasant: 'Allah Allah! (for God's sake), the state of the peasant is dreadful here'.[41] He then went on to rhetorically challenge the new regime, stating 'now that the light of freedom and liberty has come upon us, is it still possible to allow land to be sold to Najib al-Asfar? Do you not see [that] the Zionist movement [is behind this]? Are you blind to the Zionist movement?' The words of *al-Hadara* were heeded, and, just two months later, it was reported that Istanbul had refused to sell the Baysan tract of land, or for that fact any of the lands in Syria and Palestine, as it is was rumoured that Asfar was planning to buy up all of the former lands of Abdülhamid II in that region.[42]

For the Palestinians, the possible sale of the land, whether to the Zionists or Najib Asfar, was of growing concern, something which is documented both in the Ottoman archives and the local Palestinian press. The Ottoman authorities were well aware of this due to the influx of numerous petitions dispatched to the capital. The issue continued to plague relations between the government and the Palestinians; the latter group came to include not only Baysan's local population but also the notables of Palestine's southern cities. Asali recalled the words of former Ottoman lawmaker Atıf Bey, who once legislated that the peasant has preferential status over the owner of the land. In other words, even if land is purchased by a new owner the peasant should not be removed from it. Lastly, he reminded the government of the fact that peasants are on the land, and this fact should not be ignored when the lands are being sold to foreigners and companies.[43] Later, following the Daran example below, the Baysan's case will be discussed more in detail, a case that by 1913 had become a major point of contention between Palestinians and the central government.

Palestinian Emigration: The Case of Daran

In a December 1912 article published in the newspaper *al-Mufid*, we learn that: 'the people of the country emigrate to America, while the Zionists immigrate into our country: one day, if things go on like this, the Arab in his own country will become worse off than an orphan at the tables of the stingy'.[44] In fact, scholars working on Palestinian population numbers, both contemporary and historically, show that fears of a diminishing Palestinian population in the face of Jewish immigration was not unfounded. Perhaps what is more surprising is how historians of modern Palestine have not factored this into their historical analysis. While the statistics do not break down how many emigrating Arabs were actually from Palestine, even if these were considerably fewer in number than the emigrating Syrians and Lebanese, a small number of Jews arriving in Palestine could be enough to offset the balance between the two communities.

During the period 1860–1914, the regions of Syria (Palestine included) and Lebanon witnessed a massive emigration of their peoples to the Americas, which was estimated at 330,000 in total with about 15,000 leaving annually during the period 1900–14,[45] and if we look at the period from 1860–1914, it could have reached up to 600,000 emigrants leaving the region.[46] With such high numbers, which do not even include the large numbers of immigrants – Armenian and Turk – going to the Americas, it is a bit surprising that the Ottoman authorities did not pay more attention to it, even if Ottoman consuls abroad were alarmed by it.[47] This of course also must have included the emigration of peasants away from their rural communities, and not just to urban arenas within Palestine; this peasant immigration became of increasing concern to village leaders.

Similar to the Syrian emigration, Palestinians leaving the country were thought to be overwhelmingly Christian and not Muslim, but the 'overwhelming' aspect of this assumption turns out to be incorrect. Karpat shows us that from among the overall Ottoman emigration 15–20 per cent were Muslim.[48] During the migration to the Americas there are also numerous documented cases of Muslims taking on Christian names, with some even converting to Christianity in order to make their migration process and acclimation to the new lands easier.[49] At the height of World War I, Arthur Ruppin, a Zionist representative, wrote a report on Muslim migration.[50] Ruppin begins by describing the known emigration from the predominantly Christian principalities Bethlehem, Beyt Jala and Ramallah; however, he goes on to mention a report produced by the American consul of Jerusalem that states in 1913 3,000 mostly young men, of whom 30 per cent were Christians, 35 per cent Jews and 35 per cent Mohammedans, left Palestine from the district of Jerusalem.[51]

In addition to the migration abroad, Muslims (and Jews) were migrating to Jaffa from other cities, such as Hebron, Gaza and Jerusalem, including both peasants and merchants.[52] In fact, according to the Muslim population census conducted by the Ottoman state, this migration affected all the neighbourhoods in Jaffa, and, along with foreign workers (such as Egyptians), made upto 21 per cent of the combined populations of five central neighbourhoods.[53]

In addition to Ruppin's work on emigration, his early references show that Muslims in Palestine suffered from a relatively high infant mortality rate,[54] and an overall higher mortality rate due to epidemic diseases.[55] In a September 1913 speech to the 11th Zionist Congress in Vienna entitled 'A General Colonization Policy', he stated the following:

> We shall have to come to terms with the fact that the Jews of Palestine, who number one hundred thousand in a total population of seven hundred thousand, will have to wait several decades before they become a majority, this is in spite of the fact that their natural rate of increase seems to be higher than that of the non-Jews of Palestine. At the beginning of the Zionist movement the opinion was widely prevalent that Palestine was an empty country, and it is possible that all our policies have until now been based on erroneous assumptions. Since then we have had to unlearn and learn much . . .[56]

What emerges here is that key Zionist leaders such as Ruppin foresaw that despite the fact that the Jewish community comprised the absolute minority, it was certainly in their reach to become the majority within 'decades'.

This would be achievable not only through Jewish immigration, but relied also on Palestinians leaving, and a high Jewish birth-rate to counter the Palestinian birth-rate, which, as noted before, suffered from a high infant mortality rate. From the cases below, it is clear that Palestinians were also aware of the fact that continued emigration put them in danger of becoming a minority within their homeland.

Peasant Tribulations and Emigration

In a 1911 telegraph dispatched to Istanbul, Palestinian urban notables from Gaza stated their concerns over rampant corruption, the loss of land and the emigration of peasants. In this document we also see the growing despair and a new-found expression of identity with the Land of Palestine and the need to protect it:

> Azmi Bey, and his relations with Jerusalem's notables and Gaza's kaimmakam (head administrator) and mayor, and the members of its administration, and its former Mufti, who is currently residing in Constantinople, and other notables of Jaffa and Beer Sheeba [have set as their purpose] to steal the money of the umma, [and] to embezzle the treasury money. Blood has been shed, disgrace has occurred, public order has been occupied, security no longer exists, and the present continuous emigration [of Arabs] needs your immediate attention ... In conclusion ... what is going on in the district in general and Gaza in particular ... will increase ... Palestine is a dear land [*filastin bilad 'aziza*], home of the Prophets and religion [*din*], protect her in the name of God, faithful men of the state, help us with a just investigation.[57]

Just two years later, we see once again a growing Palestinian urgency to press the Ottoman administration to act on the 1913 Daran Petition. In this, a group of village leaders, *mukhtar*s, voiced their fears of emigration and loss of land at the height of a clash that took place between the Jewish farming colony of Rehovot (Daran) and the adjacent Arab village of Zarnuqa, which left an Arab and a Jew dead.[58] Like the petition above, the Daran Petition also originated from the southern region of Palestine. Importantly, since the first settlers arrived in the region, establishing Rehovot in 1890, clashes between the new Jewish settlers and the local Arab population would become commonplace with the locals writing numerous similar petitions before 1908, quite similar to the ones examined here.[59] Not surprisingly, earlier that year the British consul discussed the rampant corruption in the Gaza district, when a Jewish settlement was established as the result of a twenty-pound bribe paid to a 'very high official', and that 'a great deal of bribery is going on, as the Jews now seem to experience no difficulties in the acquisition of land whereas last summer the Authorities steadily refused to allow any transfers to be made to them'.[60]

In the Daran Petition, after praising the Sublime Porte, the *mukhtar*s set off in assertive language uncommon among the bureaucratic and notable classes. The tone of the petition, coupled with the fact that it was written in Arabic with no Turkish translation, must have made it clear to Istanbul that the source was a more uneducated group of leaders. Their status was recognised by the signers themselves, who pleaded that 'in the execution of law, there should be no differentiation between a peasant (*fallah*) or a city dweller (*madani*), between rich and poor, and between a Muslim, a Christian, and a Jew . . .' and that:

> The Jews discussed herein have extended their oppression upon the people of our villages, they have committed murder, plundered and displayed acts of disgrace in a way that it is impossible to describe . . . the terrible agony and the disturbance is reaching such a point that even God has not heard of such things. If this oppression continues we will be forced to emigrate from our land despite our love (*muhabbatna*) and loyalty (*sadaqatna*) towards it.[61]

They go on to accuse, along with the new Jewish immigrants, 'foreign Circassians', who, while serving as guards, carry illegal weapons and cause havoc, beating and robbing passers-by, who for the most part are among the peasantry (*fallahin*).

This group of *mukhtar*s and local imams bring forth the voice of the Palestinian *fallah*, who not only perceived the Jewish immigrants as 'foreign' but also the Circassians, who were Muslim. This is significant since their opposition was not directed towards the Jewish population because of their religion or ethnicity, but was based on their actions and land acquisitions. No less important, this document provides the chance to hear the voice of the Palestinian peasant, a rarity when dealing with the Ottoman period. Lastly, it provides evidence of the growing dependency of the *mukhtar*s on the *fallahin*, who were coming to terms with the fact that if the *fallahin* were leaving the land, their own existence would be endangered.

Ted Swedenburg has addressed the issue of interdependence between the different strata of Palestinian society in his noteworthy article on the Palestinian peasantry in the Great Arab Revolt of 1936–9.[62] His background discussion concerns the breakdown of the patron–client relationship between the landowners and peasants during the late Ottoman era and its continued effects during the Mandate period. According to Swedenburg, as a result of the 1858 Ottoman land law, 'notable patrons used their power and influence to assist their peasant clients in dealing both with the state and with other groups . . . In return, peasants supported their patrons in political struggles'. He writes that this 'hierarchical relation between notable and peasant appeared to involve a high degree of mutuality and reciprocity'.[63] However, this reality was shaken by Zionist immigration and the displacement of peasants, which left the notables without the patronage to which they had grown accustomed.

The Internal Security department of Istanbul's Ministry of Interior seems to be where peasants' complaints were forwarded, such as the Daran Petition. In another case, the Internal Security department contacted Jerusalem's governor Mecid Bey, along with Jaffa's commissioner, about an alleged clash between Jewish settlers and Palestinian peasants.[64] In a July 1914 telegraph, Istanbul demanded an investigation in relation to newspaper reports of a local Muslim who, while crossing an orange grove owned by Zionists, 'was hung to a tree by his feet [by Zionists], flogged, and then apprehended and tortured'.[65] Interestingly, the archival dossier contains the draft and final enquiry, revealing a split within the Istanbul government over how to deal with Palestinian complaints. Originally, the order inserted a harsh warning to the Zionists, 'beware Zionists! (Turkish: *Siyonistler'e zinhar*)'. However, in the final draft, these words were omitted.[66]

While details of the incident were not in the text in the Ottoman documents, the Hebrew press covered it, basing their story, which strikingly resembles the case above, on an Egyptian paper. In the early months of 1914, Jerusalem's governor Mecid Bey, questioned by a journalist about a 'poor *fallah*' who was beaten in Tel Aviv then placed in a 'special prison', was asked whether it was true that a large number of notables of Jaffa had sent him a telegram concerning this. The governor replied:

> I wrote the Commissioner of Jaffa about conducting an investigation stressing the seriousness of this. However, following this, I received word from him denying any matter relating to the residents of Tel Aviv: There was no prison found, as claimed. And if it would have been found it certainly would have been destroyed.[67]

The case of the beaten peasant once again confirms some points crucial to this work. First, similarly to the Daran Petition, there was a break between the local Ottoman administration and the local notables. Where the local notables were convinced that a crime had taken place, the government completely disregarded it. This story would eventually reach Istanbul, only to return once again to the governor, with no guarantees that it would be treated with the seriousness the local Arab population demanded.

The Final Straw: Palestinians Unite

By 1913, the Palestinians had begun to unite to combat the land sales and the continued migration of peasants from the land, and from Palestine in general. Especially evident was their frustration with the Ottoman government, demonstrating a growing sense of urgency in their demands that Jewish immigration be halted, which emerges both in the local press and in petitions that were directed to Istanbul. Further, in the 1914 parliamentary elections these issues became the centre of campaigns among some of the candidates.

In spring 1913, after almost three years of tension between the Palestinians and the Ottoman government over the possible sale of the Baysan *çiftlik*, once again Baysan would make the news headlines. However, given the previous Fula incident in northern Palestine and the growing sense of Palestinian frustration with developments in the southern region, as portrayed in the Daran Petition, the Baysun land sale was a testament to the fact that Palestine in all of its regions was under imminent danger of being lost to the growing Jewish migration. So much so that in one article in *Filastin*, the editor called for Palestinians to unite and create a national fund, similar to the Jewish National Fund, which would collectively purchase land that was under threat of being purchased by the Zionist movement. What is remarkable is that the Palestinians finally did establish a fund to buy lands; however, this only came to fruition first with the founding of the Arab Land Fund, which was briefly in existence in the early 1930s, and then again with the Arab National Fund established in 1944, during the latter part of the British Mandate. The fact that it was conceived in the late Ottoman Empire is unknown to most historians and once again illustrates how collective Palestinian action dates back even before World War I.[68]

An editorial in *Filastin* addresses this issue and expands on how Palestinians should take control of their own destiny:

> the private lands (*al-aradi al-miriyah*) in our land are extensive and if Jews (*Bani Israil*) are able to buy it, our lives will be threatened from a political, social, and economic aspect. Nothing is left for us to do except defend the land; and it is not possible to defend it other than with arms; and our armed men are indeed righteous journalists; and from this weak point . . . we will benefit from . . . the formation of a national Palestinian company, which will be formed partially with the help of the established families in Nablus, Jerusalem, Jaffa, Haifa and Gaza.

He goes on, 'if we collected from [each of] the cities tens of thousands of lira, the company would have fifty to sixty thousand liras [for this purpose].' Further, 'we will encourage the government to ensure the right of sale of the remaining lands goes to the peasants and if the Children of Israel wish to accept Ottoman citizenship, we shall not refuse them . . .'[69]

Just two months later, in another call to protect Palestine a concerned reader submitted a letter to *Filastin* that called on the wealthy ones from among the Palestinians to establish a national organisation to prevent 'the Zionist wave' from taking more lands, by purchasing the lands themselves.[70] Importantly the calls to protect the land were only one aspect and this article shows us how Palestinians realised the need to claim the homeland, by pressuring the government to open a port in Jaffa, in addition to schools and a hospital. The author, 'Isa al-Safri, made a passionate call, stating that the Palestinians had to rise from their sleep and awake from their indifference. The challenge was not just posed by Zionists but also by the Ottoman government's lack of ability to invest in Palestine as well. He, however, noted that most were not aware of the threat to Palestine, arguing that even when Palestinians 'see their homeland sliding into the depths of disaster' they will not lift a finger.

Palestinian notables, from Jaffa, Gaza and Jerusalem, petitioned the Istanbul's Office of the Caliphate (*Makam-ı Celil-i Hilâfet*), the prime minister and the interior minister. In the petition, Said al-Husayni, the Jerusalem MP, addressed the dire situation, comparing the pain the Ottomans were enduring during the Balkan Wars to that of the Palestinians. 'Just as the general security as a result of the Balkan Wars has been struck in the heart of the Ottomans, so, too, the conditions of the people of Palestine have suffered . . . especially when the Zionists are purchasing some Palestinian lands . . .'[71] The petition goes on to state that the Zionists have succeeded in purchasing lands, and that this time the government is exploring the prospects of selling the Baysan land to the 'Asfar Company' (the above-mentioned Najib Asfar), which is causing general worry. The notables then called on the government to rule in 'the name of justice', in order to prevent damage to the Ottoman state.[72]

One article from *Filastin* in early 1913 also used the comparison between their situation to that of the defeats the Ottomans endured on the battlefield. For example, 'Arif al-'Arif, someone who years later would become a renowned Palestinian journalist and politician, did not mince his words about the danger the Zionists posed. Upon lands being sold in the village of Kefariya and Abu Shusha he wrote that

> if this situation continues and the Zionists [continue] taking over our land, village by village, town by town, so eventually Jerusalem will be sold in its entirety and Palestine in its totality. If we do not [take steps] to prevent this

matter, the state's fate in [Palestine] will be no different from its fate in Libya and in the Balkans.[73]

While it is impossible to understand the reaction of the Istanbul government, the comparison between the Palestinians and the Ottomans suffering in the Balkan Wars was certainly bold, with thousands of Muslim refugees pouring into the capital and a long list of Ottoman casualties; so much so that perhaps such an exaggerated claim could have sparked even outrage among some of Istanbul's officials, or a sense of exaggeration. However, the comparison was central for the Palestinians to show their true anguish in light of continued land sales and Jewish immigration. Further, it stands as a historical reminder that it was during the Balkan Wars that relations between the Ottoman government and the Arabs began to sour. According to Jacobson, the year 1912 served as a breaking point – or in her historical narrative a starting point – 'because of the effects the Balkan wars and the loss of so much territory had on the Ottoman Empire as a whole, and in particular on intercommunal relations within the Arab provinces'.[74]

In another letter, the Jerusalem governor explained to the Ministry of Interior that there were rumours that the Baysan land was going to be sold to a foreign company and that this needed to be reconsidered due to the fact it was among the most fertile territories in the Jericho district. He went on to explain more importantly that the land is an integral part of the Holy Land, reminding the government in Istanbul that the 'Holy River', referring to the Jordan River, runs close to the above-discussed sales.[75] The fact that the governor spoke about the holy aspect of the land only strengthens the fact that he was becoming more aware of the local population's worries that European and Jewish encroachment was also infringing on its 'holiness', which according to the governor could break the status quo between the different religions causing greater problems. In the next chapter, this discussion will be placed into the context of the perceived desecration of the Haram al-Sharif compound, after it was violated by a British archaeological team.

Most interestingly, featured in the Ottoman documents in relation to the possible sale of lands in Baysan are petitions sent by locals who provide an innovative voice, appealing to the Ottoman authorities to look at the greater ethical issues surrounding the sale of lands. This seems to mark a new strategy, much different than in the case of Fula where the local population's voice was almost non-existent, with notables and politicians in the Arabic press lobbying against the sale of huge tracts of land. Here, we find four petitions defending the peasants who have lived there 'from time immemorial' and that a total of 45,000 residents who were to be affected by the sale were in a state of despair. Among the four telegraphs sent to the authorities, we have signatures from among the *mukhtar*s, the heads of clans (*ashiret*) and even among farmers themselves (seemingly to be from among the peasants) who were in search of justice. Interestingly, these petitions are less inflammatory than those the notables dispatched, and focus much more on ethical questions on the relation between state and citizen and the sense of betrayal at the land being sold to foreigners.[76]

Mobilising for the Homeland

By 1914, a new sense of urgency, even one of desperation, emerged among Palestinians concerning the growing Jewish hegemony. During the spring and summer, *Filastin* came out with a series of articles focusing on the Zionists' growing efforts in Palestine in finance, agriculture, industry, trade and real estate.[77] From Jerusalem, Jaffa and Haifa, to the neighbouring lands of Egypt, Syria and Lebanon, news that Palestine was under threat from Zionism captured headlines. This included now even more moderate outlets, such as *al-Quds*.

In early July, a 'General Summons to Palestinians' appeared in three papers in Syria and Palestine: *al-Iqdam*, *al-Karmil* and the well-known Arab nationalist organ in Beirut, *Fatat al-Arab*, and carried the title 'The Dangers of Zionism'. It was also translated into Hebrew, appearing in both *HaHerut* and *Moriah*.[78] The open call to all Palestinians was done by a Palestinian, an anonymous author, who simply signed the document as 'a Palestinian'. The article provides a special window into how a local Palestinian nationalism was being carved out within a greater Arab nationalism.

> Oh people of the Land, we are calling you in the name of the grieving land, the one of mourning, in the name of Arabia, Syria, our land Palestine, which has fallen to misfortune. In the name of everything valuable to you. We are making a general call from the depths of our hurting heart . . . we are calling you as Caliph Omar ibn al-Khattab, who was the one who conquered Syria and Palestine, is watching over you from the distance of thirteen generations, and is yelling out to you: Awaken! . . . Have mercy on your land! Hold on to it with your bare teeth! Are you leaving the land even though God has ordered you not to? Have you not heard the words of the Prophets forbidding you to leave the land? . . . if you do so, then you are not Muslims! . . . We are addressing you just as the just ruler Saladin is standing in front of you from a distance of seven generations!

The narrative is striking and the absence of the Ottoman rulers is perhaps even more so. Here the conquest of Palestine by the Caliph Umar, and the second by Saladin, reiterates that Palestine is about to fall to foreign rule for a third time. It is the first time we also see the invoking of the caliph, providing a religious perspective, with him coming alongside Saladin, whose name, as we have seen, is regularly invoked. While the focus on saving Palestine is placed specifically on the Palestinians, the importance of Syria and Arabia stands as a reminder that Palestinians, while identifiable as a separate group, feel loyalty also to the greater Arab nation. In this narrative, we witness the reoccurring theme of Palestinian migration from the land, with the author saying that leaving Palestine is not only a betrayal to the cause, but one to the religion as well. The narrative goes on:

> Do you want to be slaves and servants to a people who are well-known already in the world and in history? Do you wish to be slaves to Zionists who have come to remove you from your land, claiming it is theirs? I call upon God and his Prophets to exclaim they are liars. They resided in the Holy Land and were expelled by God and forbidden to return . . . [so why are the Zionists] longing to reconquer it after 2,000 years? The danger is already at its height. They have purchased most of your country and over 300,000 have arrived just as thousands [among you] are leaving to America and other places; [in fact] trade and industry are already in their hands, in the future they will control agriculture, and then they will conquer everything that is within it . . . [the Zionists] not only rule over us, but also to expel us from the country. Muslims are you satisfied with this? Yes, you! Palestinians! Syrians! Arabs! Are you satisfied with this? . . . They [the Zionists] need to know that there is a nation in this country, and that they will not be able to enter as long as we are here!

Up until now, Palestinian narratives we have seen have worked hard to distinguish Jews from Zionists. However, this narrative has a new tone of anti-Semitism, hinting at them being a hated people worldwide. In one previous passage it calls Jews 'the lowest and the most despicable of peoples'. The religious imagery in the text highlights the author's attempts at capturing the hearts of Muslims and declaring that not only is it their national homeland, but also one dear to Islam. This paragraph also reveals once again levels of belonging in terms of local populations and identity, with the statement that the Palestinians are not alone in the struggle; however, it is clear that they will be its sole victims if they lose their homeland.

The text ends with six steps the Palestinians can take to lay claim to the homeland. It is possible to categorise them into two groups. The first set turns to the government, demanding that it puts an immediate stop to the inward flow of Jews, and to do its utmost to stop the sale of lands to Jews, and to middlemen who purchase the land and then turn it over to Jewish ownership, such as was the case with the Fula land sale. The second category is an assertive call to Palestinians to take their future in their own hands, and through hard work and loyalty, to save the homeland from the enemy. Most of all these points, the text states, will be achieved through education, promoting Arabic in schools, assurances that Palestinians themselves would not collaborate or sell lands to Zionists, strengthening industry, and to have 'mercy on the fellah and to respect him'.

The call by the lone 'Palestinian' was heeded by the Jerusalem notables and parliamentarians who had long left off bringing the debate to the halls of the Ottoman Parliament. In fact, it appears that the notables were now aligning with the much more outspoken voices of the Palestinian and Syrian press, and this is key to understanding how different segments after years of a brewing conflict were starting to merge into one national voice. The document below, strongly resembling the 'General Summons', clearly shows that even these notables, who were among the most loyal of Ottoman citizens, were beginning to lose faith in the Empire's ability to curb Jewish immigration.

In July 1914, Said al-Husayni, who had just been re-elected to Parliament, dispatched to his fellow Arab parliamentarians a copy of a petition originating in Jerusalem [hereafter: the Jerusalem Petition] which had been submitted to the Sublime Porte:[79]

We have become frightened that the Zionist people's calamity which has become as clear as the sun, is a nightmare that has befallen the Land of Palestine. This should cause a warning that in the very near future it will become clear that this is such a [great] set of disasters that it will be impossible to reverse. Every day hundreds of Zionist immigrants are arriving in Palestine. In the face of this the wretched ones from among the people of Palestine are migrating. The government is acting quite indifferently to this situation. The al-Aqsa Mosque which is the keepsake of Salah al-Din al-Ayyubi and the first qibla has practically been handed over to the Jews with consent . . . we protest this with all our hearts. Since the Constitutional period the Zionist people have seized the opportunity and more than 300,000 have arrived in Palestine and in the event that it is not possible to reduce this number we request that significant and rational measures be taken by the government in order to keep it at this number. [Signed left to right, top to bottom, A=Arabic, T=Turkish, U=not legible]:
Muhammad in the name of the Trade Company (Shirkah al-Tijariyyah) (A)
Farid in the name of the Palestine Youth in Damascus (Sham'da Filistin Gençleri) (T)
Arif in the name of the Palestinian Economic Society (al-Shirkah al-Iqtisadi-yyah al-Filastiniyyah) (A)
Raghib in the name of the Society for Prevention of Alcoholic drinks (Al-Jamiyyah al-man' al-muskirat) (A)

President Salih in the name of the Brotherhood Association (Jamiyyah al-Ikha')
(A)

President Shafiq al-Khalidi in the name of the Islamic Community (al-Jizyah al-Islamiyyah) (A)

Ali Nashashibi in the name of the Jerusalem Youth (Al-Shabibah al-Qudsiyyah)
(A)

Jamal in the name of the Society of Literary from among the Notables

Amin in the name of the Palestine Youth in Egypt (Misir'da Filistin Gençleri)
(T)

Ishaq in the name of the Palestine Youth in Beirut (Beyrut'te Filistin Gençleri)
(T)

Ahmad in the name of the Palestine Youth in Istanbul (Der-i Saadet'te Filistin Gençleri) (T)

and Muhammad Yusuf al-'Ilmi, Rifa'at Abu al-Saud, Faiz al-Haddad, 'Abd al-Qadir al-'Afifah (U), 'Abd al-Rahman al-Nuri, Rafaat Husayn, 'Abd al-Salam al-Husayn, Imam Sahada, Abu al-Saud, Dawud al-Husayni, . . . (U), 'Uthman Zaki, and Imam Masjid al-Aqsa 'Ali al-Jama'i.

While the Jerusalem Petition is striking in many aspects, it particularly stands out on four main issues: a) the Palestinian perception of Jewish immigration, b) the continual problem of Palestinian emigration, c) the disappointment of Palestinians with the central government and d) it provides us evidence of a Palestinian identity and organised movements. In terms of Jewish immigration, the first obvious point is the exaggeration of the numbers of Jewish immigrants in the statement that 'every day hundreds' of Zionists were arriving and that since the Constitutional Period, more than 300,000 had arrived, which is also stated in the General Summons. However, the fact that this number was also cited in the open letters mentioned above beckons us to look deeper into this claim. Mere speculation suggests that the notables were consciously exaggerating the number of Jewish newcomers in order to highlight the extent of immigration to an administration in Istanbul that did not seem to have a clear understanding of how significant it had become. In any case, we know there was a sharp influx of Jews arriving parallel to the issuing of the petition since the Ministry of Interior notified Beirut and Jerusalem that 'a large group of Jews made up of mostly Romanians are being transferred (*hicret ettirilmekte*) with foreign passports under political pretences'.[80] The Ministry concluded that 'the entrance of Jews with foreign passports should be strictly forbidden', but should not apply 'to ones with Ottoman citizenship and Ottoman passports'.[81] We also have the case of 150 Russians arriving in Palestine during the same time period, despite being refused a visa at the Ottoman embassy in Odessa.[82]

Returning to the Jerusalem Petition, as we saw in previous petitions, it also emphasised the emigration of Palestinians from Palestine. Certainly, with the exiting of Palestinians, together with the influx of Jewish immigration, Palestinians began to imagine a reality where they would be a minority in their land. Unlike former petitions, this one blamed such emigration on Jewish immigration alone, and did not take into consideration other previous claims of corruption or violence.

With all their efforts failing, Said al-Husayni proposed that 'in the event that it is not possible to reduce this number [of immigrants] we request that significant and rational measures be taken by the government in order to keep it at this number'. This position starts a trend which would become apparent during the British Mandate: rather than calling for the expulsion of Jewish immigrants, Palestinians demanded that the government abruptly halt any additional immigration, while accepting the fact that a large Jewish population would remain.

This petition is even more important due to the fact that it provides the historian of Palestine with the names of social, political and economic organisations which were based solely on their local Palestinian identity. One example of this is the Palestinian Economic Company, which clearly conveys that the Palestinians already believed before World War I that Palestine should not only serve as a reference denoting an identity, but also was an economic unit.

Then we learn that there was an organised Palestinian youth movement with representation throughout the Middle East, most likely student organisations. For example, some of the main people signing the petition were part of a group called 'Palestine's Youth' (Turkish: Filistin Gençleri) in Syria, Egypt, Beirut and Istanbul. Also mentioned was Jerusalem's *Qudsiyya* Youth Organisation, which did not need to denote Palestine since they were in Palestine, not like their counterparts.[83] While we have little information today concerning who exactly the Palestine Youth organisations were, it was reported in *HaHerut*, in an article entitled 'the Arab Movement and Zionism', that indeed new organisations defending Palestine were emerging throughout the Ottoman Empire, in Istanbul, Beirut, most cities in Palestine and also in Egypt. However, this article reported about a different organisation called the 'Society for the Resistance against Zionists', which was made up of both Palestinians and Syrians residing at the time in Cairo.[84] The aim of this group was to gather support among Arabs at large; it would seem that the same Palestinians in this group were the ones who joined together as the 'Palestine Youth' as well.

The petition infuriated Jerusalem's governor Mecid, who believed that the Jews were working in good faith. In his letter to his superiors, he claimed that the letter was written by a 'malicious group', set on trying to create a 'Jewish–Arab' conflict; in fact, this was the first time we see the divide between Jews and Arabs referred as 'a conflict'.[85] This fact cannot be overlooked since the governor did not see the Zionist movement as a separatist one, but rather as a group modernising Palestine, a land vital to Ottoman interests, and working under the umbrella of Ottoman patriotism.

The governor obviously must have felt betrayed by the fact that he also first received the dispatch from Istanbul, the notables having completely bypassed his authority. In fact, Palestinians directing complaints directly to Istanbul rather than working with the local authorities as intermediaries seems to have developed into a trend by this point, as we see with the Daran Petition, the case of the Greek Orthodox Patriarch's report on the threat of British imperialism and, lastly, a common note sounded in the reports relating to the Haram al-Sharif incident (both appearing in the upcoming chapter). With the spread of technology, the once far-off capital became much closer, empowering the local citizen even as it challenged the local administration, and creating a new sense of tension between the two.

While Said Bey was presenting his petition to his Arab counterparts, Jerusalem's British vice consul's internal report was echoing the Palestinians' complaints, stating

> the government has lately shown themselves extremely favourable to the Zionists. Amongst other things, they have completely abolished all restrictions on Jewish immigration and land purchase. At the same time, the lot of Ottoman subjects becomes increasingly hard to bear, so that the natives are streaming out of the country as fast as the Zionists are coming in.[86]

Certainly, this internal British report confirms that even if the Palestinians exaggerated the numbers of Jewish immigrants, during the spring of 1914 a new wave of such immigrants were arriving, and Palestinians were leaving in large numbers as a direct result of this.

The vice consul also reported that the Ottoman government had temporarily suspended *Filastin* based on an article hostile to Zionism. He remarks that the article 'faithfully mirrors the growing resentment among the Arabs against the Jewish invasion', and as a result of this, 'assaults upon Jews in the outlying districts are increasingly frequent and it is conceivable that the jealousy created by the threatening economic preponderance of the Jewish element may become a source of serious embarrassment for the government'.[87] These remarks also give potency to Governor Mecid's words that foresaw a future Jewish–Arab conflict in Palestine.

The Ottoman governor was uncompromising towards Palestinian demands and even seemed uninterested in addressing their needs. This fact was also mentioned in the General Summons, and the dismay with the Ottoman authorities had already been highlighted in April in an article in *Filastin*, which was also responding to the suspension of the newspaper due to its anti-Zionist sentiments. This article was dispatched to London by the British ambassador to show the growing tension between Jews and Arabs.[88]

> It seems that in the opinion of the Central Government we have done a serious thing in drawing the attention of the nation to the danger threatened by the advancing tide of Zionism, for in the course of last week the Local Authorities received a telegram from the Ministry of the Interior ordering the suppression of our paper 'Palestine', and our committal for trial as having committed in our campaign against Zionism and our appeal to the national spirit an offence which they term 'sowing discord between the elements of the Empire'. This is mighty well; still better is the acknowledgment by the government of the Zionist Society as one of the elements of the Empire, to which cause she shows more devotion than the Zionists themselves. They cry in their meetings, declare in their conferences, and announce it in the highways and byways of Palestine, nay from the very housetops, that they are a political party whose aim is to restore Palestine to their nation and to concentrate them in it, and to keep it exclusively for them. Then comes the Government saying, 'No, you are on the contrary one of the elements of our happy Empire, and he who opposes you is in our sight a criminal bent on causing strife between those elements.' How, we wonder, did the Government learn that the Zionists form one of the elements of the Empire? How can she shut her eyes to the fact, universally known, that 'Zionist' is not synonymous with 'Jew'?

The article goes on to accuse the Zionists of successfully creating divisions between the Arab population and the local Jews who had lived there before the arrival of the new Jewish immigration. According to *Filastin*'s editor,

> up until ten years ago the Jews were a fraternal native Ottoman element, living and intermixing with the other elements in harmony, interchanging business relations, inhabiting the same quarter, sending their children to the same school, and shadowed by one banner and one crescent.

This was ruined by Zionists who were 'German revolutionaries and Russian nihilists, and vagabonds of other countries'. He then goes on to complain that they have built their own neighbourhoods and now boycott the Arabic tongue, and have only worked to progress Hebrew, a 'dead language, which is useless to the world except as a weapon of Zionists, and prevents natives from frequenting their schools and mixing with their children'.

The Palestinians' frustration during 1914 cannot be separated from the fact that the Ottoman governor Mecid Bey had made clear his support for Zionist projects in Palestine. During 1908–14, the Palestinians often witnessed governors of Jerusalem sending positive signals to the Jewish Yishuv. In fact, there were times when parts of the Jewish community simply attributed the positive attitudes to 'political flattery', as seen in the case of the mutasarrıf Muhdi, following his visit to Rishon LeZion and Petah Tikvah. In this incident, quoting a Jewish periodical, *The New York Times* reported that the Jews were promised autonomy in Palestine and that this was 'indirectly confirmed by a cablegram from Constantinople'.[89]

Among the Ottoman governors, Mecid Bey stood out as particularly favourable to the Jewish Yishuv. In March 1914, an interview with him appeared in Egypt's *al-Iqdam* newspaper, and was reprinted in Jerusalem's Hebrew paper *HaHerut*, under the title 'What are they saying about us?'[90] Despite being interviewed by an Arab who was antagonistic to Zionism, Mecid praised the Zionist project, suggesting that the indigenous population learn from the Jews and their achievements such as the newly founded city of Tel Aviv and other Hebrew settlements. This angered the interviewer, who argued that the Arabs were not able to learn from the Jews since the Jews did not hire them. It was in this spirit that *Iqdam*'s interviewer pressed on, eventually accusing the government of favouring the Zionists. Finally, Mecid lost his temper, stating that 'the government is not ignoring the indigenous population and is paying close attention to the laws of the State' and 'if the government noticed any damage caused by the Zionists, then of course they would protest'. When questioned about the government selling land to the Zionists, Mecid replied that the 'government does not forbid the settlement of foreigners in any part of the [Empire]', and 'aspires solely for the union of nationalities and different ethnic groups that are in its land and will not place any pitfalls in their way'. Not surprisingly, the newspaper *HaHerut* praised Mecid for this to no end, declaring that his words struck down every claim the anti-Zionist movement had at its disposal.[91]

What is especially important about Mecid Bey was not only that he served during one of the most crucial years, but he was also the longest-serving governor during the Young Turk period, stationed in Jerusalem from March 1913 to the end of 1914. Moreover, his presence was all the more important due to the fact that the two governors preceding him only served four months each. What is clear is that Mecid Bey perceived the indigenous population much in the same way that the Jewish population viewed them: as backwards and under-developed.

To understand Mecid Bey's prejudices towards the rural, mostly peasant, population, it will be useful to consider Ussama Makdisi's argument on Ottoman Orientalism, which he defines as a 'complex of Ottoman attitudes produced by a nineteenth-century age of Ottoman reform that implicitly and explicitly acknowledged the West to be the home of progress and the East, writ large, to be a *present* theater of backwardness'.[92] He concludes by reminding us that it is impossible to 'speak of Western Orientalism without taking into account the fact that Western Colonialism, within which the former is embedded, has created myriad other Orientalisms'.[93] While most scholars like to show how Zionists believed they were bringing progress to Palestine, here we see that some Ottoman officials adopted similar attitudes to the Jewish community, whom they perceived as developing the land and bringing progress to it. One could even argue that some of the Ottoman bureaucracy looked positively on the Jewish settlements, believing that Jewish immigration was a modernising force.[94]

Zionism and the Elections

Parallel to the Palestinians becoming conscious of the growing Jewish hegemony, during the spring of 1914 Ottoman parliamentary elections were held and the debate over the future of Zionism was widely covered in the local press. In one case, interviews with Palestinian candidates were featured in the Egyptian newspaper a*l-Iqdam*, and parts were subsequently reproduced in *Filastin* and a more extensive translation in *HaHerut*, entitled 'The Prominent Muslims and Zionism'.[95] In this article, the five candidates from Jerusalem were questioned about their stance concerning the spread of Zionism in Palestine. Their answers make it clear that despite pervasive and growing opposition to Zionism, Palestinians' take on Zionism varied in detail, and like any group acting within a political system, these candidates had their limits, especially in light of the fact that they were also dependent on the Jewish vote.

In addition to this, these interviews shine light on the other issues that were of interest to these politicians, similar to what we have already discussed above, such as the poor economic conditions of the Palestinian peasant, and the growth of education. The candidates interviewed were: Said al-Husayni (former Member of Parliament), Raghib al-Nashashibi (a member of the *Meclis-i Umumi* (Jerusalem District Council)), Hassan Salim al-Husayni (former mayor of Jerusalem), Musa Shafiq al-Khalidi and Greek Orthodox candidate Khalil al-Sakakini.

Former parliamentarian Said al-Husayni stated, 'I will work on matters concerning the tithe tax and land, the *vergi* (Turkish: taxes in general), educating the people, holiness (*hitkadshut*), and also the Zionist question.' For him, the most pressing question was strengthening the status of the peasants, which was related to the question of Jewish migration: 'We need to support the hand of the peasant in their farming in such a way that he will not be cut off from his land and that the Zionists will not receive any part of it.' He continued by warning readers that if the situation did not improve, 'peasants will be forced to sell [the land] to the Zionists at a pathetic price, and then after some time they will have nothing left and will be forced to be employed by [the Zionists] as day workers'. He then called upon the government to provide assistance to the peasants by investing in modern agricultural tools and to establish vocational schools to induce prosperity in the Land. Said ends by stating that Zionism was a threat to the state, both politically and economically, explaining that he was astonished at the government's lack of attention given to the Zionist problem, describing it as being in a state of 'sleep' concerning the issue.[96]

Importantly, Said al-Husayni also reminded the reader that he would propose to Parliament that a religious school for higher education be established in Jerusalem to serve Muslims from different cities and countries, which would strengthen Islam in Jerusalem and would be comparable to Al-Azhar, the renowned institution of Islamic sciences in Cairo. The article's author noted that Said Efendi spoke in great detail about this project. This is important because this topic was only briefly covered in *HaHerut* due to the fact that it seemed to have been of little interest to the Jewish community.[97] However, in the next chapter it will become clear that the establishing of an institution of higher education was inherently connected to strengthening the Palestinian hold over Jerusalem vis-à-vis the threat of European colonialism and the Zionist movement.

The next candidate interviewed, Raghib al-Nashashibi, was the only one to stress the need to differentiate between foreign Jews and Ottoman Jews, stating:

> I am not against the Ottoman Jews, but only the foreign Jews from among them. For the Ottoman Jew, they have the same rights as us . . . [and] if the foreign Jew wishes really to attract our hearts towards him, then he would adopt Ottoman citizenship, would study the language of the state in order that he would understand us and we would understand him and we would both work for the good of the homeland.

But he goes on to give the foreign Jew a stern warning, 'if the foreign citizen has come to fight us with the weapon of his citizenship and will hate our sons and brothers and will go against our laws (*hoqim ve mishpatim*) then we will be forced not to take this quietly.' In closing, he promised that, if elected: 'I will do everything possible and will work day and night to remove the damage and danger presented to us by the Zionists and Zionism, without harming the feelings of our Ottoman Jewish brothers.'[98] This emphasis on differentiating the Ottoman Jews from the foreign Jews was especially important for him since he had been publicly accused of being an anti-Semite a year prior. This was over disputed election results for Jerusalem's District Council. The conflict, discussed in Chapter 4, centred around Ottoman loyalist Jew Albert Antebi, who lost the race to Raghib and claimed his competitor set out on an anti-Semitic campaign against Jews and even intimidated them from voting.[99]

The next two candidates took a much more conciliatory stance in relation to Zionism than the first two and in some instances almost the opposite. Hasan Efendi Salim al-Husayni, a former mayor of Jerusalem, perhaps more than any other candidate, revealed a unique perspective on the Zionist movement:

I do not see any danger from the Zionist movement since it is not a political movement but rather a settlement movement. And I am sure that not even one wise Zionist worth an opinion would consider the ideal of the establishment of a Jewish government in Palestine (*Falastina*)[100] . . . The Zionists have come to this state to live in it. They are educated and they are cultured, and they do not go boastfully, and they are united [people]. And out of justice and humanity we should not hate and despise them. Rather the opposite, we should try to become like them, learn from their doings so that it will give us a good lesson and intelligence and by doing this we will give an important thrust forward to our agriculture and sowing.

Yet he ends with the acknowledgment that

in spite of all this, we need to pay attention to them, and if we continue on our path and they on theirs then all the land will be passed over to them. Our peasant is poor and weak and the poor one is likely to forfeit his property for his survival. Therefore, the government needs to pass a new law in Palestine in relation to the selling of lands and to set regulations to have limits in accordance with our status in the land.[101]

While it is impossible to know, this candidate almost appeared as if he was courting Jewish voters.

Musa Shafiq al-Khalidi, the last candidate, presented a somewhat nuanced version of the argument above, recognising that the Zionists were contributing to the advancement of Palestine, but warning that 'the danger that comes from Zionism is greater than the benefit it can bring', and that

the Zionists possess a high culture and a real education and our land is empty
and barren and has nothing, no education and no culture, and because of this
[the Zionists] are alienated and strong in their status and we are weak and feeble
and it is natural that the weak cannot stand up to the one who attacks him.[102]

Importantly, despite his use of 'state' in a political sense, it is clear from
the context that he is referring to the Land of Palestine, and not the
Ottoman Empire. Following this, Khalidi returned the discussion to education, which was obviously connected to his words about the Jewish
community and Palestine. He stated that there was a general need to
open more schools for Muslims and to increase the low salary of their
teachers.[103]

As for the fifth candidate, Khalil al-Sakakini, *HaHerut* did not see fit to
quote him at all, reporting that he 'expressed himself in a similar fashion
and that he declared that it is upon the government to pay due attention to
the Zionists and help the advancement of the indigenous population'.[104]

What is clear from these interviews is that all the candidates were
united in their conviction that the Zionist movement was proving harmful
to the peasants and that it had reached a crucial stage. If concrete measures
were not enacted, the very existence of the peasants would be under
imminent threat, or, as one candidate suggested, they would turn into
'day workers'.[105] This leaves little room for interpretation; the Palestinian
peasant would become a cheap source of labour for the Jewish colonies,
or they would be forced to migrate to other regions, such as urban centres,
or out of Palestine, in order to make a living.

In addition to this point, what emerges in these interviews is that some
of the candidates foresaw that the Jews posed a threat to the notables'
hegemony, and it is in this context that Musa Shafiq al-Khalidi's following
words seem hauntingly prophetic: 'and if we remain stagnant . . . then of
course the day will come, in the near future, that they [the Jews] will hold
the reins of the leadership of our country and we will remain without any
support and defense in the land.'[106]

In this chapter we have seen that by 1914 there was a clear sense
of a common bond among many Palestinians regardless of their social
and religious affiliations, and that they were uniting to confront issues
such as the continued Jewish migration, British imperialism, Palestinian
emigration and the poor state of the peasants. As demonstrated above, the
Palestinian notables were forced to reconsider their previous interdepend-
ent relations with the peasants. With the Young Turk Revolution, and
the arrival of the Jewish colonial settlements, the former patron–client
system of notable protection of the peasants from government institutions

would be replaced by a new system of representation in the Ottoman Parliament. However, this was only a minor result of the mass changes taking place in the Palestinian countryside. The more radical result was the recognition that both urban and rural groups needed to unite to combat the proliferation of the colonies, with the notables adopting new strategies of monopolising the rural communities. This process was not only in reaction to Zionism, but also to British imperialism, which, in southern Palestine, placed both urban notables and peasants alike close to British-controlled Egypt. Sources from the Ottoman archives exhibit the peasants' difficulties and disenfranchisement, and highlight the fact that Palestinians had youth organisations throughout the Ottoman lands and Egypt, with a clear emphasis on their awareness of being in real danger of losing control of their land. With the knowledge of the Palestinian emigration, and other demographic considerations, the Palestinian notables recognised that their hegemony in the land was under threat and that drastic steps needed to be taken to reverse this trend.

However, and more importantly, through these events we see that by the Second Constitutional Period, there was a clear sense of 'Palestinian identity' among the Arab population of Palestine. This point has been neglected in the past, and the history of Palestine has been blurred by the over-emphasised assumption that Palestine was geographically a part of *Bilad al-Sham*. Importantly, while the Palestinians most likely perceived themselves as belonging to a greater entity, for them Palestine was Palestine, and Syria was Syria. In the following chapter, it will become clear that the Palestinian notables embarked on concrete plans to strengthen their hold on Jerusalem in light of the growing European and Jewish presence.

The Palestinian new sense of self not only resulted from the growing dominance of Zionism, and the looming British threat, but was also linked to the Ottoman administration's widespread corruption. In fact, what we find in some of the Ottoman archival documents is that the Palestinians were gradually becoming alienated from the Ottoman state as a result of their lack of trust in it and its institutions.

As Palestinians were being forced to leave their land, some peasants even chose to leave Palestine and emigrate abroad, a situation that most scholars have limited to the period of the British Mandate. However, this actually began in the late Ottoman period. Only when one understands to what extent emigration posed a threat to the Palestinian countryside, will it be possible to understand how the Jewish community, despite their minority status, posed a challenge to Palestinian hegemony in Palestine. This emigration is also important to consider since it created a sort of 'practical nationalism' among the Palestinian peasants, meaning that once they were forced to leave the land, they discovered this connection not only with that land, but with Palestine in general.

Notes

1. *Filastin*, 15 July 1914, p. 1. I would like to extend my special thanks to Emanuel Beška, who was able to locate this poem for me, which I originally had found in the Hebrew press, as explained below.
2. *Moriah*, 31 July 1914, p. 2.
3. *Moriah*, 31 July 1914, p. 2.
4. DH.ŞFR 1332.Ca.22, 40/39; 18 April 1914.
5. Mandel, *The Arabs and Zionism before World War I*, p. 8.
6. Doumani, 'Rediscovering Ottoman Palestine'.
7. Ibid., p. 3.
8. Khalidi, *Palestinian Identity*; Porath, *The Emergence of the Palestinian-Arab National Movement, 1918–1929*.
9. Khalidi, 'The Formation of Palestinian Identity', in *Rethinking Nationalism in the Arab Middle East*, p. 171.
10. A good example of a Palestinian who, it could be argued, was an important link in understanding this phenomenon is 'Isa al-'Isa. See Khalidi, *The Iron Cage*, pp. 90–104.
11. The notion of *Palestinianism* builds off what Khalidi defined as a 'local patriotism', which 'could not yet be described as a nation-state nationalism, for the simple reason that the prerequisites for modern state nationalism did not yet exist'; Khalidi, *Palestinian Identity*, p. 32.
12. *Filastin*, 10 September 1913.
13. Rashid Khalidi documented that in the newspaper *Filastin*, in May 1914, the editor referred to the Palestinians as *al-Umma al-Filistiniyya* (the Palestinian Nation). Unfortunately, this edition is not available in the archives. See Khalidi, *Palestinian Identity*, p. 155.
14. According to Ruth Kark, in addition to the *effendis* purchasing land in the 1858 Ottoman land reform, they also succeeded in obtaining a monopoly on the land, by bribing administrative officials and having the public land registered as private (*mulk*), or as a religious endowment (*waqf*). Kark, *Jaffa*, pp. 247–8.
15. Kark, *Jaffa*, pp. 247–8.
16. Khalidi, *Palestinian Identity*, p. 110. Rashid Khalidi originally stated this claim in 1985, in a paper he presented at the Middle East Studies Association in New Orleans; quoted in Muslih, *The Origins of Palestinian Nationalism*, p. 72.
17. For more on the Dinshaway incident, see Cleveland, *A History of the Modern Middle East*, p. 101; for more on the Dinshaway incident and its relation to Egyptian nationalism, see Fahmy, *Ordinary Egyptians*, p. 92.

18. Lockman, 'Imagining the Working Class', *Poetics Today*, p. 181.
19. For a look at peasant life in Palestine, see Reilly, 'The Peasantry of Late Ottoman Palestine', *Journal of Palestine Studies*, pp. 82–97.
20. *Filastin*, 17 January 1913.
21. Ibid., 11 June 1913; quoted also in Khalidi, *Palestinian Identity*, p. 57. Also, see Ayalon, *Reading Palestine*, pp. 140–1. For a fascinating look on how Menashe Meirovitch, an Ashkenazi immigrant, and *Filastin*'s editor 'Isa al-'Isa collaborated on a column promoting the peasant cause, with Meirovitch using the pen name 'Abu Ibrahim', and posting as a Muslim peasant, see Dolbee and Hazkani, 'Impossible Is Not Ottoman: Menasha Meirovitch, 'Isa Al-'Isa, and Imperial Citizenship in Palestine', *IJMES*, pp. 241–62.
22. Fahmy, *Ordinary Egyptians*, p. 36.
23. Beška, 'Political Opposition to Zionism in Palestine and Greater Syria', *Jerusalem Quarterly*, pp. 54–67; Beška, 'Shukri al-Asali', *Asian and African Studies*, pp. 237–54.
24. Beška, 'Shukri al-Asali', p. 241.
25. *Ha-Or*, 29 May 1911, p. 3.
26. DH.MUI 1328.Ca. 3, 93/41.
27. PRO FO 795/2321, 26 July 1909, pp. 247–8. In the Ottoman sources, it does not go into detail exactly why it was returned but does mention that it was returned as a result of complaints.
28. DH.ŞFR 1332.C.27, 41/63; 23 May 1914. BEO 3583/268718 1327.C.6; 25 June 1909.
29. For more on Shukri al-Asali, see Beška, 'Shukri al-Asali'.
30. Beška, 'Political Opposition to Zionism in Palestine and Greater Syria', p. 242.
31. Khalidi, *Palestinian Identity*, p. 109.
32. Beška, 'Shukri al-Asali', p. 242.
33. *Al-Quds*, 17 March 1911, issue 223.
34. Kark and Frantzman, 'Bedouin, Abdul Hamid II, British Land Settlement, and Zionism', *Israel Studies*, pp. 49–79.
35. *Ha-Poel Ha-Tzair*, 18 July 1913, p. 3.
36. *Ha-Tzvi*, 1 July 1909, p. 3.
37. *Ha-Tzfira*, 6 November 1910, p. 2.
38. Beška, 'Shukri al-Asali', p. 243.
39. Ibid.
40. *HaHerut*, 23 December 1910, p. 1.
41. Ibid.
42. *Ha-Tzvi*, 2 February 1911, p. 3.
43. *HaHerut*, 23 December 1910, p. 1.
44. *Al-Mufid*, 18 December 1912, p. 3. This segment of the article appears in Khalidi, *Palestinian Identity*, p. 128.
45. Issawi, *The Economic History of the Middle East, 1800–1914*, p. 269. (This is Issawi's introduction to the excerpt of Arthur Ruppin's work.)

46. Karpat, 'The Ottoman Emigration to America, 1860–1914', *IJMES*, p. 185.
47. Ibid.
48. In his article on Ottoman emigration, Kemal H. Karpat also highlights how it is incorrect to assume that the majority of Syrian emigration was predominately Muslim, showing statistics that at times place Muslims more than Christians. See Karpat, 'The Ottoman Emigration to America'.
49. Karpat, 'The Ottoman Emigration to America,' p. 183.
50. Ruppin, 'Syrien als Wirtschaftsgebiet', in *The Economic History of the Middle East*.
51. Ibid.
52. For more on the topic of migration and the city of Jaffa, see Kark, *Jaffa*, pp. 135–203.
53. Kark, *Jaffa*, pp. 141–3.
54. Ruppin, *Syria*, p. 9; Ruppin, 'A General Colonization Policy', in *Three Decades of Palestine*.
55. Ruppin, 'A General Colonization Policy', p. 63.
56. Ibid., p. 62. The other interesting aspect of this quote is the statistics that Ruppin provided in respect to the population of Palestine. As we see, this number contradicts the 'official' numbers, as discussed in Chapter 1, which claim that the Jews were only one-tenth of the population. If Ruppin's numbers are taken into consideration, they allow us to understand that, while the Palestinians might have exaggerated the numbers, for those living in Palestine there was no clear picture of what the population was in exact terms.
57. DHID 1329.Za.13, 23/6; 5 November 1911; Documents 19, 21, 23 and 24.
58. Ben-Bassat, *Petitioning the Sultan*, pp. 169–70. See this source for a translation of the Daran Petition, which is documented as 'appendix 10', pp. 223–5.
59. Ibid., pp. 164–70.
60. PRO FO/2377, p. 104.
61. DH.EUM.EMD 1331.L.5, 30/5; 6 September 1913.
62. Swedenburg, 'The Role of the Palestinian Peasantry in the Great Revolt (1936–1939)', in *Islam, Politics, and Social Movements*.
63. Ibid., p. 175. For a general decline in the status of *mukhtar*s vis-à-vis the peasants, see Freas, 'Ottoman Reform, Islam, and Palestine's Peasantry', *Arab Studies Journal*, pp. 196–231.
64. DH.EUM.EMN 1332.S.17, 85/49; 11 July 1914.
65. Ibid. There are incidents where a Palestinian merchant was 'driven out of the *Israeli* colony of Tel Aviv', and other Arab merchants being barred from entering the Jewish city. See *Filastin*, 7 June 1913, p. 3.
66. DH.EUM.EMN 1332.S.17, 85/49; 11 July 1914.
67. *HaHerut*, 25 March 1914, p. 1. In one case, a year earlier, there were reports that an Arab merchant had entered Tel Aviv to sell the Turkish drink Boza, and was driven away by the residents. *Filastin*, 7 June 1913.
68. *Palestine Post*, 28 December 1932, p. 3; *Jewish Telegraphic Agency*, 'Arab

National Fund Established in Palestine to Acquire Land; Launches $400,000 Campaign', 28 January 1944, available at <http://www.jta.org/1944/01/28/archive/arab-national-fund-established-in-palestine-to-acquire-land-launches-400-000-campaign> (last accessed 27 May 2019).

69. *Filastin*, 12 July 1913, p. 1.
70. Ibid., 10 September 1913, p. 3.
71. DH.ID 1331.Za.20; 2 October 1913.
72. Ibid.
73. *Filastin*, 25 January 1913, p. 3.
74. Jacobson, *From Empire to Empire*, p. 2.
75. DH.ID 1331.Za.20, 10 May 1913.
76. Ibid., 2 October 1913 (see documents 39–45).
77. DH-KMS 1332.R.3, 47/4, 11/15; 8 February 1914.
78. *Moriah*, 19 July 1914, p. 3; 20 July 1914, pp. 2–3.
79. DH.EUM.4.Şb 23/5; 11 August 1914. The document that exists in the archives is the accompanying letter to the Arab parliamentarians. Unfortunately, the copy sent to the Sublime Porte itself is missing.
80. DH.ŞFR 1332.C.27, 41/63; 23 May 1914.
81. Ibid.
82. DH.KMS 1332.C.27, 18/14; 23 May 1914; DH.ŞFR 1332.C.27, 41/59; 27 May 1914.
83. While we know little about these organisations of Palestinians abroad, they are referenced one other time in a newspaper article in *al-Karmil* in September of the previous year; see *al-Karmil*, 13 September 1913, quoted in Mandel, *The Arabs and Zionism before World War I*, p. 173.
84. *HaHerut*, 27 July 1914, p. 1.
85. DH.EUM.4.Şb 23/5; 11 August 1914, p. 1.
86. PRO FO 200, 30 April 1914.
87. PRO FO 196, 30 April 1914.
88. PRO FO 195/2459, 29 April 1914, pp. 198–9.
89. *New York Times*, 13 September 1912.
90. *HaHerut*, 25 March 1914.
91. Ibid.
92. Makdisi, 'Ottoman Orientalism', *The American Historical Review*, pp. 768–96 (italics in original).
93. Ibid., p. 795.
94. Sa'di, 'Modernization as an Explanatory Discourse of Zionist-Palestinian Relations', *British Journal of Middle Eastern Studies*, p. 26.
95. *HaHerut*, 29 March 1914, p. 1.
96. Ibid.
97. Ibid.
98. Ibid.
99. DH.UMVM 1332.M.22; 21 December 1913.
100. This translation is interesting since the original Arabic must have been

Filastin. Therefore, instead of translating it to the more accepted Jewish translation, *Eretz Israel*, they translated it to the Hebrew *Falastina*.

101. *HaHerut*, 29 March 1914, p. 1.
102. Ibid.
103. The fact that 'wealthy ones' were funding education shows us that philanthropy was not only essential for the Jewish Yishuv's survival, but also for the Palestinians. I stress 'Palestinian' instead of Muslim since the 'wealthy ones' donating money could have been Palestinian Christians.
104. It is unclear, and deserves future research, as to why Khalil Efendi was not at all mentioned when the abstract of the interviews was published in *Filastin*.
105. *HaHerut*, 30 March 1914, p. 1.
106. Ibid.

3

The Haram al-Sharif Incident and its Aftermath[1]

> That Palestine holds a place of special importance from the point of view of the history of religion needs no special explanation and is obvious.
>
> The Governor of Jerusalem, Mecid Bey Efendi, 1913[2]

In the spring of 1911, an English exploration team carried out an archaeological dig within the Holy Compound of Haram al-Sharif, which houses the Dome of the Rock (Figure 3.1), and the al-Aqsa Mosque. As explained in the book's first chapter, the compound is one of Islam's holiest places. As one can imagine, any archaeological work within the Haram al-Sharif was bound to strike up fears among the local Palestinian population, who, it can be argued, see themselves as the guardians of the holy site. The 'Haram al-Sharif incident', as documented in a dossier in the Ottoman state archives, highlights also the Palestinians' growing frustration with the Ottoman local administration, and the Ottoman state as a whole, for its inability to protect one of Islam's holiest sites.

Shortly after the dig began, rumours began to spread about the English archaeological team stealing holy relics. This threw Jerusalem into turmoil and led Palestinians to march in protest and call a general strike. Simultaneously, Jerusalem's notables, led by the Khalidi and Husayni families, dispatched numerous telegrams to government ministers and municipalities throughout the Ottoman Empire presenting their case. In solidarity with their counterparts, the notables of Nablus and Gaza joined those in Jerusalem, creating a Palestinian coalition that confronted the local Ottoman administration.[3]

The Haram al-Sharif Incident

During the late nineteenth century, Jerusalem witnessed the opening of the British Palestine Exploration Fund (PEF) and the French École Biblique

Figure 3.1 The Dome of the Rock, Jerusalem. Jacob Wahrman Collection, National Library of Israel, <http://beta.nli.org.il/he/archives/NNL01_Wahrman002716403/NLI_Photo#$FL7833040>

et Archéologique. This marked a general trend, where Europeans became more and more interested in studying the Holy Land, which often induced local fears. As a result, the PEF was repeatedly forced to defend itself against accusations among Palestinians that it was on a mission to discover treasures.[4] In light of this, the PEF reiterated that they abided by Ottoman laws and that many of their findings remained within the Ottoman Empire, located in the Imperial Museum in Constantinople.[5] The PEF's honorary secretary, J. D. Crace, said that 'we seek to obey the law of the land while acquiring knowledge of history, and we are not "treasure-seekers"'.[6]

The English exploration team that arrived in Palestine in 1909 was a private venture and had no connection with the PEF. Nonetheless, the seeds of fear had been sown and the head of the dig, Captain Montague Parker, well understood the sensitivity of the situation. In fact he did his utmost to keep the plans secret since his team actually was on a treasure hunt. Parker belonged to a wealthy aristocratic family, and his brother, the Earl of Morley, was leader of the Liberal Party and a senior member of the

Figure 3.2 Clip of *al-Quds* newspaper, The Institute for Palestine Studies (Ramallah) and the Center for Palestine Studies, Columbia University, <http://www.palestine.mei. columbia.edu/>

British cabinet. Parker first learned about Jerusalem's prospective treasures from Henrich Juvelius, a Finnish scholar of ancient Jewish history, who was travelling throughout Europe searching for benefactors to finance his treasure hunt. Juvelius claimed to have deciphered a secret code concealed within the text of the Old Testament, which would lead them to the Ark of the Covenant and treasures of the First Temple.[7] After meeting with Juvelius, Parker left his post in the British army to dedicate all his time to research.[8] Eventually, he was able to raise the sum of £25,000 from donors, both in Great Britain and the United States, to pay for the mission.[9]

The next part of the venture brought Parker, Juvelius, and a compatriot of Parker's, Captain Hoppenrath,[10] to Jerusalem to designate land where Juvelius believed the treasure existed.[11] After surveying the area south of the Haram al-Sharif and just outside the city walls, they concluded that their excavations should take place on the Hill of Ophel, located adjacent to the village of Silwan (Siloam). Significantly, it was the same place where an archaeologist by the name of Charles Warren had excavated forty years previously, and discovered a system of shafts and subterranean passages, which date back to the period of the First Temple. From this point, known as Warren's shaft, and from Hezekiah's tunnel, Juvelius believed that it would be possible to find passages that led under the Haram al-Sharif.[12]

With the finances secured and the land surveyed, Captain Parker set off for Istanbul to receive permission from the Ottoman authorities to begin the dig. In November 1908, just months after the Young Turk Revolution, Parker signed a contract with Ottoman Prime Minister Kamil Paşa and Finance Minister Ziya Paşa.[13] This contract guaranteed that 50 per cent of all profits would go to the Ottoman government, and in return the government would assist Parker in buying land in Jerusalem necessary for their excavations.[14]

Despite the contract, Parker's representative in Jerusalem, Captain Hoppenrath, encountered problems when trying to purchase the privately owned land. Jerusalem's governor, Subhi Bey, oblivious to the deal struck in Istanbul, supported the land owners against the government and believed that a commission should be set up to investigate the matter. In light of these setbacks, Parker returned to Istanbul, and was successful in convincing the new prime minister and finance minister, Hilmi Paşa and Rıfat Bey, respectively, to intervene on his behalf; they sent an order to Jerusalem's governor to immediately expropriate the land and to sell it to them at a reasonable price,[15] with the finance minister even supplying a false report claiming the land was needed to build a hospital.[16] Upon the recommendation of Ziya Paşa, the former finance minister, Parker hired an Armenian by the name of Hagop Makasdar as an intermediary and translator to accompany them to Jerusalem.[17] Lastly, in order to protect their own interests, the Ottoman government sent two commissioners, Abdülaziz Mecdi Efendi from Karesi, and Habip Bey from Bolu (both MPs), to 'supervise' the work.[18]

After receiving the land, the excavation team finally began their work in August 1909.[19] They set up their base in the village of Silwan, and at first the team encountered local opposition, but this petered out once it became obvious that the team would employ hundreds of local workers. Their work also resulted in enlarging Silwan's water supply, which the locals also welcomed.[20] Once, when their work was suspended in the winter of 1909–10 due to poor weather conditions, they opened up a soup kitchen that offered hot meals to their workers and village residents.[21] The project's merging together of archaeology, infrastructure works and philanthropic acts remind of us other foreign missionaries, such as the American Colony, that were involved not only in helping the local population but also contributing to the urban development, such as its work on installing a telephone system.[22]

By securing the area and allowing only a limited number of people to enter the excavations, forbidding access even to Jerusalem's representatives of the Ottoman Parliament and of the British consul, the team was able to maintain a low profile.[23] Among the people who were allowed in was Hughes Vincent, a priest who belonged to the École Biblique et Archéologique. Parker had Vincent join their work in order to put a stop to the rumours surrounding the secrecy of the dig, and more importantly for his archaeological expertise, since neither Parker himself, nor others on the team, had much knowledge of how to conduct an exploration of this type.[24] Vincent even upheld the scientific nature of the excavations and defended Parker's team in a book published immediately following the Haram al-Sharif incident.[25] Nonetheless, Parker's main purpose in embarking on the dig was the finding of long-lost treasure, with the archaeological motivations coming second.

Captain Parker's project continued intermittently for about two years, with the contract being renewed twice (once because of the damage done to the excavations by harsh weather conditions).[26] In the winter of 1910–11 rumours began to spread that Parker was attempting to dig under the Haram al-Sharif and to 'come up in the sacred area'.[27] Undeterred, by April, the team had decided to move the majority of their operations within the Haram al-Sharif compound itself, where they began work immediately in two main areas. The first location was at the Stables of Solomon, southeast of the Dome of the Rock, where they had hoped to enter a tunnel that would lead under the Dome itself. However, their way was blocked by cisterns and they were not successful. The second site was situated on the opposite side of the Dome, where they entered what is known as the 'rock tunnel'. Once in, they followed it for seven metres, finally reaching a spot located directly under the Sacred Rock itself.[28]

Realising the potentially hostile reaction of Jerusalem's Muslim community, work was carried out only during the late hours of the night under tight security, with Ottoman gendarmes guarding the site. Even so, after nine nights of continuous work, the local population learned of this violation of their holy site on the night of 12 April when Mahrumi Efendi – a caretaker of one of the area's holy sites, the Haram – noticed that one of the compound's gates was open. Upon entering, he came across twelve people standing next to two sacks of soil and after he enquired about their presence, they allegedly threatened him. Following Mahrumi Efendi's visit, the assistant administrator of the district's estates (*liva-i evkaf ikinci katib*) learned about the incident and arrived to investigate in person, concluding that the expedition team's intentions were to open one of the Haram's tunnels. At this point, rumours about holy relics being stolen began to spread rampantly, provoking outrage throughout Palestine.[29] The Istanbul newspaper, *Tanin*, published unconfirmed reports from Palestine's local press that the stolen relics could possibly be of significant religious importance, such as the Ten Commandments, Moses' staff or King Solomon's ring.[30] Others believed that stolen items even included the royal insignia of the House of David.[31] Even though most of the British and American press categorically denied any treasures were stolen, in one *New York Times* article it was reported that despite not finding the Ark of the Covenant, it was believed that the explorers had found 'Solomon's crown, his sword, and his ring, and an ancient manuscript of the Bible'.[32] According to Gustaf Dalman, who was the Swedish consul and an archaeologist affiliated with the Palestine Exploration Fund, it was highly unlikely that they found any treasures since these tunnels had previously been explored by Captain Warren and a French archaeologist.[33] Further, he added that it is 'improbable that any treasure worth naming could lie concealed in a place that had been so often ransacked by Romans, Jews, Moslems, and Christians'.[34]

However far-fetched these reports may have sounded, there was a deep conviction among Palestine's Muslims that holy relics had been stolen, which was prevalent both among the lower and educated classes alike. According to the British consul, 'even among the more educated Moslems the idea seems to prevail that something of value has been removed, as this being so, it is not surprising that among the peasantry the wildest statements should be current'.[35] This belief was reinforced by the fact that immediately following the incident, Captain Parker and his team set off for Jaffa with the intention of boarding their ship and leaving Palestine, amidst rumours that the holy relics were in their possession. This was denied by Azmi Bey, Jerusalem's governor, who nonetheless ordered Jaffa's local administration (*kaymakamlık*) to search the ship, where nothing of any importance was found.[36] Further, the British vice consul reported that all their bags had been previously searched at the Customs House.[37] Captain Parker, however, left without no threat of detainment, and he reiterated that 'all the antiquities we found in the Holy City have been left in the hands of the Turkish government'.[38] Although no documents mention the reason for this, it is likely due to the fact that he was a British subject (and thereby not subject to Ottoman law) and, as previously mentioned, he had familial ties to a member of the British Cabinet. Therefore, any detention would have sparked a diplomatic crisis between Britain and the Ottoman state.

With the expedition team gone, the Palestinians' anger was first redirected towards Azmi Bey and his administration. The notables accused the governor of being responsible, a charge that he adamantly denied.

Jerusalem notables also pointed an accusing finger at the central government in Istanbul, since Captain Parker's team had originally received permission from the Sublime Porte to carry out the excavations. They were also enraged by the fact that Ottoman gendarmes were guarding the Haram al-Sharif while the excavation work was underway.[39] Not surprisingly, adding to the Palestinians' fury, during the excavations in the Haram compound, the two local Ottoman commissioners were on leave in Istanbul.

At the outset of the incident it was reported that some of Jerusalem's Christian communities had feared a backlash, while some Europeans also feared they could be targeted.[40] However, the British consul did not believe that there was 'any ground for this alarm as Moslem irritation has so far been directed against the Governor'.[41] While it was reported in the Istanbul newspaper *Tanin* that demonstrations were to be held in front of British consulates in Jerusalem, Jaffa and as far away as Aleppo,[42] this seemed to not have materialised since there was no information about this in the British consular reports. Almost a month later, reports did surface of small incidents of British subjects being targeted; however, these turned out to be minor ones with the original assessment of the consul holding true.[43] One amounted to an English tourist being refused entry by a group of armed *fallahin* near Bethlehem, and another was when two 'English ladies' were sketching the al-Aqsa Mosque, with permission of the governor, but were politely turned away by the head of the compound, the *Evkaf*.[44] However, there is no doubt that the Palestinians had reached a new level of mistrust for the British, adding to the already prevalent fears of British intervention in Palestine.

Especially significant was that the Haram al-Sharif incident coincided with the Nabi Musa celebrations, a local Muslim tradition, which concludes halfway between Jerusalem and Jericho at a shrine identified with Moses' tomb,[45] attracting pilgrims from all over Palestine who march in processions from their cities of origin to the shrine.[46] In fact, Captain Parker had chosen this period to dig in the Haram al-Sharif compound precisely because most Muslims were on pilgrimage. However, with pilgrims returning, the Ottoman administration was confronted with an increasingly tense situation.

The excavation caused a great upheaval and one that was seen by the local Arab population as a 'boundless act of desecration [of their holy site] and a blow to the honour of their homeland', which was reported in Jerusalem's Hebrew newspaper *Moriah*.[47] Protests arose throughout the city and surrounding areas,[48] and the military authorities posted patrols in every street,[49] as the population was 'aroused to the point of rioting'.[50]

Marches were held, a general strike was called, and about 2,000 angry demonstrators, including both townsmen and *fallahin*, gathered in front of the *Saray*, the seat of the Ottoman government; calls to kill the governor and Englishmen were even heard. Demonstrations were also held in the Haram al-Sharif compound itself against Sheikh Khalil, the main guardian.[51] The crowd motivated their anger at the governor since it was rumoured that he had received a $25,000 bribe – the largest of a whole slew of bribes dealt out to other officials – allowing the team entrance to the Haram.[52]

The height of these protests seems to have occurred at the Friday prayers, when the Istanbul governor, Azmi, showed up to take part and was received with 'curses from the fanatical mob', also spitting on him,[53] and 'was mobbed in the street for supposed complicity in the profanation and hooted as a "pig"'.[54] It was also reported that the mosque's caretaker had his beard and moustache shaved in a public act of humiliation. The Hebrew newspaper *HaHerut* estimated present at the communal prayer were a large group of peasants – more than ten thousand – who were from the villages surrounding Jerusalem and had returned from the Nabi Musa pilgrimage. On the same day, a quarrel between two people escalated into a manifestation of rage against the authorities, with the Ottoman police firing shots in the air to restore order. As thousands of people poured out of the compound, a stampede ensued, with people screaming that a massacre had taken place, prompting storeowners to close their shops.[55] Police and military forces were soon sent out along the roads 'to stop and assure the fleeing people that nothing was the matter, lest alarming reports should unsettle the country'.[56] They also forced the store owners to reopen their shops, leading to the obvious conclusion that they had closed in protest, and not just due to the chaos unfolding during the Friday prayer.[57]

Importantly, throughout the incident, there were no reports that the Jewish community ever felt their security threatened. However, the Hebrew *Moriah* did mention that the Sunday following the Friday prayers, Muslims attacked the Western Wall, which was located in 'their quarter', attacking the Sephardic caretaker, and destroying the benches. This, however, was not reported in any other of Jerusalem's Hebrew press, pointing to the fact that it was an isolated event.[58] In fact, just about two weeks later, the Jerusalem correspondent for *HaTzfira* justified the Arabs' anger over the incident, stating 'all the residents from among all the religions and nationalities are angered and disturbed' over the incident that was unusually serious in scope. However, it once again brought up the incident at the Western Wall, stating that had it not been for the intervention of the local authorities it could have turned into a "small pogrom".[59]

As for the Christian community, the British consul, H. E. Satow, reported to his senior in Istanbul, Sir G. Lowther, that the Christian population had fears that the Muslims might 'vent their wrath' upon them; however, he stated that 'I do not believe that there is any ground for this alarm, as Moslem irritation has so far been directed against the Governor'. He added that 'in any case the garrison has, as is usually the case at Easter, been temporarily strengthened'.[60]

Jerusalem's governor tried to downplay the extent of the unrest, denying that shops were closed in protest and attributing the closings instead to the Nabi Musa celebrations. But the Ottoman regional military commandant (*mir-i alay*), Ali Rıza Bey, denied this, and in a letter to the Office of the General Affairs of the Army, he drew a very different picture. Here he expressed genuine concern over shops closing their doors and the general feeling of tension, and he reported that in order to 'maintain public security, his forces had to exert themselves night and day'.[61]

From the start, the public outcry put Azmi Bey on the defensive. Some reports even state that Azmi's life was in danger and that for the first time the Ottoman governor did not participate in the Nabi Musa celebrations.[62] In order to quell the unrest, Azmi ordered an investigation to be jointly headed by the regional commandant, the public prosecutor, Jerusalem's mayor, the mufti, the public instruction administrator (*maarif müdürü*), the police chief and the main scribe of the *Evkaf* (Islamic foundation).[63] However, this did little to reassure the local population that the truth would be revealed, and many asserted that the investigation's purpose was simply to cover up the extent of Azmi's involvement in the affair.[64]

News of the investigation did not quell the tension and Azmi Bey expressed his concern about the growing anger of the local population in a letter to the Ministry of the Interior. Without mentioning their names directly, he accused some of Jerusalem's notables of unfairly judging the incident by not waiting for the investigation's result and stated that their actions would not be tolerated. He went on to accuse different groups from among the general population (*ehali*) and Bedouins (*'urbani*), who were 'taking advantage of pilgrimages', whether to Mecca or Jerusalem, in order to incite the masses to hold demonstrations (*icra-i nümayiş*) against the government.[65]

Azmi Bey also had four people arrested who he claimed were responsible for allowing the expedition team to work within the compound. The first arrested was Hagop Makasdar, the previously mentioned intermediary and translator, who also held British citizenship. Despite the Catholic Armenian Bishop's request to the British consul to help secure his release, he opted not to interfere, 'feeling that it would be both useless to do so, as the matter was in the hands of the Commission and that any intervention on my part might give rise to false impressions'. He added that Makasdar's case 'seems a hard one, as, whatever he may have done, he was only acting as a subordinate'.[66] Also arrested were the official caretaker of the Haram compound (*kayyum-i baş*), Sheikh Khalil al-Zanaf and his two sons.[67] Zanaf denied this accusation and placed the blame on Azmi saying that Azmi had ordered him to let the team into the compound.[68] On 6 June, Zanaf and his sons were sent to Beirut, together with the above-mentioned Makasdar and two gendarme officers to stand trial,[69] where later they were found guilty and executed.

While Azmi Bey was busy trying to put this case behind him, Jerusalem's notables, representing more than ten families, and led by the Husaynis and Khalidis, began a two-tiered campaign to remove the Ottoman governor. First, these notables dispatched official telegrams to the prime minister, Parliament, the interior and war ministries and to the governor in Beirut.[70] The first letter was sent out on 19 April, and even though the majority of signatures were from among the Husayni family, when reporting this letter to the minister of the interior, the prime minister noted that it was signed by Musa Shafiq al-Khalidi and his counterparts.[71] These petitions were reprinted in Jaffa-based *Filastin*, and, according to the Hebrew newspaper *HaTzvi*, the newspaper directed much of their anger at the Jerusalem governor and the head of the gendarme.[72]

Secondly, Jerusalem's notables sent letters to their counterparts in other cities in Palestine, such as Nablus, warning them of the imminent danger posed by archaeological expeditions. These letters of warning are mentioned in the governor of Nablus's report to Istanbul on 18 April, just one week after Mahrumi Efendi came upon the open gate at the compound. In his report, the governor of Nablus mentions that the notables of Jerusalem sent a telegram to the Nablus municipality that was addressed to 'the Islamic people'.[73] According to the British ambassador, the Khalidi family opted to correspond with the authorities in Istanbul, while the Husaynis preferred reaching out to their counterparts in the Empire, in what seems to have been aimed at placing pressures on Istanbul.[74] While there is no evidence of this, the fact that this struck at the hearts of Muslims, both in Jerusalem and Nablus, and in other cities in Palestine, news of the incident seems to have reached the general public during Friday prayers, being conveyed in the *khutba*, the weekly sermon. From other reports, we know that in Hebron the local Muslim population was also greatly moved, as well as the sheikhs of Bedouin tribes east of Jordan.[75]

The news also reached other cities in Palestine by way of the local Palestinian Arabic press: the local Arabic *al-Quds* covered it in every issue for about two months (Figure 3.2). In the breaking news stories it also included an open letter to the sultan, calling for justice, addressing him in Turkish, and also included in it dispatches to the different offices in Istanbul.[76] The newly founded newspaper *Filastin* based in Jaffa, and Jerusalem's *al-Nafir*. Unfortunately, copies of the newspapers cannot be found for the period when the incident first occurred;[77] however, despite this, there is extensive evidence that the press played a decisive role in educating the masses about the incident. For example, in their complaint to the Sheikh al-Islam (*meşihat penahi*) and to Parliament, Nablus's notables mention that they gathered information about the incident from the press.[78] Moreover, in an article commemorating *Filastin*'s six-month anniversary, the editor proudly mentioned that 'the issue that we went into most detail about was the Azmi Bey and the Haram al-Sharif question and we do not think that any other paper has written as much about this as the *Filastin* newspaper has'.[79] This is significant since, as mentioned earlier, the owners and editors of *Filastin*, Yusuf and 'Isa al-'Isa, were Christian and the paper had a large Christian readership in addition to Muslims. The fact *Filastin*'s editors took pride in covering the story extensively demonstrates that the Haram al-Sharif incident was a rallying point for all Palestinians regardless of whether they were Christian or Muslim.

This incident, and the opening of an Islamic school of higher education, discussed later in the chapter, demonstrate *Filastin* was not only leading the battle against the Zionist settlement, but was also active in making its voice heard in Jerusalem and beyond. This was important since its anti-Zionist rhetoric, while appealing to the masses in the Jaffa region, was less critical to the everyday life of the Jerusalemites. The denizens of Jerusalem did not feel the immediate effects of the Jewish rural settlements, which by this time had become a daily reality in the villages surrounding Jaffa, and even in the city of Jaffa itself.[80]

The other newspaper that covered this event was Jerusalem's *al-Nafir*; while copies of *al-Nafir* are not available, we learn about its coverage from Jerusalem's Hebrew newspaper *HaHerut*, which reported how the incident was unfolding in the Arabic press.[81] Also, the Istanbul newspaper *Tanin* reported that it based its news reports concerning the incident on local newspapers.[82] The government also used the local press to express their side of the issue by publishing a declaration whose purpose was to calm the nerves (*tatmin-i efkar*) of the population.[83]

Moreover, once word reached Nablus, its notables joined Jerusalem in expressing their anger over the incident.[84] In a letter to the Islamic High Court and the Ottoman Parliament, Nablus's notables demanded that the government locate the missing artefacts belonging to Muslims, and they described how the incident had 'broken the hearts of the people of the Nablus region'.[85] Although there was no evidence of civil unrest in the city as the events in Jerusalem unfolded, the authorities must have been aware that there was a strong possibility that unrest could spread to other regions.

Since the *sanjak* of Nablus was under the jurisdiction of Beirut, it is not surprising that the administration in Beirut was especially concerned about developments in Jerusalem. We learn this first from a letter from Beirut to Istanbul, where the deputy governor reports to the Ministry of the Interior about the case after learning about it from the Beirut mufti, who, as happened in Nablus, received news of this from a telegram sent by the Husaynis and Khalidis.[86]

Once the news reached Gaza, its notables also joined in, although in contrast to their peers in other cities, these leaders took advantage of the charged atmosphere to present wider complaints about the failings of the local Ottoman administration. On 23 April, notables from Gaza, representing the Abu Khadra, Fayyad and the Surani families, complained to Istanbul about the local administration's corruption and pro-Zionist tendencies.[87] These telegrams (which appear below), like the ones from Jerusalem, were simultaneously sent to numerous government offices,[88] but these were much more critical in tone and give us a further glimpse into how highlighting their attachment to Palestine became an inherent part of their collective struggle. Their long list of accusations reflects not only the great animosity they had towards the Ottoman administration, but also for other local Palestinian notables who collaborated with it:

> The current state of the present government in this district, which encompasses Zionist ambitions and falls on the Egyptian border, which is full of ancient relics, is unconstitutional. And especially during the time of the current governor Azmi Bey, and his relations with Jerusalem's influential ones and Gaza's kaimmakam and mayor, and the members of its administration, and its former mufti, who is currently residing in Constantinople, and other influential ones of Jaffa and Beer Sheeba [whose purpose is] to steal the money of the *umma*, [and] to embezzle the treasury money. Blood has been shed, disgrace has occurred, public order has been occupied, security no longer exists, and the present continuous emigration [of Arabs] needs your immediate attention . . . In conclusion . . . what is going on in the district (of Jerusalem) in general and Gaza in particular . . . will increase . . . Palestine is a dear land [*filastin bilad*

'*aziza*], home of the Prophets and religion [*din*], protect her in the name of God, faithful men of the state, help us with a just investigation.[89]

By mentioning that the district 'falls on the Egyptian border, which is full of ancient artefacts', the Gazan notables appear to have been linking what was happening in their region to the Haram al-Sharif incident. Just as treasures had fallen into foreign hands in Jerusalem, it was implied that if the land was sold to the Zionist movement, that this could happen in Gaza as well. Further, as documented in the previous chapter, Palestinians also were concerned with the growing number of bribes being paid to Ottoman officials by Jews to purchase land for new settlements, which in 1911 saw a sharp rise.[90]

First, with the British occupying Egypt since 1882, Palestine had become a frontier community, and these Gazan notables must have been aware of the special importance as guards of the homeland. On numerous occasions since 1903 the Zionist movement had also tried to purchase land in the Rafah and al-Arish of the Sinai Peninsula, not far from Gaza city. However, this was out of the authority of the Ottoman Empire, and was regulated by the British, who occupied Egypt and kept a strong hold over the Sinai. Just as Jerusalem was experiencing the unrest due to the Haram al-Sharif incident, a land sale which had been under negotiation off and on since 1906 was about to be finalised.[91] Significantly, the purchase was brokered by the British consular agent in Gaza, Alexander Knesevich, since the British were interested in setting up a British colony which could be populated by Zionist Jews, some of whom were British subjects.[92] But this transaction was cancelled that summer after it became clear that the Egyptian government (and the British) were opposed to the idea of Jewish settlement in its territory.[93]

Following this first petition by Gaza notables, another group of notables from Gaza, representing the Sarraj, Hamdi, Abu Ghali and Mubashir families,[94] also complained to the state that 'the stealing of antiquities from Palestine does not stop with the al-Aqsa Mosque'.[95] Similar to the previous telegram, while less intensively, they also openly criticised the Ottoman administration. However, in contrast, this one adhered to the problem of European archaeology and did not mix this problem with Zionism. Rather, they informed the state of other areas that were under threat of being 'raided by foreigners', including sites in Gaza, Majdil and Asqalan – the city of Saladin.[96] Perhaps the reason this group chose not to mention Zionism outright was because they believed that the Haram al-Sharif incident stood on its own and they did not need to discuss Zionism in order to justify their other claims against the local government. However, by mentioning Saladin, they were introducing a recurring theme that was an integral part of the Palestinians' memory of their land. Haim Gerber reminds us that the 'memory of the Crusades [and Saladin] lived on in Palestine since the Middle Ages'.[97] For them, Saladin was the hero who had saved Palestine from the Crusaders. Just months before the Haram al-Sharif incident, Palestinians had rallied around Saladin in order to promote opposition to Zionist immigration since they believed that in northern Palestine, Saladin's fortress had been sold to Zionists in the Fula land sale, which, as we saw in the previous chapter, sparked one of the first cases of organised Arab opposition to Zionism.[98] This was just among the many letters written by the previously mentioned Ottoman Arab politician Shukri al-Asali, who led the campaign against Zionism in the Arabic press using the pen name Saladin. The fact that the Gaza notables also mentioned Saladin allows us to understand that whether in northern or southern Palestine, foreign intervention evoked a fear that was linked to a particular historical memory. However, in the case of Fula, following a 'civil and military' investigation, the Ottoman government in Istanbul concluded that on the land that was sold to the Jewish buyer, there was no evidence of a fortress or historical artefacts.[99]

The most remarkable aspect of both documents from Gaza is their portrayal of Palestine; in the first telegram, Palestine is described as a 'dear land' (*bilad 'aziza*) and 'home of the Prophets'. The second refers to Palestine as 'our beloved land' (*biladna al-mahbuba*). In each, it is evident that although they were concerned with what was occurring in the Gaza area, they perceived themselves as belonging to a greater entity.

Besides notifying their counterparts in Palestine, Jerusalem's notables notified municipalities throughout the Ottoman Empire, such as to Izmir, and Baghdad.[100] In the letter to Izmir, the notables provided basic information concerning the Haram al-Sharif incident, mentioning that the incident had been presented to the High Court, and expressing hope that the Izmir municipality would voice their solidarity.[101] While it is not clear whether or not these municipalities responded positively to this request, these letters exist today only because the municipalities forwarded the actual letters or provided a summary to the Ministry of Interior in Istanbul.[102]

The Ottoman State's Reaction

The Ottoman government began to comprehend the seriousness of the Haram al-Sharif incident and worked quickly to control the growing animosity felt towards them in Palestine. Because such open attacks on the state were unprecedented in Palestine it was the felt that the situation might well deteriorate even to the point that military intervention would be necessary. What is remarkable is that back in 1908, Ali Ekrem Bey, the governor of Jerusalem, had warned that Jerusalem's notables posed a threat to the government. In a letter assessing the situation in Jerusalem at the time of the revolution, he expressed his fear that the Ottoman government would face some sort of resistance from Jerusalem's notables from among the Husayni, Khalidi, Nashashibi and the Da'udi families.[103] He went on to warn Istanbul that due to Jerusalem's holy status, any small problem could turn into a serious incident.[104]

Similar to Jerusalem's governor, Azmi Bey, the authorities in Istanbul decided to open an official investigation. This idea was first put forward by Jerusalem's regional commandant, Ali Rıza Bey. In a report to Istanbul, he suggested sending a commission to replace the local commission, which had not succeeded in reducing local tension.[105] Accepting these recommendations, Minister of War Mahmud Şevket Paşa, in an official communique to the minister of the interior, ordered that an investigative team be sent to Jerusalem.[106] Along with these two ministers, Minister of Justice Necmettin Molla Bey was also in charge of setting up the committee.[107]

The investigation began on 30 April, and was led by the Trablusşam governor, Azmi Bey (not to be confused with the Azmi Bey who was the governor of Jerusalem), along with Aleppo's Wakf administrator (*Halep evkaf müdürü*), Mari' Pasha, and the regional gendarmes commander (*nizame fırkası kumandanı*), Haşim Bey, who was based in Haifa.[108]

The Parliamentary Debate

Just days before this investigation was completed, Ruhi al-Khalidi and Said al-Husayni presented the Palestinian case to the Ottoman Parliament. In the parliamentary debate held on 8 May, Khalidi pointed his finger both at the local administration and at government ministers in Istanbul. In opening the debate, Khalidi, who at times was quite sarcastic, provides important missing information:

> The issue [to be discussed] above all is a mysterious one. It starts off like . . . *One Thousand and One Nights* or *Monte Cristo*, which was authored by Alexander Dumas. Issues like this, however, can be observed in the revolutions of the Great Powers. Now, there were a few men from among the English nobility who following . . . [the Young Turk Revolution] applied to the [new] government, one of them was his excellency Captain Parker the brother of the famous Lord Morley, a member of the English cabinet . . .

However, within minutes, Khalidi turned Parliament's attention to members of the former cabinet, to Prime Minister Kamil Paşa, and to

Minister of Finance Ziya Paşa, indirectly accusing them of corruption. He uncovered the scandal by reporting that they had signed the contract, even though it should have been referred to the Ministry of Public Instruction (*maarif nezareti*) and the Museum Affairs office. According to Khalidi, the English team estimated this treasure at 100 million Turkish lira, an enormous sum considering that the Ottoman debt during this period totalled about 115 million lira.[109] The claim that the treasure was worth such a large amount was later described by *The Times* as being 'the flamboyant imagination of the Orient'.[110] Khalidi did not stop there, however, but went on to accuse Jerusalem Governor Azmi Bey and Gendarme Commander Sami Bey of secretly receiving monthly salaries from the British government.[111]

In Parliament, Minister of the Interior Halil Bey presented the government's case. Losing his patience, he cut short Said al-Husayni and, most likely to the dismay of many of the MPs present, confirmed that indeed a contract had been signed between the two parties, and that the English team was in fact searching for treasure. He went on to explain that if treasure had been found, it would have been divided between the Ottoman state and the English exploration team. However, the minister did not give details of the Haram al-Sharif incident itself, claiming that this was the work of the investigative committee.[112] Despite this, he did share with Parliament some of his outlandish ideas about who perhaps masterminded this: a man who had been arrested in Nablus, dressed like a North African (*maghribi*), who was an accused spy, and had dodged his army service. It just so happened that this man had been in Jerusalem at the time of the incident, was known to have possessed army and civil servant uniforms and, according to Beirut's governor, during the excavation he was seen dressed as a gendarme.[113]

Protesting the Ottoman administration's innocence, the minister asserted that it had acted appropriately and had nothing to hide. He also claimed that the English team did not escape from the site in order to steal treasure but was on their way to a vacation.[114]

The minister's words were contested and the heckling of MPs constantly interrupted him, the Parliament Speaker repeatedly called the members to order. Numerous parliamentarians lined up to speak and one of the Christian members yelled out, 'This issue does not only concern Islam, it is also of concern to Christians.'[115] From the text, it can be understood that the parliamentarians were angered by the fact that most of what Khalidi had accused the government of had just been confirmed. This heated debate ended with the minister agreeing to report details of the investigation back to Parliament.

Also speaking on behalf of the government was Abdülaziz Mecdi Efendi, one of the two commissioners sent to Palestine to oversee the work. After he explained why he had accepted the position, several Parliament members yelled out, 'Why was the contract kept secret?' In answer, Abdülaziz went into a long explanation about the importance of the archaeological dig, and how any treasure found there, whatever its value, would be worth quite a sum and therefore 'for the nation there would be a great profit from it'. Also, while explaining the historical importance of the site, he pointed out that other teams had already been working in the region, such as a French team supported by the Rothschild family. Moreover, he made numerous references to Zionism and how the origins of its name came from Mt Zion,[116] subtlety alluding to the fact that securing cooperation with the English exploration team meant that the holy relics would not fall into the hands of Zionists. Of particular note is his statement that Jerusalem's notables did not believe that the Haram al-Sharif was in danger of being robbed by Jews, or for that matter, Zionists, and therefore had never mentioned this.

The debate strongly resembled the 1911 debate on Zionism, uniting the Arab Parliament members regardless of party affiliation. The best example of this is that, just as they had during the debate on Zionism, Ruhi al-Khalidi and Shukri al-Asali joined forces despite the fact that Khalidi was a staunch supporter of the CUP and Asali was one of the leaders of the opposition.[117] In fact, it was believed by some that the Arabs were using this case as a point of rally against the government.[118]

Findings of the Investigation

When a state investigation team sent their seven-page report to Istanbul on 13 May, it focused only on what had happened in Jerusalem and did not question the relationship between Parker and the government. The report confirmed Jerusalem's governor accusations that the 'the caretakers and the gendarme were bribed by way of [the team's] translator [Makasdar]' and goes on to add that 'it was found that the government and bureaucrats took no part and had no information'. The committee described how both Azmi Bey and the gendarme commander, Sami Bey, had received monthly salaries from the British consulate, and this accusation eventually led to Azmi Bey leaving his post,[119] on 21 May, just a little over than a month since news first broke of the incident.[120] Leaving Jerusalem, Azmi Bey insisted that this was just to be a month's leave of absence, but it was clear that he was being replaced. Less than a month later he was officially dismissed from his position.[121] At the same time, the commission accused the Jerusalem notables of using the incident as a pretext to express their dissatisfaction with the Ottoman governor.[122] The British ambassador added upon his leaving that both Azmi and Sami were 'leading lights' among the CUP, and was quite unfriendly to Europeans and avoided private intercourse with foreigners.[123] Therefore, it is ironic that it would be the act of a foreigner that would bring his career in Jerusalem to an end.

The Ottoman government opted to punish low-level officials only, failing to implicate high-level ones in Istanbul. Surprisingly, relations between Istanbul and Captain Parker continued even after the incident. During the investigation, Parker, on his way back to London, stopped over in Istanbul in order to meet with government officials. Unfortunately, details of this visit are unknown, but the meeting itself was not kept secret since it was reported in the press.[124] Parker himself, who was under growing criticism in England, defended his work in Jerusalem but refused to comment on the Haram al-Sharif incident until the commission had published its report.[125] The case made it all the way to the House of Commons, when in early July the Under-Secretary of State for Foreign Affairs, Thomas McKinnon Wood, was addressed over the question if the British consul of Jerusalem had submitted a report of the incident and if the Sheikh of the Haram and others had been imprisoned due to the 'consequence of the action of certain British subjects who have been seeking treasures in Jerusalem'. Wood confirmed that this was not within the jurisdiction of His Majesty's Government but assured the House that an Ottoman commission took the necessary actions to put an end to the case.[126]

Second Parliamentary Debate

Three days after the report, the incident once again surfaced in Parliament. Minutes after the debate on Zionism, in which Ruhi al-Khalidi spoke in great detail on its history and aims, Acre's representative Assad Tawfiq confronted the minister of the interior's handling of the incident. The fact that Tawfiq was from a northern region is of special importance since the Ottoman documents only provide us with insight on how the incident unfolded in central and southern Palestine. Arguing that recalling Jerusalem's governor was insufficient, Tawfiq asked, 'let us say that the governor did not commit a crime but just a mistake, [then] does this not constitute a sufficient reason to immediately dismiss him?' Very importantly, Tawfiq also places the event in a global context, and explained how the fact that this event caused animosity as far as way as Afghanistan and India should alone be cause for his removal.[127]

Almost two months after the Haram al-Sharif incident first occurred, the case was finally put to rest when, on 4 June, the minister of the interior reported to Parliament that Azmi Bey had been recalled and that the case would be referred to the Beirut tribunal.[128] By the summer of 1911, following the investigation, the appointment of a new Jerusalem governor, Cevdet Bey, and the recognition that no treasure had been stolen from the Haram al-Sharif, the situation in Palestine returned to normal.[129] Nevertheless, the head of the Palestine Exploration Fund noted that, as archaeologists, they had lost the confidence of the local population as their archaeological excavations continued.[130] That autumn Parker was even permitted to return, according to *The Times*, the Turkish government having exonerated him of any wrongdoing, the excavations would be 'resumed with the full approval of the authorities in Constantinople, who have appointed officials to supervise the operations'.[131] This was facilitated by reappointed Minister of Finance Cavid Bey, who received a £600 advance to go towards the financing of such inspectors.[132] Where this money ended up is unclear, but it should not be overlooked that Captain Parker himself paid, at least in part, Ottoman government officials, which portrays a clear conflict of interest.

Upon Parker's arrival to the Jaffa port, friends advised him that due to the local opposition, it would be unwise to disembark. Moreover, Ottoman authorities indeed cut short his trip, expelling him from Palestine, due to the renewed excitement (*telaş ve heyecan*) among the 'general population'[133] that his return occasioned. This was not even taking into consideration the hostilities directed at Europeans by the local population as a result of the 1911 Italian invasion of Libya,[134] which were sparked by demonstrations held in Jaffa, Ramlah and Lydda and not only proved dangerous for Europeans, but also threatened the harmony between local Christians and Muslims, as dogs dressed with crosses were paraded through the streets.[135] It would be interesting to explore this in future research, to see how widespread anti-Christian sentiments were among the general Muslim population. However, as we have seen, in the pages of *Filastin* and *al-Quds* a clear bond between the two communities was the trend, one that would remain intact for decades to come. Concerning this event, *Filastin*'s writers came out strongly against the acts of violence and humiliation towards Ramlah's Christian population, with one highlighting the spirit of the equal status between all Ottoman citizens, Muslims, Christians and Jews, and another article highlighting the strong bonds between the Christians and Muslims in Palestine.

Reimagining Jerusalem: An Islamic University

In light of the Haram al-Sharif incident and the growing hegemony of Europeans and the Jewish Yishav, the Palestinians felt a new urgency in protecting Jerusalem. In the summer of 1911, just months after the incident, the newspaper *Filastin* ran a series of articles addressing the need to introduce a regional education centre in Jerusalem, which would be equivalent to that of Al-Azhar, the prestigious Islamic university in Cairo.[136] In an article entitled 'The Islamic Colleges (*al-Kulliyat al-Islamiyya*)', Hajji Raghib al-Khalidi gave an overview of the state of Islamic education in the neighbouring regions, including Al-Azhar, focusing also on education offered at Jerusalem's al-Aqsa Mosque, within the Haram al-Sharif compound, and suggested that it should be transformed into an Islamic centre of education. What essentially he was arguing for was to transform the already existing centre for local Muslims and to extend it out into a much greater project.[137] Further, he argued that the *waqf* (religious endowment) should be transferred from Ottoman state control and placed in local hands.

In his ensuing explanation, we receive a unique picture of how a local religious leader perceived the future of Palestine:

> Palestine is the Holy Land for the Peoples of the Book [Muslims, Jews and Christians] and for that reason it was and it continues to be subject to religious or political wars as in the history of Palestine ever since the Children of Israel occupied it until the Crusaders took control of it, which is famous and well known, but when ... Sultan Salah al-Din (who is in heaven) saw that the strengthening of the Islamic community (*al-Jami'a al-Islamiyya*) would not be possible without reclaiming this Holy Land and turning it into a centre ... After he saw that the force of the sword would not be sufficient by itself to strengthen the Islamic authority in Palestine, he turned to the power of science, and thus established schools (*madaris*), hospices (*rubatat*) and hospitals, until he transformed this Holy Land (*diyar*) into a source of knowledge (*'ulum wa 'urfan*) and followed in the practice of the Circassians and Turkmen kings ... they bought the majority of villages in this district and endowed it for religious and political purposes.

Remarkably, what is proposed here, besides Jerusalem having to be protected from Jews and (foreign) Christians, was that a practical plan needed to be implemented to protect Palestine's lands from foreign penetration, whether cultural or from their actual presence in the Land. This would entail purchasing lands in and around Jerusalem that would be endowed as Islamic lands, preventing them from being sold to foreigners. Khalidi also stated that there was a certain geographical importance to this college being located in Jerusalem, as 'it is at a middle point between Syria, the Hijaz and Egypt'.

Khalidi's fears of foreign penetration also caught the attention of the Ottoman administration, and reveals that it is impossible to separate the fear of foreign cultural penetration from the actual threat of British occupation over the Land. While in retrospect there was no way of knowing that the Ottoman Empire would fall in World War I, and that Britain would occupy Palestine in the late months of 1917, the Palestinians were aware of the possibility that one day they might lose Palestine to British imperialism, a fear that likely would have persisted even in the absence of Zionist immigration.[138] A secret 1911 report that was issued from Nablus went into detail about a secret meeting he held with the Greek Orthodox Patriarch of Jerusalem, who informed him that the Haram al-Sharif incident 'had a profound impact on both the Islamic and Christian communities', and he went on to warn 'that this deplorable act that has happened could have caused great anxiety to our State (God forbid!), which was prevented by the administration and military authorities' ability to see far into the future . . .' In this same report he also went into great detail about how the 'indigenous population' believed that the growing presence of foreigners – referring to Jews and Europeans in two separate categories – posed a threat to the local culture:

> Generally speaking, it is evident that the land's indigenous population's (*ahali-yi asliye-yi memleket*) properties and land are being lost, they are being transferred to foreigners and Jews and [it is evident] that the Ottoman language has become non-existent in the government . . . and it is clear the Arabic language is also disappearing, and that the Islamic population is to a large extent diminishing.[139]

Also causing worry to the patriarch was the influence of Protestants, Roman Catholics and Christian communities on the local population, a point that the Greek Orthodox – who were loyal subjects – could identify with. This was exhibited in their activities surrounding their religious and humanitarian work in their monasteries, schools and orphanages. He concludes that we are doing our utmost 'to win the hearts ignorant one in villages who cannot even distinguish the good from the bad, including the children of Islam who goes to [our] schools'.

The governor identified with the words of the Greek Patriarch, adding that there are now those who in Palestine from the population that 'cannot understand one word of the official language of the state, but can speak fine French and English', and that 'I [myself] have encountered Muslim youth [like this] in schools in Jaffa, Jerusalem and Beirut'. This seemed to be a safe assessment since we know that both Ottoman MPs Ruhi al-Khalidi and Said al-Husayni had briefly attended the Alliance School. Also, we see in an 1894 article that boys of Muslim notables were enrolled in the Jewish school at Haifa. The report that was commissioned by supporters of the Alliance and Anglo-Jewish school networks also named schools in Istanbul that had Muslims of good standing, and noted that their enrolment in Jewish schools was done purposely since their parents did not need to worry about the schools proselytising their children, not like at Christian missionary schools.[140]

The governor continued that even 'In Nablus, which only has a few foreigners and three to four hundred Christians, things exist such as Christian woman, who are not observing the rules of modesty and learning English together with men'. For our purposes, it is especially interesting that in order to combat the spread of the European culture, the patriarch reported to the Ottoman administration the very plan Khalidi had spoken about, opening an Ottoman university. In a plea to Istanbul, Fethi Bey stressed that 'we have to think of our future not in terms of a few years but rather hundreds, and according to this it will be necessary to determine for ourselves a new way, a new political path'. Following this, the Ottoman official continued and proposed transforming the classrooms that once housed students within the Haram al-Sharif to be transformed to what he called a 'university', not using the Islamic term, *kulliya*. He went on to point out what Khalidi also had, that it was a meeting point between Syria, Egypt and the Hijaz, and that it would be comparable to that of Egypt's Al-Azhar. Lastly, Süleyman Fethi Bey took pride in the face that this university would be taught in the Ottoman language (*lisan-i Osmani*), which was all the more crucial with the above-explained worries.[141]

The Greek Patriarch did not stop with the British cultural threat and went on to confirm that the Palestinian population held views similar to those of the central Ottoman government concerning the growing English threat:

> It is clear that the main objective of the English is to spread and establish their English population to the Mediterranean coast from Tripoli all the way to Egypt and in India, Iran, Basra, Baghdad, Al-Jazira [present-day Northern Iraq] and Palestine. And there is no doubt that in the near future, following the path from India to Egypt, that they will establish a railway.[142]

Firstly, we know from other historical sources that the British were interested in setting up a railway from Baghdad to Homs and the Mediterranean through Mesopotamia and Syria.[143] Further, this report is all the more interesting in light of the fact that just eight years later the

British would occupy both Palestine and Iraq; however, the patriarch's fears of British (and French) encroachment should not come as a surprise to us. Further, by 1911, most of North Africa had already been occupied by the British and French, and that year marked the Italian invasion of Libya, which left hundreds of Ottoman troops stuck in southern Palestine trying to cross over the Sinai in late December to reach Egypt, and then go onto Libya to fight the Italians.[144] According to British records, hundreds of Ottoman soldiers had arrived to the border, with 400 soldiers making their way south to Beersheba trying to bypass the British ban on crossing into the Sinai, and others pitching tents and preparing the large amount of camels for the journey. Among the potential military personnel was Shakib Arslan, who the British claimed was trying to gain passage as a merchant.[145] However, the attempt seemed to have failed with the British officials upholding the order that 'no persons are to be allowed to go to Egypt via the Sinai Peninsula'.

Even if many of the Jews were becoming Ottoman citizens and integrating into the Ottoman system, it is important to point out here that even before World War I the British knew that some Jews believed that one day Palestine might fall into British hands. The British consul in Jerusalem made note of the fact that the Zionists 'had always striven to secure the protection of the British flag for their institutions, being convinced that under *no other auspices* could they hope to attain their object, viz., the settlement of a Hebrew-speaking Jewish population in the land of their fathers',[146] and that there was an inclination

> among an influential section of Zionists to place as many of their institutions as possible under British protection, the principle motives for this preference being distrust of French policy and the idea that this country [Palestine] may eventually in some way come under British sovereignty.[147]

This confirms the fact that the fear that the British would one day occupy Palestine was not out of line with reality and an aspect that certainly deserves more attention in the future.

A closer examination of the Nablus governor's dispatch reveals that three of the regions mentioned were already under direct British control: Iran (the southern region), India and Egypt. The fact that the report mentioned Iraq, in addition to Palestine, was not coincidental, since there were similarities between the two Ottoman regions. First, Iraq was under the looming threat of British imperial plans; and surprisingly, and as will be discussed in Chapter 5, there were also plans to make Iraq a place to absorb Jewish refugees.[148]

Just a few years later, the topic of the university would once again emerge. In the spring of 1914, former MP Said al-Husayni addressed the foundation of the university on the campaign trail, vowing to propose it to Parliament, reiterating the role it would play in strengthening Islam in Jerusalem by serving Muslims from different cities and countries and being comparable to Al-Azhar.[149] In fact, less than a year later, just months after the Ottomans entered World War I on 28 January 1915, the school was established and named the 'Salahiyya College' (*al-Kulliya al-Sala-hiyya*), retaining the namesake of Saladin.[150] While identified historically as a post-World War Ottoman decision, the information here shows that it was a long-term plan developed by local Palestinians; nevertheless, in the end the curriculum remained under the jurisdiction of the Ministry of the *Evkaf* (Religious Foundations) in Istanbul, geared towards training *ulama'* (Islamic scholars) in religious and secular sciences.[151]

As we find in both the Ottoman report and *Filastin*'s articles, as well as in the election campaign of March 1914, the *Kulliya* took on the char-acteristics of the school proposed by Hajji Raghib al-Khalidi and found in the Greek Patriarch's report to Jerusalem in 1911. While the fate of the school is beyond the scope of this work – and deserves attention in future research – we know that at its opening many indeed saw it as a competitor to Al-Azhar, and that it served not only Palestinians but had regional and international enrolment.[152] The very fact that in 1916 there were sixty-five applicants from Damascus alone demonstrates the viability of Jerusalem reviving its importance as a regional centre of learning, and in essence strengthening the Palestinians hold over Jerusalem.[153]

As Hajji Raghib al-Khalidi was proposing in 1911 to establish a uni-versity to strengthen Islamic culture in the face of the encroachment of European culture, in the next chapter we will see that the Zionist movement was simultaneously in the midst of setting up a Jewish institution for higher education in Jerusalem, which eventually evolved into the establishment of the Hebrew University, which opened its doors in 1925. Palestinians and Jews creating institutions of higher education exclusively for their own peoples at this early date serves as a stark example of how divisions between them were already well embedded into their worldviews.

Placed in such an overall context, in the end what is most compelling, however, about the Haram al-Sharif incident is that the mistrust and anger towards the Ottomans and British it fomented in only three years came to be completely directed at the Jewish population. This switch is significant since even though the Jewish community had made up the second-largest religious group since the late nineteenth century, never did the Muslims perceive them as a major threat to their holy sites. However, as we saw in the example in the previous chapter of the Jerusalem Petition, this no longer held true, with claims that 'the al-Aqsa Mosque which is the keepsake of Salah al-Din al-Ayyubi and the first qibla has practically been handed over to the Jews with consent . . .' This is just one more way of understanding that the Palestinians were well aware of the fact that the Jewish population had transformed into a national community, regardless of their original nationalities, and that as a community aspiring to national rights, they challenged Muslim hegemony over Palestine at large.

The Haram al-Sharif incident was important to Muslims worldwide – including an Indian group arriving in the summer to investigate the matter – as it was their belief that the incident happened under the auspices of the British government, and had greatly affected people in India, especially the 'lower and ignorant' classes, and this was due to the fact that it was believed that whoever was able to get a hold of the holy relics 'will gain complete dominion over Islam'.[154]

Clearly, the actions taken by the Palestinians reiterated their perceived role as protectorates of Jerusalem's holy sites.[155] What made the Haram al-Sharif incident such a potent flashpoint was a confluence of tradition and innovation. The tradition was the simple fact that the incident coincided with the Nabi Musa festival. Therefore, pilgrims were informed of these events, and once they had arrived back home, they served as messengers revealing the alarming news to their fellow villagers and families. Innovation, on the other hand, can be found in the outrage expressed in the local press.

The Haram al-Sharif incident also provides us with a unique portrait of the emergence of a modern Palestinian collective struggle. This incident was sparked by European cultural penetration, but the local residents justifiably held the Ottoman administration responsible. The Palestinians were uncompromising in their demands for the removal of the governor. Unquestionably, what gave the Palestinians their strength, and what made it a *Palestinian* opposition, was that they united together: the notables with the masses, the educated with the uneducated, Muslims and Christians.

In terms of Palestinian history, the Haram al-Sharif incident demonstrates the complexities of Palestine during the pre-Mandate period. Moreover, it serves as a good example of how we, as scholars, while concentrating on the Palestinian–Jewish conflict, have overlooked other points of interest concerning the local Palestinian population. As scholars of late Ottoman Palestinian history, it is for us to uncover them and place them in their proper context.

Notes

1. An article based on this chapter was published in the *Journal of Palestine Studies*, in spring 2005; see Fishman, 'The Haram al-Sharif Incident: Palestinian Notables versus the Ottoman Administration', *Journal of Palestine Studies*, pp. 6–22.
2. DH.SYS 1331.10.14, 27/6; 15 September 1913.
3. Rashid Khalidi has argued previously that Palestinian modern nationalism 'was rooted in long-standing attitudes of concern for the city of Jerusalem and for Palestine as a sacred entity which were a response to perceived external threats'. Khalidi, *Palestinian Identity*, p. 30.
4. Dalman, 'The Search for the Temple Treasure at Jerusalem', *Palestine Exploration Fund Quarterly Statement*, p. 38.
5. Kark, *Jaffa*, p. 42.
6. *The Times*, 9 May 1911, p. 8.
7. For a short autobiography of Juvelius, see Landau, 'Walter Henrich Juvelius, Information Based on Finnish Sources', in the pamphlet *In Search of the Temple Treasures, The Story of the Parker Expedition 1909–1911* (Hebrew), pp. 20–4.
8. Shalev-Khalifa, 'In Search of the Temple Treasures, The Story of the Parker Expedition 1909–1911' (Hebrew), in *In Search of the Temple Treasures*, p. 6.
9. Dalman, 'The Search for the Temple Treasure at Jerusalem', p. 38.
10. Ibid., p. 35.
11. Captain Montague B. Parker, Report on Progress of F. J. M. P. V. Syndicate, p. 1 (hereafter: Parker report). According to one report, they were given a total 500,000 Swedish krona at their disposal to secure the needed land. Haram al-Sharif Dossier: Haram al-Sharif Dossier: Document, 130/4B. This seems to have been much more than estimated. The net value of the Swedish krona sum was worth almost £2 million.
12. Shalev-Khalifa, 'In Search of the Temple Treasures', p. 8.
13. Parliament report, pp. 286, 290. According to the report the contract was signed on 26 November 1908.
14. Parker report, p. 2; Parliament report, pp. 286, 290.
15. Parker report, pp. 3–4.
16. Parliament report, p. 287.
17. Parker report, p. 4.
18. Dalman, 'The Search for the Temple Treasure at Jerusalem', p. 36; Abdülaziz Mecdi accepted this position after he came to the conclusion that 'Anyhow I was going to take leave, and if this issue would benefit both the state and also allow me time off, thus I would travel and at the same time supervise this work'. Parliament report, p. 293.
19. Shalev-Khalifa, 'In Search of the Temple Treasures', p. 6.

20. *The Times*, 8 May 1911, p. 8; Dalman, 'The Search for the Temple Treasure at Jerusalem', p. 36.
21. Blyth, *When We Lived in Jerusalem*, p. 254.
22. Jacobson, *From Empire to Empire*, pp. 48 (n. 67), 196.
23. Parliament report, p. 287.
24. Silverman, *Digging for God and Country*, p. 184.
25. Vincent, *Underground Jerusalem*.
26. Parliament report, p. 290.
27. Blyth, *When We Lived in Jerusalem*, p. 254.
28. Dalman, 'The Search for the Temple Treasure at Jerusalem', pp. 36–7.
29. Haram al-Sharif Dossier: Document 2, 17 April 1911(Rumi: 4 Nisan 1327).
30. *Tanin*, 2 May 1911 (Rumi: 19 Nisan 1327).
31. PRO FO 195/2377, 21 April 1911, p. 112.
32. *New York Times*, 5 May 1911, p. 1. Two days later, the *New York Times* ran a whole page article on the incident, *New York Times*, 7 May 1911.
33. While Gustave Dalman does not state in his work that he was the Swedish consul, this is mentioned in the Haram al-Sharif Dossier: Documents within the Haram al-Sharif Dossier.
34. Dalman, 'The Search for the Temple Treasure at Jerusalem', p. 38.
35. PRO FO 195/2377, 26 May 1911, p. 165.
36. Haram al-Sharif Dossier: Document 4; PRO FO 795/2377, p. 129.
37. PRO FO 195/2377, 6 May 1911, pp. 128–9.
38. *New York Times*, 9 May 1911, p. 4.
39. Parliament report, p. 289.
40. *The Times*, 4 May 1911, p. 5.
41. PRO FO 195/2377, 21 April 1911, 111B.
42. *Tanin*, 7 May 1911 (Rumi: 24 Nisan, 1327).
43. PRO FO 195/2377, 26 May 1911, 165b.
44. Ibid.
45. According to Muslims, Moses was buried in the Holy Land, differing from the Jewish tradition.
46. Khalidi, *Palestinian Identity*, p. 151.
47. *Moriah*, 21 April 1911, p. 2.
48. *Tanin*, 7 May 1911 (Rumi: 24 Nisan, 1327); PRO FO 795/2377, 111B.
49. Vester, *Our Jerusalem*, p. 214.
50. *New York Times*, 4 May 1911, p. 6.
51. PRO FO 195/2377, 21 April 2911, pp. 110–12; Blythe, *When We Lived in Jerusalem*, p. 257.
52. *New York Times*, May 14 1911, C3.
53. Ibid.
54. *New York Times*, 4 May 1911, p. 6.
55. PRO FO 195/2377, 21 April 1911, pp. 110–12; Vester, *Our Jerusalem*, p. 214.
56. Vester, *Our Jerusalem*, p. 214–15.

57. *HaHerut*, 24 April 1911, p. 2.
58. *Moriah*, 25 April 1911, p. 2. The Haram al-Sharif incident was covered in great details in *HaHerut*, *HaTzvi* and *Moriah*. For a summary of the incident in its entirety, see *HaHerut*, 16 May 1911, pp. 1–2.
59. *HaTzfira*, 10 May 1911, p. 2.
60. PRO, FP 195/2377, 21 April 1911, p. 111.
61. Haram al-Sharif Dossier: Doc 31, 22 April 1911.
62. *The Times*, 4 May 1911, p. 5.
63. Haram al-Sharif Dossier: Document 2, Nisan 3.
64. Parliament report, p. 288.
65. Haram al-Sharif Dossier: Document 11.
66. PRO FO 195/2377, 12 May 1911, p. 134.
67. Haram al-Sharif Dossier: Document 4; Dalman, 'The Search for the Temple Treasure at Jerusalem', p. 37.
68. Parliament report, p. 293.
69. *HaHerut*, 7 June 1911, p. 3.
70. Haram al-Sharif Dossier: Documents 35, 38B, 41, 42 and 46. The sadrazam was Ibrahim Hakkı Paşa, the interior minister was Halil Bey, and the minister of war was Mahmud Şevket Paşa.
71. Haram al-Sharif Dossier: Document 44.
72. *HaTzvi*, 3 May 1911, p. 2.
73. Haram al-Sharif Dossier: Document 7, 18 April 1911.
74. PRO FO 195/2377, 26 May 1911, p. 165.
75. Ibid., 6 May 1911, p. 129.
76. *Al-Quds*, 20 April 1911.
77. Copies of both *Filastin* and *al-Nafir* for the period March–June 1911 cannot be located. For example, *Filastin* was published during this period but today the microfilm collections available in the Hebrew University's collection (which is used by most universities in the United States) only begins from July 1911, three months after the event occurred, and six months after the paper's first publication. Today, this edition is published online: <http://web.nli.org.il/sites/nlis/en/jrayed> (last accessed 30 May 2019).
78. Haram al-Sharif Dossier: Document 9, 27b.
79. *Filastin*, 15 July 1911, p. 1.
80. Khalidi, *The Iron Cage*, pp. 90–3.
81. *HaHerut*, 12 May 1911, p. 3.
82. *Tanin*, 2 May 1911 (Rumi: 19 Nisan 1327).
83. Haram al-Sharif Dossier: Document 33.
84. Among the notables who signed letters of protest were members of the Abdu, Hammad, Nablusi, Tamimi and Tuqan families.
85. Haram al-Sharif Dossier: Document 9, 27B.
86. Haram al-Sharif Dossier: Documents 8, 10 and 33.
87. This letter was signed by Rashid and Salim Abu Khadra, 'Abd al-'Azim and 'Abd al-Qadar al-Fayyad, and Ahmad and Muhammad al-Surani. While I

have not found information about the al-Fayyad family, information concerning both the Abu Khadra and the al-Surani families can be found in
the reference listed below. The Abu Khadra family had representatives
during different periods of time in Gaza's municipality and held different
administrative positions (p. 21). The al-Surani family was well known,
with some of them serving in various positions, such as 'Amr serving as
the mayor of Gaza, and Musa Efendi, who was once a member of both the
Lajnat al-Awkaf al-Mahaliyya and the Meclis al-Baladiya; the family was
also well known in trade (pp. 273–8). Al-Tabba', *Ithaf wa-A'izzah fi Tarikh
Ghazzah*, pp. 21, 273–8.

88. This set of letters was sent to the prime minister's office, the Ministry of
Interior, the Sheikh al-Islam and the Ministry of War (Documents 19, 21,
23 and 24).
89. Documents 19, 21, 23 and 24.
90. PRO FO 195/2377, p. 104.
91. PRO FO 195/2377 no. 28. This Haram al-Sharif Dossier: Document appears
in Eliav, *Britain and the Holy Land 1838–1914*, pp. 375–8.
92. Eliav, *Britain and the Holy Land*, pp. 375–8.
93. Ibid., p. 378.
94. Al-Tabba', *Ithaf wa-A'izzah fi Tarikh Ghazzah*, pp. 219–20, 29. Little information is given on the al-Sarraj family (pp. 219–20) and the Abu Ghali
(p. 29).
95. Haram al-Sharif Dossier: Documents 17 and 19.
96. Ibid.
97. Gerber, *Remembering and Imagining Palestine*, p. 67.
98. Mandel, *The Arabs and Zionism before World War I*, pp. 106–7; Khalidi,
Palestinian Identity, pp. 31, 111, 139.
99. DH.I.UM 1331.S.6, 26/4–8, no. 21 (25 January 1912).
100. Haram al-Sharif Dossier: Documents 10, 29 and 81–3.
101. Haram al-Sharif Dossier: Document 29.
102. Haram al-Sharif Dossier: Document 52.
103. This family was from a branch of the Dajani clan.
104. Ali Ekrem Bey, *Moshel Hayyiti be-Yerushalayim* [A Governor in Jerusalem],
pp. 193–4.
105. Haram al-Sharif Dossier: Document 31, 21 April 1911.
106. Haram al-Sharif Dossier: Document 32, 22 April 1911.
107. Haram al-Sharif Dossier: Documents 34, 37, 39 and 45.
108. Haram al-Sharif Dossier: Document 26. See also PRO FO 195/2377, 6 May
1911, p. 129.
109. Parliament report, p. 291; highlights of the debate were also covered in
Moriah, 19 May 1911, p. 2.
110. *The Times*, 16 September 1911. This article is a feature column about the
Haram al-Sharif incident.
111. Rıza Nur was a member of the oppositional *al-Ahali* (People's) party, and

in 1910 was arrested for conspiracy against the government, but was later released due to pressure placed on the government by fellow Members of Parliament. See Kayali, *Arabs and Young Turks*, p. 98.

112. Parliament report, p. 290.
113. Ibid., p. 291.
114. Ibid.
115. Ibid., p. 292.
116. Ibid., p. 294.
117. Khalidi, *Palestinian Identity*, pp. 83–4.
118. *HaTzvi*, 18 May 1911, p. 2.
119. Haram al-Sharif Dossier: Document 116.
120. *HaHerut*, 22 May 1911, p. 3.
121. *HaTzvi*, 15 June 1911, p. 2.
122. Haram al-Sharif Dossier: Document 116.
123. PRO FO 195/2377, 22 May 1911, 153–153b.
124. *The Times*, 8 May 1911, p. 8.
125. Ibid.
126. Ibid.
127. Parliament report, 16 May 1911, p. 579.
128. *The Times*, 5 June 1911, p. 5.
129. According to the British consul, Cevdet Bey arrived on 18 July 1911. He formerly served as the mutasarrıf of Bengazi. PRO FO 195/2377, 22 July 1911, p. 261.
130. Dalman, 'The Search for the Temple Treasure at Jerusalem', p. 39.
131. *The Times*, 23 September 1911, p. 3.
132. Captain Montague B. Parker, Report on Jerusalem Excavations, 25 June 1912, p. 1.
133. *The Times*, 30 October 1911, p. 6; Haram al-Sharif Dossier: Document 137.
134. *New York Times*, 12 November 1911, p. 4.
135. PRO FO 195/2377, pp. 354–5, 366–8.
136. *Filastin*, 19 July 1911.
137. Rashid Khalidi explains in his book *Palestinian Identity* how this served as an important learning centre for the local Muslim elite; Khalidi, *Palestinian Identity*, p. 37.
138. DH.ID 1329.Ca.15, 34/18; 14 May 1911, 3/1–2.
139. Ibid.
140. *The Jewish Chronicle*, 12 April 1895, p. 7.
141. DH.ID 1329.Ca.15, 34/18; 14 May 1911, 3/1–2.
142. Ibid.
143. Khalidi, *British Policy Towards Syria and Palestine*, p. 129; see also Khalidi, 'The Economic Partition of the Arab Provinces of the Ottoman Empire before the First World War', *Review*.
144. PRO FO 1951/2377, p. 417.
145. Ibid., pp. 413–14.

146. PRO FO 195/2452/621, 29 January 1913, p. 2.

147. PRO FO 195/2459, 12 March 1914, p. 2.

148. Haddad, 'Iraq Before World War I', in *The Origins of Arab Nationalism*, pp. 120–50. Hasan Kayali notes that 'During the 1909–1910 and 1910–1911 annual parliamentary sessions three issues of imperial significance concerned the Arab provinces directly: the Lynch concession, Zionist settlement, and the war with Libya'. See Kayali, *Arabs and Young Turks*, pp. 99–100.

149. *HaHerut*, 29 March 1914. p. 1.

150. Strohmeier, 'Al-Kulliya al-Salahiyya, A Late Ottoman University in Jerusalem', in *Ottoman Jerusalem*, part I, chapter 5. Strohmeier traces the origin of this university back to World War I, and provides us with a unique glimpse of its beginnings and its curriculum. However, the documents found in the Ottoman archives and the Palestinian press contradicts his findings that this Jerusalem institution was a 'direct product of the First World War and the progress of the war determined the fate of the school'. The Kulliya was inspired by the madrasa that was endowed by Salah al-Din al-Ayyubi and was founded in 1187 on the grounds of the Crusader Church of St Anne, remaining in Islamic hands up until Sultan Abdülmecid relinquished it to France in 1856.

151. Strohmeier, 'Al-Kulliya al-Salahiyya', p. 58.

152. Ibid.

153. Ibid. We also know from Strohmeier's research that among the students of the Kulliya, some would later reach high positions throughout the newly established Arab states, and that its faculty included some of the most influential Arab thinkers of the period. For example, among the student body we find the names of Ishaq Musa al-Husayni, a University of London graduate and later a professor at both the American University in Beirut and the American University in Cairo, and we also find Yusuf Yasin, who would serve as foreign minister to Abd al-Aziz Ibn Saud. What is most striking about the school's faculty is that they represented some of the most influential Arab nationalists of the period. Among them was one of the founders of the renowned *Fatat* organisation, Rustum Haidar, who served as the school's inspector of education. Haidar received this position after working as a teacher in a *lycee* in Beirut. Also on the faculty was Abd al-Qadir al-Maghribi, one of the founders of the Arab Academy in Damascus. Among the Palestinians serving on the faculty were Amin al-Uri(?), Musa Budairi and Husam al-Din Jarallah. Among the prominent Jerusalemites, Is'af al-Nashashibi taught Arabic literature, and Khalil al-Sakakini presented lectures. Lastly, Asad al-Shuqayri, the Ottoman MP of Acre, was closely affiliated with the school. Surprisingly, Strohmeier made no mention of Hajji Raghib al-Khalidi, who originally proposed establishing the school almost four years before its opening.

154. PRO FO 195/2377, 22 July 1911, p. 258.

155. *Filastin*, 20 July 1911; *The Times*, 24 July 1911, p. 6. According to *The Times*, Kawaja Hassan Nazami of Delhi, who served as the secretary of the All-Indian Sufi Conference, led a delegation to Jerusalem to investigate the alleged 'sacrilege at the Mosque of Omar'. It was also reported in *HaHerut*, 31 July 1911. This was also recorded by the British consulate in Jerusalem, who stated that Indian Muslim leader came due to the 'dismay aroused in Moslem circles in India by the reports received as to an alleged sacrilege in the Mosque'. PRO FO 195/2377, 22 July 1911, p. 258.

4

Palestine's Jewish Community Unites[1]

Nahman Efendi! Remember first and foremost you are a Hebrew, and an Ottoman Hebrew, just like a Greek is an Ottoman Greek, or an Armenian is an Ottoman Armenian. Only then, if you do not forget this, you will serve as an honour to your people and your brothers![2]

This excerpt from Jerusalem's Zionist newspaper, *Ha-Tzvi*, provides a window into a not-so-distant past when Jews in Palestine saw no contradiction in their being Zionists on one hand and proud Ottoman citizens on the other. The open letter, submitted to the newspaper on the occasion of the Jewish soldier Nahman Karniel being promoted to a corporal, brought great joy to the Jewish community in Palestine – not only to the Ashkenazi colonists from the Jewish settlement of Zikhron Ya'akov, where the soldier was from, but to the Jewish Yishuv at large. In addition to *HaTzvi*, the Sephardic newspaper *HaHerut*, and the non-Zionist *Moriah*, spread the news of Karniel's achievements to their readers as well. What Nahman could not have known when he joined the army was that upon his finishing his year service in Jerusalem, he would be recalled to fight in the 1911 war in Libya, the 1912–13 Balkan Wars and also to serve his homeland during World War I. His fate, however, would be very different from Karmi Eisenberg, the other Ottoman Zionist soldier discussed at the end of this chapter. Unlike Eisenberg – who died as an Ottoman prisoner of war in Russia, never having the chance to return to Palestine, which by then was already under British occupation – Karniel lived to tell his story.[3]

The above quote praising Karniel as a proud Ottoman Hebrew points to how the Jewish community (both in Palestine and throughout the Ottoman Empire), like other non-Muslims, was negotiating its new found Ottoman patriotism, ushered in with the 1908 Young Turk Revolution, with its own growing communal nationalism. Similar to the Greeks and Armenians, adopting the civic-Ottomanism of the post-Young Turk Revolution would provide them with a greater amount of cultural autonomy, even if this did come at the price of military service. One Armenian newspaper article summed this up by stating that military service was even a prerequisite of maintaining equal status, stating 'equality cannot prevail until every subject equally participates in the defense of the empire'.[4]

Lastly, even if Hebrew by 1911 clearly was the emerging dominant language of the Jewish Yishuv, with it increasingly connecting the different communities into one linguistic camp, many Jews would have most likely disagreed with the nationalist wording of this text. True, Zionism had become a dominant force among both the Sephardim and Ashkenazim of the Yishuv, but, as it will be discussed below, most Jews must have found being referred to as 'Hebrews' too nationalist in tone. In fact, for the mostly observant Ashkenazi and Sephardic Jews of Jerusalem, and the Yishuv at large, this certainly must have sounded preposterous to many. However, for the new generation of Jews raised speaking and reading Hebrew, this was an extension of their new-found nationalism within the Empire.

Similar to the study of Palestinians, often the history of the Jewish community in Palestine, the Yishuv, has been blurred by projecting the historical realities of the British Mandate and the first years of the Israeli state backward onto the period of the late Ottoman era. Even if an essential part of understanding Israeli history is taking into account the role of Ashkenazi immigrants of the Second Aliyah, the truth is that they only made up a sliver of the overall Jewish population. In fact, when reading traditional histories of the Yishuv, one receives a skewed picture as if the Labour Zionists of the Second Aliyah were the dominant group behind the Zionist project and that the local Sephardic community, or those Ashkenazi Jews of the First Aliyah, who were born in the land and raised as proud Hebrew-speaking Ottomans, played a little role in paving the way to the construction of a national community in Palestine.

Recently, a growing number of scholars have started to reassess this blind spot; according to Guy Alroey, 'Zionist historiography stressed the pioneer ethos and regarded cooperative-agricultural settlements as the glory of the Zionist endeavor and the source of its success.' This historiography highlighted the 'young socialist immigrants' of the Second Aliyah, even though they made up only about 2,000–3,000 people, in comparison to 35,000 other immigrants heading to urban centres.[5] This claim also needs to be placed into the context of Anita Shapira's earlier comments about how Israeli history has neglected the contributions of the First Aliyah. I would add that the official Israeli history also distorted moments in history to retain the inevitability of a Jewish state; in other words, official history in Israel was written to highlight the contributions of a small group in solidifying the path to statehood, even though they themselves were not aware that statehood would be the eventual outcome. For example, while Israeli children learn in school that the first prime minister and founding father of the Jewish state, David Ben-Gurion, studied in Istanbul, the history they study does not expand on his complicated existence there as a law student and an organiser of a Hebrew student union. They do not learn that he was in the Ottoman capital in order to integrate into Ottoman politics, and by no means was lobbying on behalf of an independent Jewish state in Palestine. He like others had no magic crystal ball that would show that within less than a decade the British would invade and the Balfour Declaration would be issued. With his narrative in Istanbul of integrating into the Ottoman system going against the inevitability of statehood, it remains to be taught as a random fact, without any utility given to it.

For many Ashkenazi Jews in Palestine, adopting Ottoman citizenship and expressing their loyalty to the Ottoman state allowed them to realise their dream: Jews living in *Eretz Israel* within a semi-autonomous system where they could develop a 'Hebrew' culture. This indeed can be described as a local Zionism that was in a great sense removed from the Zionist Organization programme of establishing an independent Jewish state. Up until 1914, Arieh B. Saposnik correctly assesses that the Yishuv was only 'remotely concerned ... with the kinds of political objectives that might have exercised Zionists in Cologne or Berlin'.[6] In fact, I would add that following the Young Turk Revolution, much of the Yishuv was actually more concerned and connected with what was happening in Istanbul than they ever were connected to Berlin. What it is often forgotten in the narrative of the Yishuv is that they too were living within an Ottoman world, which inherently bound them to Ottoman law, politics and society.

The movement towards adopting a national Jewish identity within the framework of Ottoman citizenship captured the hearts and minds of both Sephardic and Ashkenazi residents, regardless of whether they were born in the Land, or had recently immigrated. These Zionists, who were influenced by their Ottoman non-Muslim compatriots and Arabs working towards cultural autonomy,[7] succeeded in shifting the official policy of the Zionist Organization, which aligned international Zionism with the Yishuv's local Zionism. The trend to work within the Ottoman system in fact was so influential that the Zionist Organization in Berlin eventually transformed its own agenda, backing away from the Herzl's goal of first seizing an international charter, even before immigration. In 1911, just three years after the Young Turk Revolution, the Zionist Organization leader, Max Nordau, declared that Zionism is

> a movement having for its aim the settlement of as many Jews as possible as free citizens in Palestine, with guarantees that the Turkish government shall not be at liberty to expel them nor to subject them to any restrictions not imposed on other inhabitants of Palestine.[8]

This was also explained by the British Zionist Norman Bentwich, who argued that the real work of Zionists 'consists in promoting Jewish settlement in Palestine, and reviving Jewish culture in the Hebrew language'. He goes on to state that 'the Young Turks will not obstruct us when they see our true intention', and that the

> Turkish authorities will encourage autonomous Jewish settlement. You must recollect that the idea of a Jewish state, in the proper political sense of the word state, connoting independence [and etc.] has long been given up by the Zionists. We want a nationalism of culture, not a political nationalism [such as an independent state].[9]

The merging together of the aims of the local Jewish community in Palestine together with those of the Zionist Organization, which was greatly responsible for creating institutions to support the Yishuv, cannot be underestimated in transforming the small Jewish community into a hegemonic force, which was only strengthened even more through the Yishuv's support of the Ottoman state.

It was in this context that the Yishuv, which was made up of multifaceted religious and ethnic communities, began to transform into a national community, which would set out to claim the modern homeland, placing them in direct competition with the local Palestinian population. In fact, while one cannot can deny the Sephardi/Ashkenazi divide that existed within the Yishuv (and later within Israel), during the late Ottoman period, local Zionism was strengthened by the multiplicity of the different groups, and was by no means only an Ashkenazi initiative. Claiming the homeland by the different groups was not a coordinated project, but rather one strengthened by the multiple initiatives of each group, and many subgroups. For both Ashkenazim and the Sephardim, the claiming of the homeland was not about staking out territory with clear borders and ceding from the Ottoman Empire, but was about building an autonomous home. For them the borders of this homeland, the *moledet*, were etched out in their minds and were not drawn on maps.

The Arabic–Hebrew Language Divide

The claim that an overwhelming part of the Sephardic population did not see the Palestinians as part of their collective future stands in contrast to recent work that has portrayed a strong commonality between Palestine's Sephardic population and the Palestinians. This is based on new research that claims that the two communities were closer because they lived in close proximity, shared a common culture and possessed Arabic as a common language.[10] In her ground-breaking work on Jerusalem during World War I, Abigail Jacobson states, 'A great majority of the Sephardi Jews were fluent in spoken and written Arabic, even though for many of them Ladino was the mother tongue.'[11] Moreover, some scholars have gone so far to define the community as Arab Jews. According to Menahem Klein, 'Before nationalism brutally separated the two words "Arab" and "Jew" and required the inhabitants of Palestine to count themselves as one or the other, there were people who thought of themselves as Arab Jews.'[12]

This chapter scrutinises this claim and agrees with Arieh Saposnik, who asserts that:

> To be sure, the ability to converse in Arabic and a closer familiarity with local Arabic culture tended to set Sephardim in Palestine apart from most Ashkenazi Zionists. It is by no means clear, however, that this cultural familiarity neces-sarily bred more accommodating views [of the Palestinian population].[13]

This chapter argues that there is not sufficient evidence to show that beyond specific urban spheres within Jerusalem, the Arabic-speaking Sephardic Jews were somehow closer to Palestine's Muslim and Christian communities.[14] No less, it is important to remember that it was not only the Sephardim who maintained relations with Arabs; certainly, there were Ashkenazi Jews as well who spoke Arabic and lived among Arabs, a topic that remains greatly unexplored. For example, Moshe Sharett was fluent in Arabic (and Turkish) and served in the Ottoman army in Syria during World War I, up until even after the 1917 Balfour Declaration had been issued.[15]

It is important to remember that the Sephardic community, like the Ashkenazim, was composed of people from a multitude of backgrounds and did not possess a united culture or language; also, for the ones who did speak Arabic, they spoke a multitude of dialects, which often dif-fered from the local Palestinian dialect.[16] There were also those Sephardic Jews who were migrating to Palestine from Ottoman lands; they were not setting out to create a 'new Jew' as some of the more radical Ashkenazi Zionists aimed for, but, nonetheless, were not from the local community.

Rather, they were Ottoman Ladino-speaking Jews, who were moving from one Ottoman city to another, and with the Ottoman Empire losing major Jewish-populated cities like Salonica, the number of Jews reaching Palestine would only grow. In fact, one study completed by the foremost Ottoman scholar on migration within the Ottoman Empire, Kemal Karpat, describes a steady stream of Ottoman Sephardic Jews to Palestine, both from the Balkans and the Crimea.[17] Nevertheless, these Jews coming from Ottoman lands would have offset the number of Sephardic Jews speaking Arabic, complicating the question of divisions within the Sephardic community.[18]

One research study completed by Arthur Ruppin in 1907 also sheds light on the apparently low number of Jews speaking Arabic as their mother tongue. Focusing his study on three Hebrew kindergarten classes in Jerusalem, he found that out of 305 children attending them, only 7.1 per cent spoke Arabic as their mother tongue, which was a distant third to Ladino (39.3 per cent) and Yiddish (38 per cent); following Arabic, the other languages listed were Bucharic, Persian, Georgian, the Moroccan dialect and Bulgarian.[19] His findings are strengthened in the pages of *HaHerut*, where intellectuals and community members often debated and discussed the status of Arabic within the community.

In 1910, the extent to which the Jews in Palestine knew Arabic was the subject of a discussion in Jerusalem's *HaHerut* newspaper. In a letter addressed to the Ottoman Jewish community of the northern city of Safad, education supervisor and leading notable Salah al-Din Hajji Yusuf questioned why Jews did not learn Arabic. He argued that the large Jewish community in Safad should have had official communal representation in the local courts but that this required knowledge of Arabic. Yet, he stressed, 'there is not a single Jew in Safad that knows Arabic . . .' and this was the reason the administration was forced to appoint a Christian, even though the city's Jews outnumbered its Christians. Referring to Jews as 'my brothers of my homeland', Yusuf finally made a compassionate call to learn Arabic:

Why is it that you are lazy? When will you finally treat the learning of Arabic as an equal? This is the language of the land, and as Ottomans you have the right to participate in legal matters and the rest of the government's administrative tasks. You can only benefit from these rights if you know the language of the state [Turkish] and only then can you work for your homeland, and to benefit from it as your supreme councils do as a result of your knowledge of other languages. I especially direct this call to my friend Mr David Yusuf Efendi [editor of *HaHerut*] . . . who knows the Arabic language well, that he alert his brothers and his fellow people to the urgency of this and to the great pleasure they will reap by knowing Arabic and to point to the benefit the Ottoman Jews will obtain by doing so . . . I know the love this respected editor has for his land (*artso*) and homeland (*moledeto*) and his will for the development of the state (*medina*). I hope that he will help me with this Holy Work for the good of our homeland.[20]

We can infer from this that learning the language of the state, Turkish, was not sufficient for this author. Clearly, what he was pointing to in this account was that Jews preferred to learn Ottoman Turkish instead, deeming Arabic unnecessary. This trend should not be surprising as the Ottoman administration encouraged all populations within the Empire to study Turkish, the language of the state. Furthermore, with much of the Ottoman administration in Palestine not speaking Arabic, and obviously, not Hebrew, Turkish was essential for the Jewish Yishuv to exist. In fact, the British consul once commented on the fact that Azmi Bey, the governor of Jerusalem, prided himself on the fact that he did not know a European language, in addition to not knowing Arabic either.[21] For Arabs within Syria and Palestine, the fact that some Ottoman administrators did not know Arabic turned into a point of contention between them and the Ottoman state; in fact, the administration's stringent policy of learning Turkish (while not knowing Arabic) led some Arabs to accuse the government of promoting a 'Turkification' project.[22]

Salah al-Din Hajji Yusuf was correct in his assessment that the editor of *HaHerut* was interested in advancing the study of Arabic among the Jewish community, but where Hajji Yusuf stressed the need to focus on Arabic, the editor placed equal importance on learning Turkish.[23] In response to Yusuf's letter, the editor assured him of his good intentions in an editorial that began, 'It is with great pleasure that the call of this enlightened gentleman . . . was placed on the front page of our newspaper due to the greatness of urgency that we find in this topic.' He goes on:

> As Ottoman Jews, who recognise their duty towards their land [Palestine] and dear homeland [the Ottoman state], we have not missed the chance to take part in all the opportunities and in every matter for the good of our homeland, which is very dear to us. We feel that it is a religious duty, being that we are true sons of the homeland . . . the languages of the Land [Palestine] and of the state are the first conditions and what is necessary in order to realise the brotherhood and the uniting of all the Ottoman nations into one single strong and healthy perspective.

From this excerpt, it is clear that *HaHerut*'s editor was sincere in his call to the Jewish community to learn both the language of the 'Land' and the 'State'. However, what needs to be taken into account is the practicality of it, or, more bluntly, to question whether he was *in sync* with his population's wishes. The fact that so few actually spoke Arabic or Turkish, combined with the call to learn the languages, seems to point to the fact that there was not such a demand arising from within the Jewish community. Further, given Istanbul's push for all of its citizens to learn Turkish, there must have been even less of an incentive to learn Arabic. The fact that the Jewish community was a relatively closed community should not come as a great surprise and it bears a striking resemblance to Istanbul's Jewish community. There, among a great part of the Jewish community, 'Turkish and other regional languages were occasionally defended but rarely employed . . . [E]ven the most secular of Jewish students showed little interest in learning Turkish, a language that, in any case Jewish teachers proved unqualified to teach'.[24] In fact, it seems that outside of some intellectuals, most Jews did not possess a high proficiency in Turkish,[25] something that continued over into the Young Turk period as well.[26]

No less interesting in the pages of *HaHerut* was the debate over the need for a Jewish Arabic newspaper, put forth by a group of intellectuals, such as Nissim Malul and Shimon Moyal, which repeatedly emerged during a three-year period (1910–13). Crucial to the discussion is that the original idea of publishing such a newspaper was never about the need to supply information to the Jewish community in Palestine, but rather was to combat the growing anti-Zionist discourse in the Arab newspapers in Syria and Palestine, which presented a 'great danger' to the Jewish Yishuv and the Zionist project.[27] The mission of the paper was to transform this negative stance, which included Malul writing pro-Zionist articles for the Arabic press (with articles appearing in Beirut and Cairo).[28] The language used by Malul and others defined this mission as a 'war', which demanded from them a 'conquest' of the Arabic press, which bears a striking resemblance to the language of the Second Aliyah, which called for a 'conquest of the land and the labour market'.[29] This conquest could be achieved by 'a special Israeli power', 'strengthened by extensive organisation and planning, defending the Yishuv and its Hebrew element'.[30] Perhaps most noteworthy about the debates was that in all their fervour to counter the Arab press, *HaHerut* 'never engaged [directly] with the substance aired in the Palestinian Arab press', which was brushed off as being motivated by anti-Semitism.[31]

The big dreams they had of an Arabic newspaper that would cover events with numerous offices spread throughout the Empire were dashed with the realisation that there was not a sufficient number of Jews in the Yishuv proficient in Arabic to carry out such a project. In one estimate,

Malul stated that there were only about 10–15 Jewish journalists whose Arabic was good enough to fulfil such a goal.[32] Haim Ben Attar, the editor of *HaHerut*, put it more bluntly by asking if such a newspaper is realistic considering that there are very few Jews in the Yishuv who know how to read and write Arabic, and for the ones that do, they already filled important positions.[33] Avraham Elmaliah, the former editor of *HaHerut*, believed that the newspaper should follow the model of the Zionist press in Istanbul such as *Le Jeune Turc*, one that was supported by Zionists but relied on influential Turkish writers (see next chapter). In other words, for his paper to be able to convince the local Palestinian population of the benefits of the Zionist community, it would need to employ Arab Muslim writers since Jewish authors would be disregarded by the overall population. The newspaper finally saw light for a short period in 1912, and then once again in 1914, under the editorship of Shimon Moyal. However, by then, the divide between Jews and Palestinians had reached a point of no return and the fact that the newspaper remained Zionist placed them within the camp of the Jewish Yishuv at large.

Within this greater debate, an interesting discussion emerged concerning the importance of teaching Arabic and the essence of Jewish–Arab relations, which has received special attention by scholars working on the Young Turk period. These scholars have correctly assessed that Malul's call for a 'shared homeland', in addition to the importance he attributes to the study of Arabic, provide a refreshing look at Jewish–Arab relations. His voice is a unique one, but the question is if this almost lone voice, and if the group of intellectuals promoting Arabic, can be seen as representative of the Sephardic community at large.

Nissim Malul, Shimon Moyal and others, such as Moyal's wife, Esther Azhari Moyal, indeed were different and unique – their world extended beyond the Yishuv, and in reality, they were *actually* not part of Jerusalem's Sephardic population. Malul, even if born in Safad, was raised in Egypt and in his formative years, he took part in the fascinating changes it encountered in Egypt during the years before World War I. Moyal, too, was in Egypt during those years, and during his lifetime had lived in Beirut, studied medicine in Istanbul, made his way to Cairo and then back to Jaffa, where he had been born. He was joined by his wife, Esther Azhari, who already was well known in the literary circles of Beirut, and then in Cairo. One could thus argue then that they were actually trying to apply to Palestine the experience of many Egyptian Jews in the pre-World War I period. Certainly, more work needs to be done on this very small but interesting group of Jewish intellectuals. What is certain, however, is that this elite group of intellectuals' support for cultural Zionism was uncompromising and fit very much into the world of the Ottoman Young Turk period; and, it was this point that connected the cosmopolitan lives of the likes of Malul and the Moyals to the Jewish Yishuv. Certainly, their close ties with the Egyptian world of journalism also seemed to have limited their understanding of the Palestinian community as well, which, for all the discussions about a shared homeland, they were never able to forge strong ties with Palestinians.[34]

The Revival of Hebrew

Within a couple of years following the Young Turk Revolution, the Sephardic community of Palestine underwent a linguistic cultural revolution; Hebrew began to transform from a written to a spoken language, the dominant language, with the language of the state (Turkish) coming in second, and only then the language of the Land (Arabic). The strengthening of Hebrew served as the main factor in creating the new Jew in *Eretz Israel*, uniting the local Sephardic community with even the most radical Ashkenazi immigrant. Thus together these two overarching communities, which included within them numerous more communities, came to identify language as a source for unity, an important step in the transformation into a national community, one that would stand juxtaposed to the overall Palestinian population. The Young Turk Revolution nurtured this cultural nationalism and turned *millets* into national minorities, allowing them to embrace their national language while professing loyalty to Istanbul; this was *renegotiating the Millet system* in action.

At this juncture it is important to dedicate a few words to the revival of Hebrew in general, which will help explain how it was able to become the language of choice by most Jews within the Yishuv in such a short time. In fact, Liora Halperin, in her work on the Hebrew language during the British Mandate era, argues that 'the story of Hebrew revival normally ends around 1914, by which point a series of organizational victories had ensured that the main institutional structures of the Yishuv would be Hebrew speaking, and had practically become a "Hebrew society"'.[35] Halperin notes that the route to institutionalisation of Hebrew can be traced back to the founding of Eliezer Ben-Yehuda's Hebrew Language Committee in 1890, and the Hebrew Teachers Federation in 1903. Concerning the developments in the post-Young Turk era, she highlights the 1910–11 decision of the leftist labour organisation Po'ale Zion to publish its journal in Hebrew rather than in Yiddish, and the 1914 capitulation of the German-financed technical school, later known as the Technion, to implement Hebrew as the language of instruction, something which will also be addressed below.[36]

While these markers serve as important milestones in the development of Hebrew as a common language (and one that was quickly turning into an 'official' language of the Yishuv), this could only have been possible by the multiple communities within the Jewish Yishuv making a decision to adopt it as the language of their choice.

By 1911, the revival of Hebrew had already been well set in motion. This was highlighted in an article at that time in *Die Welt* written by the Zionist leader, Dr Ozjasz Thon, who believed that in Palestine the Zionist movement's greatest contribution was the revival of the Hebrew language:

> In no particular sphere has Jewish activity in Palestine, during the last 25 years, produced such positive and enduring results as in that of Jewish culture, particularly in regard to the revival and development of the Hebrew language. The revival increases from day to day almost visibly.[37]

For some Jews, the transformation to speaking Hebrew was seen as a mission. For example, a front-page advertisement for Hebrew studies in *HaHerut* clearly expressed this under the title 'Hebrews, Learn Hebrew!'.[38] For some, learning Hebrew meant transforming the Jew into a 'Hebrew', which was 'counterposing the "new Hebrew" to the "old Diaspora Jew"'.[39] Yet, *HaHerut*'s running of the ad did not indicate that the editor agreed with this extreme nationalistic interpretation, for on the very same page he wrote an editorial disputing it entitled 'After all we are Jews!'. He opens by stating, 'Recently a strange question has arisen: What Are We, Hebrews or Jews?' He then continues:

> For many people this question sounds ridiculous. The ones that hate us in the places we live show us that in reality indeed we are Jews. Ask the Russian Hooligan and he will answer that you are 'Jidim', and the Frenchman would answer . . . that you are a 'Juif' and the Ashkenaz (German) will call us by the name of 'Juden' and the grandchildren of our uncle Ishmael will call us by the simple name 'Yahudi', because we really are Jews. And, it is so simple and known that it would never have dawned on us to bring this to our readers' attention.[40]

Following this interesting introduction, the editor embarks on a long essay, first explaining that it was necessary to discuss this topic after the newspaper *HaOr* had published a quote by the above-mentioned Dr Thon, who, in honour of Eliezer Ben-Yehuda (recognised as the father of modern Hebrew), stated that with Ben-Yehuda 'the Jew died and the Hebrew was born'. In reaction to this, the *HaHerut* editor argued that throughout Jewish history there has been no precedent for this, concluding with the nationalist statement,

The Jew has never died and never will. There is nothing '*galutit*' [used in this instance as a derogatory term pertaining to exile] in the word Jew, just as there is nothing 'liberating' in the word Hebrew . . . It is the Jews that fought for their freedom, until the Hasmoneans, and the Maccabees were proud of the name Jew and did not exchange it for another.

This *HaHerut* editorial is a prime example of how the Sephardic community was in the midst of transforming their communal identity, and even if they did not adopt a radical idea of Hebrew nationalism, the fact the editorial was in Hebrew, and not in Judaeo-Spanish or Judaeo-Arabic, was a testament to *HaHerut*'s mission to print a language that transcended much smaller sub-communities in Jerusalem, 'as a paper for the general Jewish and Hebrew-speaking audience in Palestine'.[41]

However, this process was not just happening among the Sephardim but also extended to parts of the local Ashkenazi population, with Hebrew serving as a uniting factor. In a 1913 essay entitled the 'Revival of the Hebrew Language', Arthur Ruppin provides a frank, meticulous portrait of the rapid development of Hebrew among Palestine's Jews, for whom it was well on the way to becoming the lingua franca:

most of the Jewish schools have adopted Hebrew as the language of instruction, while it is gradually becoming the mother tongue of the Jewish youth . . . Hebrew is the only language in which all Jews can make themselves understood, coming as they do to Palestine from every country of the world; whatever their mother-tongue, be it Arabic, Russian, Spaniolisch (Ladino), or Yiddish, they can all understand at least a little Hebrew. Thus Hebrew is a bond of union between these Jews . . .[42]

As Hebrew started to take over as the dominant language, the Jewish community in Palestine saw the Arabs' success in promoting their mother tongue as a model. In July 1913, *HaHerut* spelled this out in a front-page article entitled 'The Victory of the Will'.[43] This page-long call for the Jews to unite begins with the following recognition that

the will of the Arab people to live as a people that possess rights and demands . . . that have fought so hard against the great current that stood in their way . . . the Arabs have fought to a great extent against Turkish influence in their sub-districts and districts. The Arabs have fought in great detail to bring a radical change in their professions . . . And they had a huge and difficult task: They faced war on two fronts, the first was that there were those Arabs who stood in opposition to them . . . and on the other front stood the Central government.[44]

Halfway through, the focus moves to the situation of the Jewish community:

And what have we done? Have we organised? Have we joined all our factions into one single faction, into a massive organisation that encompasses all the different groups from among us, an organisation [*histadrut*] that encompasses, that has the strength to defend our spiritual and material values . . .?

Declaring that the Jewish community must answer these questions in the negative, the piece concludes that

> the *Hebrew Public* in *Eretz Israel* divides into different groups, and each of these groups have different aspirations and there is no one that will come and arouse in them the needed desire; the desire that will unite all of them and will arouse mutual aspirations – an aspiration to live in the Land of Israel, what we are obliged to do.[45]

In closing, the editors issue a final warning and at last highlight a sense of urgency in arousing these greater aspirations:

> The Arabs are gradually organising and occupying for themselves a social and political status within the districts of the state. Today, they have succeeded in their first steps, and tomorrow they will succeed in establishing a wide-ranging autonomous home (*shilton bayit*) throughout all the districts of Syria and Arabia, a government in which [the Jews] will need to be subdued and bound to its discipline.[46]

This editorial is probably one of the first realisations by the Jewish community that the area of Syria and Palestine could become an autonomous region ruled by the local Arab population. As a result of this reality, it was even more important that the Jewish community work within the Ottoman system. Clearly, by embracing the Ottoman Empire, the Yishuv was in effect strengthening their power in Palestine vis-à-vis the Arab population.

This article was written in the midst of what *HaHerut* defined as a 'cultural war', which revolved around the language of instruction of the new school for higher education, the Technion, which was due to open in the northern city of Haifa in 1913–14. As this institution was to be focused on the sciences, the founders, who were political Zionists, believed German should be the language of instruction, while the new Yishuv demanded Hebrew. In fact, the newspaper *HaHerut* covered this debate closely and vehemently protested the language of instruction being German, with numerous articles emerging from the summer of 1913 to the spring of 1914. This case is just one more example of the trend towards the foundation of a Hebrew-speaking community in Palestine.

From Multiple Communities into a Collective Yishuv

During the post-1908 period, the Palestinian community began to unite: Christian and Muslim, peasant and notable, regardless of residence in Jaffa, Gaza, Jerusalem or Haifa. Over the same period, we can say that the Jewish community was also transforming into a political community, with them now using nationalist terms to describe themselves. The major driving force behind this was the emergence of Hebrew as the main language of the Jewish Yishuv.

The years between 1908–14 is when the Jewish community took the steps that led to their transformation into a national community. This crucial period in Zionist history has been greatly overlooked in the historiography of the period. As the 'war' over the use of Hebrew as the dominant language of the Yishuv was set in motion, the Sephardic community was slowly parting from any ties they might have had with the Arab population, with more aggressive calls arising for the Jewish Yishuv to unite. On 22 August 1913, for example, the editors of *HaHerut* published a critical essay on the state of the Yishuv and the threat posed by the Arab population. This piece, entitled 'Us and Them', provides an interesting outlook on how the editor of *HaHerut*, a Sephardic Jew, perceived the Arab population in general, and even more how he perceived his own community, the Jewish community at large.[47] In fact, the essay provides ample evidence demonstrating that the Sephardic Jews, similar to their Ashkenazi immigrant compatriots, were just as inclined to adopt an extreme type of nationalism.

The editor begins with a confession that the Jewish community has gravely underestimated the Arab population's potential in realising their national goals. They have opted to treat the Arab community as a stagnant one, unable for centuries 'to rise from its spiritual inferiority' and reach the stage of a national consciousness. The editor goes on to say

> true, when the Arabs were on their own, they did not reach such a sophisticated level of development and ability to generate wonders [such] as other peoples. They have not possessed any intelligent scientific talent. They have not contributed any sophisticated creation (work of art). Their ability to create is deficient and flawed. Yet, despite this, they possess great desire and a healthy sense of nationalism.

From here, the editorial continues to explain how the Arabs have reached a stage where dormant nationalism could be sparked, which would have implications for the Jewish community:

> Without noise and disturbance they [the Arabs] take to their matters, make plans, organise, strengthen their status in the Land [of Israel], expand and

strengthen their influence; and us, ah, we shake up worlds for things that have never happened . . . we only know how to sacrifice [Jewish] victims, we only know how to spread power and blood, yet without bringing [the Yishuv] to fruition. We only know to ridicule others and to say about those that show signs of [national] rebirth (*tehiya*) that theirs is a pseudo-rebirth, when [in actuality] we ourselves did not know how to organise and to show signs of a genuine rebirth . . .

What is remarkable is that, often, Palestinian nationalism, and to some extent Arab nationalism, has been described as a reaction to the Zionist movement, but what this text and the one previously discussed ('The Will of the People') portray is that actually Jewish nationalism was to some extent influenced by Arab nationalism.

The rise of Hebrew and nationalism among the Jewish community was noticed not just by Zionist leaders, but also by Palestinians and the British consulate.[48] The Palestinians' concern was addressed in the newspaper *Filastin* (discussed also in Chapter 2), which was temporarily suspended by the Ottoman authorities because it was deemed to be inciting sentiment against the Jewish population. The offending article was also reported to London by the local British consulate who supplied the translation:[49]

> till ten years ago, the Jews were a fraternal native Ottoman element, living and intermixing with the other elements in harmony, interchanging business relations, inhabiting the same quarter, sending their children to the same school, and shadowed by one banner and one crescent. Then these accursed Zionists, composed of German revolutionaries, Russian Nihilists, and vagabonds of other countries, came with their cry: 'O Jew, remember you are a nation: keep yourselves apart' . . . they [Zionists] started in the first place to build special quarters for themselves, to which they gradually attracted their compatriots who were living amongst the Mussulmans and Christians, sifting them out like wheat from bran; then they boycotted the vernacular Arabic tongue, and it is no more heard in their homes and streets; then they confined the teaching in their schools to their own dead language [Hebrew], which is useless to the world except as a weapon of Zionists, and prevents natives form frequenting their schools and mixing with their children.[50]

The notion of 'Us and Them' is central to understanding how at least an important segment of the Jewish community perceived the local Arab population. Surveying the Hebrew press at the time is remarkable. Even though the Palestinians made up more than 85 per cent of the general population, they were for the most part ignored. In the newspaper *HaHerut*, for example, the Arab community surfaced mostly in reference to acts of violence, with Arabs being depicted as bandits 'pouncing upon' (*hitna-plut*) Jews. These depictions of the 'masses' resemble how some Ottoman administrators perceived Palestine's peasant population as a '*present theater of backwardness*'.[51] The fact that the Jewish community opted not to include the Arab peasants and rural groups within their worldview vividly recalls the typical attitude of the 'coloniser' versus the 'native'. However, these perceptions were not only held by Ashkenazi immigrants but also the local Sephardic community to a great extent, as we see in these examples. So, even if Sephardic Jews often had close urban ties with their urban non-Jewish neighbours, within the Sephardic (and Ashkenazi) press, we see that the overall Arab population was dehumanised to an extent, something that continued throughout the British Mandate, and one can argue, even until today.[52] Put simply, the Hebrew press during this period did not address the root causes of the violence visited by Arabs upon Jews. Placed in this context, it is easy to understand how the Jewish community in Palestine was quite oblivious to the national aspects of the conflict over the land. For many Jews, the Arabs simply lacked any control over their lives and were trapped into years of indifference, seriously lagging behind other nations in their development.[53]

A classic example of how the 'uneducated' Arabs were portrayed in *HaHerut* can be seen in a November 1913 article entitled 'Another Victim in the Galilee'.[54] Based on a telegram detailing the event, sent to *HaHerut* from the northern city of Tiberias, it was reported that a young man, Moshe Barsky, who had set out to bring medicine to his sick sister, was attacked between the two Jewish settlements of Degania and Melahmiya. His body was only found after members of the Degania Kibbutz set out on a search for him, with members of the kibbutz concluding that he had been 'jumped and killed by Arabs'. Though Barsky was clearly a victim of low-level robbery, the killing was placed in the context of ethnic strife. At the time of his killing, and the publishing of the news in *HaHerut*, few could imagine that Barsky would become legendary, etched into the national Jewish consciousness, where he is eulogised as dying 'in the service of the Yishuv and the Israeli state'.[55] In addition, while this one newspaper article described Barsky as a victim, in other similar incidents the Jewish victims were often described as martyrs.

Reacting to another incident, in which a group of non-Jewish Americans were attacked by 'Arabs' also in northern Palestine, *HaHerut* printed a letter describing it as 'an event of lynch and murder'. The letter continues, 'However this time it is not a Jew . . . [In] day light, on Monday evening, seven Americans, who are teachers at the American College in Beirut, were about to climb Mount Tabor when four Arabs from the village of Lubia jumped them.' Moreover, this was the same village whose residents were suspected of killing the Jewish guardsman.

The last example I will provide to show how Arabs were portrayed in the Sephardic Jewish press comes from a reader in Haifa. Unlike the previous cases, this time the Arab who killed the Jew was not anonymous, but rather was a customer of the man. In this case, the Jew, Eliyahu Baron, was reported as being a 'martyr', and similar to the Degania case, 'died a slow death'. After a scuffle broke out between them, the Arab 'kicked the Jew, causing him to fall to the ground . . . the fall was so harsh [that] the Jew fainted and remained dying until the evening . . .' and 'the Muslim immediately escaped'.[56]

What we see from these few examples is that the late Ottoman period bears a striking resemblance to the years of the British Mandate, and in some ways to Israel's post-Mandate relations with its Palestinian minority; that is, the Jewish Yishuv during the late Ottoman period was a self-segregated community, and had little interest in or interaction with the Palestinian majority. In fact, for the most part, the Jewish community viewed the Arab community at large through a narrow lens that focused on violence and mistrust. Therefore, in descriptions of how events unfolded during violent interactions, the Jew was more often eulogised as a martyr, a national figure, who would be remembered as someone who forfeited his life for the Yishuv. Perhaps more important also was that in this coverage, in Palestine's Hebrew press, regardless if it was Zionist or anti-Zionist, Sephardic or Ashkenazi, the killing of a Jew was covered as Jew versus Arab, having been placed within an ethnic context.

The Jerusalem Election Dispute

Even if the Jews cooperated on a daily basis with their urban Arab notable counterparts, the Jewish and Arab populations were growing highly suspicious of each other. This was particularly evident during the 1913 local council elections that created a divide between the communities, with both sides accusing the other of acting out of nationalist motives. The two men at the centre of the controversy were the Jewish Albert Antebi and the Muslim Raghib al-Nashashibi. Antebi was perhaps the most influential character in Jerusalem's Sephardic community, born in Damascus in 1873 and serving as the first director of the Jewish Colonisation Association, and later, he served as the director of the prestigious Alliance Israélite Universelle (a position he left in 1913).[57] Nashashibi, a member of one of Jerusalem's most prestigious notable families, and graduate of Istanbul University, was serving as the district engineer for Jerusalem when the election took place.

When the election results were announced on 8 June 1913, the Jewish community received a great blow, with none of their members winning a seat, with Nashashibi receiving one more vote than Antebi. Immediately, the elections were shrouded in scandal, with Antebi disputing the results on the grounds that as a public official, Nashashibi should have been disqualified from participating in the elections. Yet, according to Nashashibi, he had resigned from his position two days before the elections, and Albert Antebi had interfered in order to prevent his resignation from arriving on time.[58]

The ensuing debate over the elections provides us with a unique picture of how divided the Jews and Arabs of Palestine had become. Both sides seized this opportunity to vent their fears and suspicions concerning the other, with Antebi accusing Nashashibi of being anti-Semitic, and the Arabs openly speaking about the danger of a Zionist serving on the council. This was despite the fact that Albert Antebi had declared that he was a staunch opponent of Zionism, a common stand among francophone Jews in the Empire. However, it is important to remember that even if Antebi was not a political Zionist, his ties to the home office in Berlin meant he was never against Jewish migration to Palestine as a whole, but rather only against having an independent Jewish state. Also, it is important to highlight here that a similar attitude was held by Istanbul's Chief Rabbi Haim Nahum. Even if he was publicly a staunch anti-Zionist, he was responsible for closing down *Filastin*, interpreting their anti-Jewish immigration stance as 'anti-Semitic,' an issue he personally brought to the attention of Interior Minister Talat Bey.[59]

The front page of *HaHerut* described the election defeat in an editorial entitled 'Our Weakness', stating that 'there is no need to prove how important the General Council is for us, the Jews, the *Eretzisraeliyim* . . .' and that it was important 'to defend our public and national interests and to protect our rights and demands . . .'[60] The wording is yet another sign of how the Ashkenazim and Sephardim were uniting into one faction, the people of the Land of Israel, *Eretzisraelis*, a term that could be seen as the first step in transforming the 'Jew' into one that defined his belonging to the homeland in a modern way. In other words, this word can be seen as the Hebrew version of 'Palestinian' used, however, to exclusively denote a Jewish resident of the Holy Land.

In Jerusalem's Arabic newspaper, *Munadi* (in a news item reported in *HaHerut*), Albert Antebi was accused of being a Zionist, despite his numerous declarations that he was an anti-Zionist, and his possible dangers to the Palestinian community are described in the following words:

If Mr Antebi, with the power he has in the Zionist settlement in *Eretz Israel*[61] and his capital and influence, had been elected to the council . . . and will set foot in the council, then we will need to cry about our future and we will not be able to know how long this will last until the government switches the bureaucracy to people that understand freedom and what nationalism means. How long will the [Arab] people's rights be disregarded?[62]

Frustrated with his loss, Antebi petitioned the Ottoman state, explaining in a letter to the minister of interior why Raghib al-Nashashibi should be disqualified.[63] It should be noted that Antebi addressed the Ottoman minster in French, with a Turkish translation provided. This is significant since Antebi was a proclaimed Ottomanist, and unlike the immigrants to the land, he was born in Syria; in other words, it was not a given that local Sephardic Jews had a strong command of Turkish (as previously discussed), despite possessing Ottoman citizenship and maintaining a strong loyalty to the state.

His letter, which focuses on six points, begins by explaining the technical side of things, claiming that Nashashibi did not resign from his position in time and that the notification of his resignation was done in such a way that would have allowed him to retain his former position had he lost.[64] Antebi then goes on to a much harsher accusation that he had been subjected to an anti-Semitic campaign, citing 'irrefutable testimonies' that he believes prove the electors were intimidated and pressured to prevent the election of a Jewish member:

> We are the majority in terms of population and in terms of tax-payers even if our properties are minimal. As a result of two anti-Semitic letters of blackmail (*deux petites fueilles antisemites de chantage*), a thousand intimidations are used to prevent the election of Jewish members in the elected assembly. And when at random a Jewish member is legally elected and designated they create a thousand anti-Semitic manoeuvres to eliminate him. We have the duty of paying and of serving but not the right to deliberate and to participate in government work like our Latin, Greek, Armenian or even Syrian compatriots who are fewer in numbers yet better represented.[65]

In closing, Antebi makes a personal statement on behalf of all the Ottoman Jews:

> I have served the public cause with devotion for the last eighteen years, a past of sincere liberalism which I will defend against autocracy in these most dangerous times. I love the struggle for every sacred cause and the sacrifice does not scare me. Like all Jewish Ottomans, I love my country and serve my *patrie*, sacrificing everything for its happiness, tranquility and prosperity, which only immutable justice can assure.[66]

The investigation into the election dispute continued for almost six months before coming to a close, with Nashashibi securing his position

on the local council and the Jews left without representation. For our purposes, this case portrays a much more complicated situation than what has
been demonstrated in recent works on the Sephardic community vis-à-vis
the local Arab community. In this election, distinct lines of nationality had
already been drawn by both sides and it proved to the Jewish community
that if they did not unite they would surely lose out. At the same time,
it provided the Palestinians with a new vigour and demonstrated that by
uniting they had succeeded in dominating the local council despite the
large population of Jews.

A Jewish University: Jerusalem as a Centre for Modern Education

As we saw with the Palestinians, the Jewish community in Palestine
also envisioned Jerusalem as a centre of education for Jews outside
of Palestine as well. This idea took hold in the Yishuv just as the
Palestinians also began to imagine Jerusalem as a base for higher education; of course, it would be wrong to think that these two communities
were unaware of the other's activities. Around the turn of the century
both Zionists and non-Zionist Jews had been proposing the establishment of some type of institute of higher education in Jerusalem.[67]
However, it was only in 1913 that the Zionist Office decided to take
action. In order to achieve this, they sent their representative, Benjamin
Ibry, to Jerusalem in the winter of 1913 to purchase land for the building
of this institution.[68]

Mr Ibry was a Russian Jew who was naturalised in London in 1912.
After spending less than a year in Great Britain, he travelled to Palestine,
where he applied for a fresh passport from the British consulate in
Jerusalem. The British consulate immediately identified him as a Zionist
representative, a fact that he denied, claiming that he was interested in
purchasing land 'for himself and various friends not specified who are
anxious to take a share in the Jewish colonisation movement'. According
to the British Consul-General P. J. C. McGregor,

> as he [Benjamin Ibry] is in relations with the Anglo-Palestine Bank, I am
> inclined to suspect that he is at least in sympathy with Zionist aims and I have
> no doubt that his own aim in applying for British naturalisation was to settle
> in Palestine and engage in Jewish colonisation schemes under the protection of
> the British flag.

And, it was for this reason that Ibry was unsuccessful in convincing the
British to intervene on his behalf.[69]

Almost a year later, on 12 March 1914, the British Consul McGregor reported to London that

> according to confidential information from a person whom I have reason to regard as conversant with the doings of the Zionist leaders in Jerusalem, [negotiations] for the purchase of the house and land belonging to Sir John Gray Hill, and situated on Mount Scopus have been practically concluded, the object of the acquisition of this important site being the erection of a Jewish university.[70]

This deal was secured by way of Benjamin Ibry, who, according to the British consul, purchased the land with a 'large sum of money'. This transaction sparked British interest not only because of who Sir John Gray Hill was, but more importantly because McGregor believed that the Zionists were interested in 'securing the protection of the British flag for the institution', and therefore wanted instructions on whether to grant a title deed. McGregor goes on to say:

> there appears to be a desire among an influential section of Zionists to place as many of their institutions as possible under British protection, the principle motives for this preference being distrust of French policy and the idea that this country may eventually in some way come under British sovereignty.[71]

What is extraordinary here is that some British officials before World War I already recognised the Zionist belief that Palestine would eventually fall under British control.

Despite this, McGregor continued, expressing his doubts about handing over British support:

> What I beg respectfully to submit is that, as the avowed intention of the promoters is to establish an institution where Jews of all nationalities shall be enabled to go through a course of higher education imparted in the Hebrew language and with a purely nationalist tendency, it could hardly be considered as a genuinely British interest, and might conceivably lead to undesirable complications, particularly in the event of the Turkish government modifying its present attitudes of extreme tolerance towards the Zionist movement.

In addition, McGregor continued to question the motives of the Zionist movement, pointing out discrepancies in their narrative and conveying doubts on Mr Ibry's sincerity. First, despite Mr Ibry having denied any connection to the Zionist movement, after a meeting between them, Mr Ibry confessed that he was sent to Palestine by the Zionist Organization to purchase land. And, it was for this very reason that Mr Ibry was pushing to renew his British passport so that the land purchased for the Jewish university would be under a British name. It seems from the document that Consul McGregor was growing impatient with Mr Ibry, who was at the same time acting quite shrewdly by making clear that if he was denied the passport, he would simply have Lord Rothschild or Claude Montefiore register the land in their name. He continued in a defiant way, stating that the consul's help would simply 'facilitate matters behind the scenes', since he was 'confident of the support of His Majesty's Government'. This of course was 'provided I [McGregor] had no suspicions with regard to the aims of Zionism'.[72]

The conversation between McGregor and Mr Ibry continued and allows us to obtain a clear picture of how the British in Palestine actually held a mildly negative opinion of the Zionist movement. In fact, it highlights how the Zionist movement was in a sense 'playing both sides'. During their conversation, it was important for Mr Ibry to state that 'political Zionism was dead', and that 'the modern Zionists aimed at nothing but the possibility of settling down as colonists under Ottoman rule, for the regeneration of their [the Jewish] race'. To this, McGregor sharply pointed out that there was a contradiction in the Zionist tactics. If the Zionists were so interested in their schools being 'Ottoman', then why did they need foreign protection? To this question, Mr Ibry pointed out that the land was purchased for £21,500 and they wish to purchase another 150 acres of adjacent land, and therefore 'it was evident that such a valuable holding would need foreign protection. More importantly, the Jewish university was aiming to have it[self] affiliated with an English university such as Oxford or Cambridge'.[73] Following their conversation about the university, Mr Ibry revealed that he recently also purchased 700 dunams (191 acres) of land at Abu Shushah, the ancient site of Gezer. Besides this important archaeological site where the Palestine Exploration Fund was interested in continuing their work, Mr Ibry also noted that he had 'acquired extensive tracts of lands in other directions and had much larger transactions in prospect'.[74]

McGregor's Assessment of Zionism

At the end of the letter, McGregor supplied to his superior in London his general assessment of Zionism in Palestine. First, he reported that

> the hindrances formerly placed in the path of Jewish immigration and the acquisition of land seem to have entirely disappeared owing to the complaisant attitude of the authorities, and although the proceedings of the Zionists are enveloped in jealous secrecy, there can be no doubt that enormous sums have been spent on land throughout Palestine.[75]

In addition to the issue of land, the consul updated London concerning the growing popularity of Hebrew in Jewish schools as a result of 'national spirit' and Zionist pressure. An example of this, which is well documented in many historical surveys of Zionism, is the debate between German and Hebrew. In 1913, this debate once again resurfaced and was the cause of many Zionists pulling their children out of the German Hilfsverein. This also spread to Jaffa, 'the centre of militant Zionism rendered all the more aggressive by the presence of Russian elements strongly tinged with Socialism of an advanced type'.[76] What is more, the only English language school under British protection was the Evelina de Rothschild School for Girls run by the Anglo-Jewish association. While the Zionists threatened this school's director as well, McGregor believed that these threats were not acted on because the Zionist movement was in the process of courting the British (along with other reasons).[77] He goes on:

> I need hardly to say that Mr Ibry's presentment of the aims of Zionism as a movement devoid of all political afterthought is in contradiction with the views expressed in other circumstances by Zionist partisans, and I would add that, even if this were not so, there are signs to indicate that the protection of Zionist institutions promises to become a factor in the political rivalry of foreign Powers in Palestine. Thus, while it is true that, as Mr Ibry declared, the Zionist schools at Jerusalem are at present Ottoman, this is the case merely because most of them have but recently been established as the result of the rupture with the German Hilfsverein, and efforts are not being made to place them under French protection. This would, of course, involve a leading place being given to the French language and in other respects matters would remain as they were before.

Finally, he ends his letter by stating that, regardless of the Zionist campaign to spread the Hebrew language, it was only supported by a 'small faction', and that only 'half the time in the German and British Jewish schools is devoted to Hebrew, and the schools of the French Alliance Israélite are now proceeding to follow this example'.[78]

The cornerstone for the university was set in place in 1918, following the British occupation of Palestine, and the university would open its doors in 1925, well into the British Mandate period. However, for our purposes, this case is important for three reasons. First, it exhibits to what extent the Arab and Jewish communities were developing their communal ties separately. In other words, each group did not envision the other one as a potential constituency within the walls of its university. In the previous chapter, we saw how the Palestinians inherently saw their future university as one for Arabs, while here we see that the Jews in Palestine also envisioned one for Jews. Secondly, we see how Britain recognised that the some among the Zionist movement were vying for its support and believed that Palestine perhaps one day would fall under British control.

This in itself confirms that Palestinian fears of growing British hegemony were justified (as if the occupation of Egypt in 1882 was not enough). However, even if the Zionist movement had started to look to Britain for support, the Zionist Jewish immigrants to Palestine were still placing their hopes in the Ottoman Empire. This divide between political Zionism and that of Zionists in Palestine would only grow as time progressed.

Transforming Identities in Istanbul

With a great deal of new literature being directed towards the Sephardic Ottoman Jewish community in Palestine (and in the Empire as a whole) as one that supported the state and accepted a new Ottoman identity, there are important parallels with the Ashkenazim who were also working to integrate into the Ottoman system. In fact, while most work on the Ashkenazi Zionist movements portrays them as separatists, what emerges is a much more complicated picture, where we actually see attempts by Zionists to integrate within the Ottoman state. This coupled with the bridges being formed with the Sephardic community led to a united front where Jews asserted new powers vis-à-vis the Palestinians.

The second major wave of Jews to immigrate to Palestine dates back to 1904, accelerated following the failed Russian revolution and is remembered most by those immigrants who belonged to socialist Zionist movements. What was unique about this group was that, despite their radical understanding of Zionism and their recent immigration, their leaders understood that in order to secure their presence in Palestine, it would be necessary to make their presence known in Istanbul as well. Once there, they would meet another group of Ashkenazi Jews, this one coming from Palestine, who also believed in the need for the presence of practical Zionists in Istanbul.

It is perhaps ironic that we only now arrive at the members of the Second Aliyah, David Ben-Gurion and Moshe Sharett, the future leaders of the Yishuv during the British Mandate, and the first two prime ministers of the Jewish state. In the official historical narrative of Israel, the members of the Second Aliyah play an iconic role, with their accomplishments in solidifying Labour Zionism as the hegemonic force within the Yishuv, paving the way to the Jewish state. However, this work will not focus on their role in establishing cooperative farms, or founding the Jewish guardsmen network, but rather shift our focus to their time spent in Istanbul, a period that has been brushed off as marginal in the historical narrative. Perhaps this is the case since once one highlights their time in the Ottoman capital, it breaks the smooth narrative of Zionism and underscores the fact that the future leaders of the state did not foresee an independent Jewish state in Palestine, but rather envisioned a Jewish autonomous homeland in the greater Ottoman Empire, looking to Istanbul as its capital.

During the post-Young Turk era, just a few years after they had reached Palestine, the group of young socialist Zionists packed their bags and made their way to Istanbul, where they opted to start their political careers, studying in the prestigious law school, the *Hukuk Mektebi*, while others among them joined other schools, studying medicine, engineering and economics.[79] The young Zionists' move to Istanbul was summed up by Anita Shapira thus: 'acquiring an Ottoman legal education seemed to them a very efficient path toward large-scale political activity – the kind Ben-Gurion dreamed of.'[80]

There can be little doubt about the need to study in Istanbul if they ever had aspirations to integrate and represent Palestine's Jewish community in the Empire's politics as Ottoman citizens[81] and potentially enter the Ottoman intelligentsia and work from within.[82] For example, Ben-Gurion decided to study in Istanbul in order to learn the Ottoman administration's system and laws, since he believed he would later become an Ottoman citizen and run for parliamentary elections.[83] On the other hand, Israel Shochat stated that the HaShomer ('Watchman') organisation chose him to study law in Istanbul in 1911 so the defence organisation would no longer be dependent on Arab lawyers, whom they felt had a conflict of interest when it came to representing Jews. Yitzhak Ben-Zvi appears to be the first member of the group to have adopted Ottoman citizenship. Describing the process later he claimed he had no trouble adopting Ottoman citizenship and that this would completely break his ties with the Diaspora, and tie his fate with the Ottoman state to which his homeland was bound.[84] The social transformation did not only entail a move to a new environment but also a personal transformation, where they started speaking only Turkish in their apartments and donning tarbushes in the streets.[85]

Living in an entirely new community previously closed to them, the students' relation with Istanbul's population was particularly interesting. Yitzhak Ben-Zvi, who would later become Israel's second president, and Shochat both described the wide range of students with whom they studied. The majority of these were the children of rich Turkish *effendi*s, along with Arabs, Kurds, Albanians and Christians from a variety of backgrounds.[86] In fact, it was most likely this observation that led the group to establish the Union for Ottoman Hebrew Students in Istanbul, which mirrored other student unions which were based on the different ethnic groups living in the Ottoman capital.

Ben-Gurion, who was the general secretary of the group, described the need for the union activities in a 1913 Hebrew written report.[87] First, he stated that there was a general need for Jews to come together as they do in Western countries, which provides them with mutual support during their studies and also a way to protect their honour and national pride and to 'research the existence of the Hebrew people and personal training to prepare for its future'.[88] He then moves on to its very important role within the Ottoman context.

> Once the new government regime was declared, a few student clubs were formed in Constantinople, which were set up, understandably, according to their ethnic background. In the first years, Turkish, Greek, Armenians, Tatars and even Albanians established student clubs. Only the Hebrew students differ . . . [and] in the institutions of higher education in Istanbul, there are about 200 Jews and despite this, in Turkey's capital there is a lack of spiritual development and especially knowledge of Judaism [among them].[89]

This student union was officially authorised by the necessary Ottoman authorities and according to their chair, Shlomo Matalon, a local Sephardic Jew, this new organisation would be especially important for the Jews coming from Palestine to study there, stating that

> this would warm the hearts of people in *Eretz Israel*, and all the students coming to the capital will gain information and find a centre that will help them with anything they need. They will find a national atmosphere – even if small – and brotherly bond. We hope that our union will spark interest and practical and spiritual assistance from the Jewish public so it can fulfill its programme.[90]

In addition to working to provide better educational services for Jewish students – such as purchasing books for a library and plans to help students with financial aid – the student union took it upon itself to bring speakers who presented lectures about Jewish student life in Europe. These talks took place in such locales as the Jewish *B'nai B'rith* offices or the Maccabi Sports centre. The student union also held discussions on the wave of anti-Semitism in the Turkish press (see the next chapter), meeting with students in the Istanbul neighbourhoods of Pera, Hasköy and Galata, which ultimately culminated in official protests.[91]

Making their school and work especially difficult was the fact that the opening of the academic year in 1912 coincided with the breakout of the Balkan Wars, which eventually led to a state of emergency being declared several times in Istanbul, with many students leaving the city, as the schools closed down. Nevertheless, the student union succeeded in recruiting fifty active members and eleven supporting ones from among the local Jewish intelligentsia, and also had plans to reach out to students in other Ottoman cities, in an attempt to form an Empire-wide union.

Another source for recruiting Jewish students was at the British colleges, where Jewish students had already started to organise.[92] While most of their work was based in Istanbul, the union aimed to expand throughout the Ottoman lands and had already reached out to Jewish students in Beirut and Salonica as well.[93]

Equally important, Gad Frumkin was there to greet the students and served as the president of the union. Frumkin, born in Jerusalem and raised speaking Hebrew, was the son of Israel Dov Frumkin, the editor of the Hebrew newspaper *Havatzelet*. The young Frumkin, like so many others, saw the Young Turk revolution as a turning point for the Jewish Yishuv and thus made his way to Istanbul to study law, acting in the Ottoman capital as an unofficial representative of sorts for the Jewish Yishuv. With his impeccable Turkish he was on the one hand inherently an Ottoman, while, with his native Hebrew, he was no less a product of the new Yishuv: an Ottoman Hebrew-speaking Jew. His main thrust of work in Istanbul was serving as the head administrator of the *Netaim* company that was founded to enlarge the rural settlement of Jews throughout Palestine. After coming to Istanbul, he succeeded in registering it as a legal Ottoman business, establishing it under the Turkish name: *Der-i Saadet, Ticaret Ziruai ve Sanaai, Şirket Osmaniyesi* (Société d'agriculture et d'industrie, Constantinople).

The practical Zionists and the political Zionists in Istanbul did cooperate. One example of this was when Shochat was invited by Victor Jacobson to accompany him to a meeting with Ottoman Minister of the Interior Talat Paşa in 1912. At this meeting, it was alleged that Talat Paşa offered to sell the previously mentioned *çiftliks*, which would have opened up almost a million dunams of land to Jewish settlement. The meeting seemed to have been quite specific, with a map displayed showing the prospective lands ranging from the Galilee in the north to the Negev in the south. However, according to Shochat, the Zionist representative, Jacobson, refused the offer since the Zionist Organization (ZO) did not have the 1,000,000 Gold Francs to pay for it. However, despite this, Shochat tended to think that it was not an issue of money, even if ZO did not have the funds to pay for it, but rather that Jacobson would accept nothing less than a political charter over all of Palestine.[94] While this potential land sale in Palestine is not documented in the Ottoman archives, it seems Shochat's detailed description serves as a rare example of a meeting taking place between Zionists and a high-ranking Ottoman official. However, as we will see further down, and in the next chapter, despite attempts at developing relations, the Berlin-based ZO had only limited success in influencing Ottoman policy.

This group of Zionists had a chance to prove their loyalty to the

Ottoman Empire in the Balkan Wars of 1912 for which Shochat offered Zionist military assistance.[95] The concept of Zionists joining the Ottoman army actually dated back to 1907, when David Wolffson (the leader of (ZO) from 1905 to 1911) worked towards a settlement in which 50,000 Jews were to be brought to Palestine. These Jews would adopt Ottoman citizenship and serve in the army. To have this proposal accepted, the Ottomans demanded £26,000,000 which the Zionists would not agree to provide. Consequently, the proposed settlement was never completed.[96] Also, during the 1911 Italian invasion of Libya, the Jewish community in Palestine demonstrated on behalf of their Ottoman homeland, and set up an organisation for the purpose of sending doctors and nurses to the war front. In fact, according to a *New York Times* article, the society that was established was the Jewish version of the Red Cross, the *Magen David Adom*, and it had the support of the Ottoman government. According to the article, Jewish aid workers would replace the normal Red Cross, with the six-point star, which is a sign of the 'Shield of David'.[97]

Once the war began, Shochat, Ben Gurion and Ben-Zvi began to recruit Jewish volunteers from among Zionists in Palestine, Russia and the local Jewish population in Istanbul, to fight alongside their Ottoman compatriots. Shochat arranged a meeting with Enver Paşa and Cemal Pasha (the military governor of Istanbul) and proposed a plan to establish a Jewish cavalry division made up of fifty horsemen to fight for the Ottomans. The Ottoman officials agreed and appointed Shochat the commander, sending him to a military camp after which he contacted HaShomer in Palestine, and formed a group of cavalrymen. No sooner had they formed the group than the war ended, and the Jewish division was one of the first groups to be released.[98]

During the war other Zionists had offered medical assistance to the Ottoman army.[99] As a result, the Jewish community including the Zionists enjoyed a 'Turko-Zionist' rapprochement, which was also aided by the fact that Ottoman Jews, along with their Muslim co-patriots, were fleeing the Balkans and migrating to Anatolia. This new relationship became evident when the threat of a Greek invasion seemed likely, and the Ottomans supplied arms not only to the Muslims, but also to the Jews. The outpouring of support for these two communities even created alliances between Jewish and Muslim communities in South Africa, far from Ottoman borders.[100] Much in the way that the Great Powers drew on the Jewish communities in Europe and the New World during World War I, the Ottoman government utilised the aid of the Jews living within the Empire; for example, President of the Council of State Kamil Paşa met with the editor of *Le Jeune Turc*, and promised to meet some of the Zionists' needs if they worked towards changing European public opinion, which was suffering due to Greek claims of massacres.[101]

It is important to note that Shochat also reported the proposal for an Ottoman army Jewish division to Jacobson, seeking the Zionist Office's financial and political support. Jacobson supported the proposal and brought it to the attention of the ZO, even though he had serious reservations, believing that this division might not convince the Ottomans that the Zionists were truly loyal. Jacobson was also concerned about taking so many strong young men from Palestine where they were greatly needed – could the Zionists afford to lose them? Still, Jacobson felt they should support Shochat's proposal, since it would not disturb the ZO's activities. Strategically, Jacobson apparently understood that the Zionist movement would not suffer from this type of pro-Ottoman identification.[102]

Among the Zionists fighting in the Balkan Wars, the soldier Karmi Eisenberg (Figure 4.1) provides the best example of how local Zionism, merged with a new Hebrew culture, managed to create a new prototype of the pro-Ottoman Jew, a figure who must have stood in stark contrast to the Empire's traditional Sephardic (and much smaller Ashkenazi) populations of the Empire. The son of Aaron Eisenberg, a Russian immigrant who founded the Jewish settlement Rehovot in 1889 in the region of Daran,[103] Karmi (whose name basically means 'of the vine') was also one of the first cases of what would become a growing trend in the Zionist Yishuv: children given names related to agriculture in place of typical religious Jewish names. In many ways, Karmi represented the first generation of the growing trend of a 'native Hebrew culture'.[104]

In 1911, at the age of twenty, Karmi reached the Ottoman capital, joining his brother-in-law, Gad Frumkin, the previously discussed lawyer. Originally, he joined the student body at Istanbul's prestigious agricultural school, *Halkalı Ziraat ve Baytar Mekteb-i Âlisi*, following in the footsteps of the close family friend, Yitzhak Levi, the manager of the Anglo-Palestine Company in Jerusalem and an alumni of the school, who had left Istanbul for Palestine. However, the school seemed not to have met his taste for adventure, and Karmi was accepted to military school and by the autumn of 1912 he became the first Jewish army officer from Palestine. Karmi's motivation to join the Ottoman army was out of a belief that if the Jews joined the army, they would eventually secure the trust of the authorities, which would lead to the Ottoman Empire granting autonomy for the Jews in Palestine.[105]

It is important to highlight that the phenomenon of non-Muslims eager to join the ranks of the army was not only prevalent among the Jewish community (throughout the Empire) but also among the Armenians who,

 קצין יהודי ראשון בצבא העותומני
בנימיני בן אהרן איזנברג מרחובות קרשבא 1912

Figure 4.1 Karmi Eisenberg, an Ottoman Zionist solider. From the book *Frumkin, Gad. Derekh Shofet bi-Yerushalayim* [The Path of a Judge in Jerusalem], Tel Aviv: Dvir, 1954, p. 167

despite the massacres of 1908–9,[106] imagined a new nation where equality would be achieved through service in the Ottoman army.[107] In fact, the Jewish case seemed to have been following the greater trend among the Armenian community's stance towards the army service, with community leaders encouraging their youngsters to join.[108] However, I would like to highlight that Karmi, along with the other Jewish and Armenian recruits, did not only embody in his character a new proto-type of self-nationalism (akin to that of the Armenians and Greeks) but also a new type of Ottoman soldier; one that joined the army out of a modern sense of patriotism and not out of forced recruitment (something which certainly had to have been a foreign concept among many Muslims as well). In fact, Armenian attitudes seemed to reflect to a great extent Zionist ideology, which saw the Jews as Hebrews in order to connect them with a heroic past which was being relived at that time in Palestine. For Armenians, this was no different among some of their community; just to quote one example, there is an editorial that appeared in *Yeprad*, which was published in the eastern Anatolian city of Harput, stating that 'the blood of ancient Armenian heroes was still circulating in the veins of the contemporary Armenians'.[109] The author goes on to state that 'some thought we were traitors, enemies of state and nation. Now we hope that they see those traitors are the most fervent ones in guarding the fatherland if they are sure that they are regarded as the genuine children of the country'.[110]

It needs to be stated that overall the love for joining the army did not take hold among all the non-Muslims. In a 1910 report, the acting British consul, James Morgan, documented the recruitment of Muslims and non-Muslims from Jerusalem. Out of 110 recruits, who were set to start their army service in the Ottoman city of Adana, 34 of them were non-Muslims. The consul noted that originally 69 non-Muslims were to go but a large number of them opted out of service by paying the *bedel* fee, or running away, due to the fact that 'no enthusiasm was manifested by the non-Moslem recruits; [t]he Greeks and Latins however seemed to be resigned themselves to their lot and were content. The Jews however are far from happy and totally opposed to serving as soldiers'. It would seem that the fact Adana (today a city in southern Turkey) was a great distance from Jerusalem also must have added to the large number of Jews and Christians trying to get out of the service.[111] Interestingly enough, among the Jews who paid the *bedel*, they were equally divided among Ashkenazi and Sephardi, showing that among both groups there were those hesitant to send their children off to fight. In a report in the newspaper *HaOr* it stated that the Jewish families showed a great amount of distress over their children's recruitment:

> God forbid, however, that this was due to their sorrow that they were going to serve in the army, rather this was the first time that they had to suddenly leave their homes, their city, their land and their leaders, to a future they did not know or understand.

All this took place following an official military ceremony, and a procession accompanied by an Ottoman military band, with a procession of thousands of people bidding them farewell at the train station.[112] Interestingly enough, just as these Jews and Christians were leaving Jerusalem for the unknown, a group of Jews and Christians arrived in Jerusalem from the cities of Damascus and Safad to do their army service in the district of Jerusalem, which also calmed the fears of what army service might entail.[113] The lack of enthusiasm for joining the army among the Jewish community stands as a reminder that for all the research arguing that there was Jewish integration in the Empire, it would appear, at least in Jerusalem, that the Jewish community remained to a great deal outsiders on this issue, and even if patriotic in words, and in their hearts, this did not always equal recruitment into the army, thus making the stories of the Jewish soldiers who did join the army an even more interesting experience. This held true for Sephardic communities in Istanbul as well, where it was reported just months after Enver Paşa had praised Jewish participation, that a group of young Jews from the Istanbul Jewish neighbourhood of Hasköy caused a great embarrassment to the community by not showing up for their military check-up. Even worse, after it was claimed that the young boys had left for the US, some opted to turn themselves in, which led to searches in the neighbourhood to find the ones hiding.[114]

Returning to the story of Karmi, following the breakout of the Balkan Wars he was sent to fight, which led to great fears among his family since they had not heard from him. However, in early November 1912, a telegram notified them that he was safe at a military camp in Çorlu, in Thrace.[115] Karmi's unique case was proudly reported in the Yishuv's Zionist Hebrew newspaper, *HaTzvi*. The newspaper also highlighted the fact that he was only one of three Jewish officers in the Ottoman army, the other two Sephardic Jews from Istanbul and Salonica. Just days later, the same newspaper reported that Karmi had been promoted as a result of his remarkable performance in battle, and was awarded the prestigious Turkish title of *Gazi*. The fact that this happened around the Jewish holiday of Hanukkah did not slip past the author's attention, with Karmi being compared to legendary fighters, and the author stating 'this is the first time *Eretz Israel* has provided a hero and victor to the homeland's army', and that this recalled the heroism of the 'Maccabees', and that *Gazi* Karmi Efendi 'would serve as a role model for his brothers who will grow in numbers in the Ottoman army'. Perhaps it was Karmi and these other Jewish officers that Minister of War Enver Paşa had in mind when he met with the Chief Rabbi, Haim Nahum Efendi, and reported that Jewish soldiers showed heroism and deserved praise for their role in the Balkan Wars.[116] This mix of Jewish nationalism that we see with Karmi, meshed together with the promotion of Ottoman patriotism, proves an important example that has been overlooked in the recent histories on Ottomanism, while greatly neglected in mainstream history of Zionism.[117]

It should be noted that during World War I, the trend of Jews fighting in the Ottoman army continued, though that narrative is beyond the scope of this book. Future leaders of the Jewish state, such as Moshe Sharett, would serve in the Ottoman army until 1918, even after the British issued the pro-Zionist Balfour Declaration. The young *Gazi* Karmi Efendi ended up becoming a prisoner of war and was sent to Siberia, where he died in 1920 waiting to be part of a prisoner exchange between the newly formed Soviet state and the Ottoman Empire. Concurrent with the death of Karmi, a period in Zionist history came to an end. He would be the last and one of the few soldiers remembered as a martyr in the two new nation-states that would be established after World War I: Turkey and Israel.[118]

According to Karmi's brother-in-law, Gad Frumkin, the young Ottoman soldier also had a plan to create a Jewish majority in Palestine. Frumkin reported that even before population transfers such as the 1923 Greek and Turkish exchange, Karmi would often discuss transferring as a way to solve the question of (what to do with) the Arabs who reside within the borders of *Eretz Israel*. Frumkin quotes him as saying, 'we will buy lands in Mesopotamia (Iraq) and the Syrian plains and trade the lands of peasants in Palestine, and transfer them together with their households and livestock to these neighboring lands . . .' And, 'the peasants will receive this offer happily since the lands will be much more fertile and spacious than the ones they currently have in Palestine. In addition, this would also include convincing Jewish populations from Syria and Baghdad to leave their homes for Palestine.'[119]

For our purposes, Karmi and the students in Istanbul provide us with the key to understanding how the Zionist movement, despite its relatively small size, took concrete steps to promote its agenda as hand-in-hand with the state's ideology. In contrast to the Zionist movement outside of Palestine, which was losing hope in cutting a deal with the Ottoman government, the Zionist Jews within the Empire could not see any other reality than working with the state as citizens. However, this also included forming new bonds with the Sephardic population, first and foremost in Palestine, and then throughout the Empire, with the Hebrew language serving as the foundation of these new bonds. For the Palestinians, the Zionist presence in Istanbul also proved to be a challenge, adding to the already existing frustrations exhibited in the previous chapters.

Notes

1. Part of this chapter was published in an article format, see Fishman, 'The Limitations of Citadinité in Late Ottoman Jerusalem', in *Ordinary Jerusalem*, pp. 510–31.
2. *Ha-Tzvi* (published this edition as *Ha-Or*), 7 February 1911, p. 2; *Moriah*, 24 January 1911; *HaHerut*, 25 January 1911. The soldier was Nahman Karniel from Zikhron Yaakov, the son of two immigrants. Almost ten months after being promoted to an officer, in December we find that he also received

an award for his outstanding service. See *Ha-Tzvi*, 3 December 1911, p. 3.

3. To hear a recording of Nahman Karniel speaking about his life, including a short excerpt on his Ottoman army years, taped before his death in 1970, see: <www.yavneel.org.il/site/family.asp?fam_id=340> (last accessed 31 May 2019).

4. Quoted in Der Matossian, *Shattered Dreams of Revolution*, p. 55.

5. Alroey, *An Unpromising Land*, p. xii.

6. Saposnik, *Becoming Hebrew*, p. 179.

7. Der Matossian, *Shattered Dreams of Revolution*, p. 62.

8. *The Times*, 14 August 1911.

9. *New York Times*, 13 August 1911.

10. Jacobson, 'Sephardim, Ashkenazim, and the "Arab Question" in pre-First World War Palestine', *Middle Eastern Studies*, pp. 105–30.

11. Jacobson, *From Empire to Empire*, p. 86.

12. Klein, *Lives in Common*, p. 36. Certainly, it is correct that there were Jewish communities within Iraq and Egypt (and certainly other countries and regions) where Jews did define themselves as such; however, this case is hard to substantiate within Palestine.

13. Saposnik, *Becoming Hebrew*, p. 180.

14. An interesting case where we actually see the Jews fluent in Arabic is found in a dossier that describes tensions between the Sephardic community in Tiberias, which reached the level of state involvement. The petition addressed to the state by some of Tiberias' rabbis is in Arabic. DH.ID 1331.L.19, 21 September 1913.

15. Sharett, *Mikhtavim mehaTzva haOthmani* [Letters from the Ottoman Army], p. 158; Haram al-Sharif Dossier: Document 44. In this postcard, Moshe Sharett writes to his brother in Arabic in such a way that it is hard to distinguish his Russian background. For new studies on the extent of Ashkenazi–Arab relations, see Halperin, 'A Murder in the Grove', p. 430.

16. According to Arthur Ruppin, there were 5,000 Moroccan and Persian Jews, 1,000 Bukharans and 2,000 Yemenis in Jerusalem, and 2,000 Yemenis outside of Jerusalem during World War I. See Ruppin, 'Syrien als Wirtschaftsgebiet', p. 273.

17. Karpat, 'Jewish Population Movements in the Ottoman Empire', p. 412. Internal migration of Ottoman Jews coming from Salonica also caught the attention of the Ottoman administration; however, unfortunately, due to a misplaced file in the Ottoman archives, we do not know the extent of this 1914 migration.

18. To see primary sources and a description of a small group of Ottoman (Bulgarian) Jews who settled in Palestine in the late 1800s in the settlement of '*Artuf*, see Cohen and Stein (eds), *Sephardi Lives*, pp. 192–4.

19. Ruppin, *The Jews of To-Day*, p. 262.

20. *HaHerut*, 29 March 1911.

21. PRO FO 195/2377, 22 May 1911, 153–153b.
22. See Kayali, *Arabs and Young Turks*, pp. 82–96.
23. Here is one of the many advertisements to learn Arabic and Turkish in the Sephardic Yeshiva *Talmud Torah. HaHerut*, 11 November 1910.
24. Stein, *Making Jews Modern*.
25. Ortaylı, 'Ottoman Jewry and the Turkish Language, in *The Last Ottoman Century and Beyond*, pp. 129–39. For a detailed study of Turkification and the Jews of modern Turkey see Bali, *Cumhuriyet Yıllarında Türkiye Yahudileri*. According to Jacob Landau, few Jews had a strong knowledge of Turkish, save for a few intellectuals such as Abraham Galante and the previously discussed Moiz Kohen. See Landau, *Tekinalp*, p. 349.
26. Stein, *Making Jews Modern,* p. 79.
27. *HaHerut*, 4 November 1910.
28. Malul succeeded in publishing pro-Zionist articles in some Lebanese and Egyptian newspapers; see Mandel, *The Arabs and Zionism before World War I*, p. 132; *HaHerut*, 3 July 1912.
29. *HaHerut*, 4 November 1910.
30. Ibid.
31. Campos, *Ottoman Brothers*, p. 162.
32. *HaHerut*, 25 October 1911.
33. Ibid., 4 July 1912.
34. Some work has pointed to the fact that Nissim Malul supported 'assimilating' into the greater Arab population of Syria and Palestine, based on their reading of an article published by him in *HaHerut*, 17 June 1913. My reading is exactly the opposite; in other words, he attributed the need to learn Arabic, but refuted claims he was calling for 'assimilation'. In fact, from his piece it seems he also considers Arabic inferior to Hebrew.
35. Halperin, *Babel in Zion*, p. 8.
36. Ibid., pp. 8–9.
37. Thon, 'The Zionist Programme and Practical Work in Palestine', in *Zionist Work in Palestine*, p. 18. In the same volume, there is a descriptive account of how Hebrew by 1911 had taken hold in Palestine by David Yellin, 'The Renaissance of the Hebrew Language in Palestine', pp. 143–6.
38. *HaHerut*, 14 November 1910.
39. Even-Zohar, 'The Emergence of a Native Hebrew Culture in Palestine: 1882–1948', *Studies in Zionism*, p. 178.
40. *HaHerut*, 14 November 1910.
41. Jacobson, *From Empire to Empire*, p. 88.
42. Ruppin, *The Jews of To-Day*, p. 263.
43. *HaHerut*, 21 July 1913, 1.
44. Ibid.
45. Ibid., my italics.
46. Ibid.
47. *HaHerut*, 22 August 1913, p. 1.

48. PRO FO 195/2459, 29 April 1914, p. 199.
49. This Haram al-Sharif Dossier: Document was a secret communication from the minister of interior to the governor of Jerusalem, and was a simple notification, including one sentence about why the paper was to be suspended. It would seem further Haram al-Sharif Dossier: Documents concerning this incident will be uncovered in the future. See DH.ŞFR 1332.Ca.22, 40/39; 18 April 1914.
50. PRO FO 195/2459, 29 April 1914, p. 199.
51. Makdisi, 'Ottoman Orientalism', *The American Historical Review*, pp. 768–96 (italics in original).
52. For a discussion on Zionism and Colonialism, see Penslar, 'Zionism, Colonialism and Postcolonialism', *Journal of Israeli History*, pp. 84–98.
53. *HaHerut*, 22 August 1913. On the same exact page, there is another article about Arabs robbing Jews on the road from Haifa to Zikhron Yaakov.
54. *HaHerut*, 26 November 1913. Degania was the first *kvutzah* (communal settlement, later to be acknowledged as the first kibbutz), and was founded in 1910. For a history of the kibbutz see: <https://degania.org.il/en/> (last accessed 31 May 2019).
55. On Degania's website, he is listed among the soldiers and members who died for the cause of the Yishuv and the Israeli state. See (Hebrew) <https://degania.org.il/יזכור/משה-ברסקי/> (last accessed 31 May 2019). For more on Barsky, his life, death and the myth he would become, see Chazan, 'The Murder of Moshe Barsky', *Israel Affairs*, pp. 284–306.
56. *HaHerut*, 26 May 1914, p. 2.
57. Mandel, *The Arabs and Zionism before World War I*, p. 41.
58. Albert Antebi was involved in at least two other scandals during Ali Ekrem Bey's governorship. First, Antebi was found to have violated building regulations at one point. Second, Ali Ekrem Bey accused Antebi of 'being the moving spirit behind the campaign to ensure the election of Yaakov Meir in a manner which was both illegal and aimed at securing new rights for the Jews'. See Kushner, *To Be Governor in Jerusalem*, pp. 80, 89.
59. HaTzvi, 28 April 1914, p. 3.
60. *HaHerut*, 23 June 1913, 1.
61. While we do not have the original text from *Munadi*, it is safe to assume that in the original the word Palestine was used, and that *Eretz Israel* was simply a direct translation.
62. *HaHerut*, 23 June 1913, p. 1.
63. DH.UMVM 1332.M.22; 21 December 1913, pp. 11, 1–5.
64. Ibid.
65. Ibid., p. 3.
66. Ibid., p. 4.
67. For a detailed account of the history of the origins of the Jewish university, see Kollat, 'The Idea of the Hebrew University in the Jewish National Movement', in *The History of the Hebrew University of Jerusalem*, pp. 3–74.

68. See Shilo, 'Shi'ur be-Ziyonut-Hidate He'almuto shel "Hawajah Ibry"', *Katedra*, 1990, 58; see also *New York Times* article on the topic: 3 October 1911.
69. PRO FO, 26 February 1913, pp. 178–9.
70. PRO FO, 12 March 1914, p. 152.
71. Ibid., my italics.
72. PRO FO, 15 March 1911, p. 173.
73. Ibid., p. 174.
74. Ibid.
75. Ibid., p. 175.
76. Ibid.
77. Ibid., 176.
78. Ibid., 176–7.
79. Shochat, 'Slihot VaDerekh', in *Sefer HaShomer (The Book of Shomer)*, p. 35.
80. Shapira, *Ben-Gurion*, p. 31.
81. Ben-Zvi, *Zikronot VaReshumot (Essays and Reminiscences)*, p. 200.
82. Shochat, 'Slihot VaDerekh', p. 35.
83. Teveth, *Kin'at David (David Ben-Gurion's Biography)*, p. 252.
84. Ben-Zvi, *Zikronot VaReshumot*, p. 200.
85. Teveth, *Kin'at David*, p. 250.
86. Shochat, 'Slihot VaDerekh', p. 35; Ben-Zvi, *Zikronot VaReshumot*, p. 203.
87. The Ottoman Hebrew Student Union Report, Zionist Archives; the report is also published in *HaHerut*, 17 August 1913, p. 2. Ben-Gurion had learned Hebrew already in his early childhood in Poland, according to Anita Shapira, who tells the story of him learning it from his grandfather, and speaking it to his friends, much to the dismay of some of their elders. In his youth, in Poland, he was an avid reader of Hebrew literature, and European literature translated to Hebrew. He also prided himself on never learning Polish, which could be a stretch of the imagination. Shapira, *Ben-Gurion*, p. 5.
88. Ottoman Hebrew Student Union Report.
89. Ibid.
90. *HaTzvi*, 1 May 1912, p. 2.
91. The Ottoman Hebrew Student Union Report, Zionist Archives.
92. Ibid.
93. Ibid.
94. Shochat, 'Slihot VaDerekh', p. 36.
95. Teveth, *Kin'at David*, p. 251; Shohat, 'Slihot VaDerekh', p. 36.
96. Friedman, *Germany, Turkey, and Zionism*, p. 140.
97. *New York Times*, 10 December 1911. Unfortunately, I was unable to find more information on this. We know that Magen David Adom came into being as an organisation only much later in the Mandate period, but this news report places its roots in the late Ottoman period.
98. Shochat, 'Slihot VaDerekh', p. 36.

99. Ortaylı, 'Ottomanism and Zionism during the Second Constitutional Period', in *The Jews of the Ottoman Empire*, p. 532.
100. Sonyel, *Minorities and the Destruction of the Ottoman Empire*, p. 321.
101. Ibid., p. 312.
102. Mints, 'Ha-Shomer ve Rai'on ha-Hitnadvut ba-Tzva ha-"Othmani" [The Shomer and the Idea of Volunteering in the Ottoman Army]', in *Iyunim ba-Tkumat Yisra'el* [Studies on the Establishment of Israel], pp. 5–6.
103. Archives of the City of Rehovot (Hebrew), <http://www.rehovot-archive. org.il/Doc.asp?DynamicContentID=1546> (last accessed 31 May 2019).
104. See the following article to understand the dynamics of this new culture: Even-Zohar, 'The Emergence of a Native Hebrew Culture in Palestine', p. 178.
105. Frumkin, *Derekh Shofet Be'Yerushalayim*, p. 168.
106. The Armenian question was covered extensively in the Hebrew press in Palestine. This could prove an important source of learning more about the massacres in 1908. One massacre in the village of Yeniverdi was covered in *HaTzvi*, for example.
107. Following the abolishment of the exemption tax for non-Muslims not serving in the Ottoman army in 1909, Armenians also began to join the ranks of the army. Importantly, not only out of simply being recruited; rather, this was out of a conscious decision motivated by an ideology of serving the homeland as a prerequisite of receiving equal rights. See Kılıçdağı, 'The Bourgeois Transformation and Ottomanism Among Anatolian Armenians after the 1908 Revolution'.
108. Kılıçdağı, 'The Bourgeois Transformation and Ottomanism Among Anatolian Armenians after the 1908 Revolution', p. 74.
109. Ibid., p. 77. This appeared in the organ *Yeprad*, in an editorial entitled 'Armenian Soldiers', 15 September 1910.
110. Ibid.
111. PRO FO 195/2351, 23 September 1910, p. 228.
112. *HaOr*, 21 September 1910, p. 3; *HaHerut,* 21 September 1910, p. 3. In her record of the official farewell ceremony, Michelle Campos notes that the newspaper not only recognised the Jewish recruits by name, but also those who received a pardon by paying the *bedel* tax, in what she described as a form of humiliation. Campos, *Ottoman Brothers*, p. 156.
113. *HaOr*, 21 September 1910, p. 3.
114. *HaHerut*, 5 May 1914, p. 2.
115. *HaTzvi*, 16 November 1912, p. 3.
116. *HaHerut*, 27 January 1914.
117. *HaTzvi*, 9 December 1912, p. 3.
118. Here is the Hebrew link to the page memorialising Karmi Eisenberg on the official site of Fallen Soldiers of Israel: <http://www.izkor.gov.il/ HalalKorot.aspx?id=505307> (last accessed 31 May 2019).
119. Frumkin, *Derekh Shofet Be'Yerushalayim*, p. 168.

5

Ottomans and Zionists in Istanbul[1]

The settlement of Jews is desirable in a number of aspects. Is it not clear that the settlement of people who admire work are educated and who possess modern labour can strengthen the financial state, and culture of a land lacking people, culture and capital?

Ottoman Parliamentarian, Nissim Mazliah, *HaOlam*, 3 March 1909

The question of how Zionism was perceived in Istanbul, the capital of the Ottoman state, as well as among Ottoman bureaucrats throughout the Empire, including in Palestine itself, is an important key to understanding the divide between the Jewish and Palestinian communities.

What is clear is that at times anti-Zionist rhetoric in Istanbul was tainted with anti-Semitism, and had much more to do with changes affecting intercommunal relations in Istanbul than with local events in Palestine.

For the Jewish Yishuv, and for Jews throughout the Empire, this hampered their efforts to be recognised as a potential benefit to the Ottoman state. For the Palestinians, the fact that the debate over Zionism in Istanbul was removed from the reality of Palestine caused an even graver concern – as Palestine was slowly being lost to Zionist encroachment, the anti-Zionist movement seemed more interested in defining the future of the Jewish communities of the Empire in general, disregarding the real threat in Palestine. In fact, in some instances, the fervour of the anti-Zionist camp in Istanbul even surpassed that of the Palestinians.

Opposition to Zionism in the Ottoman State

During the Young Turk period, Ottoman Turkish perceptions of Zionism were divided into two main groups. The first group, based in the state bureaucracy, often formed their opinions as a result of their contact with the Jewish community in Palestine, meetings with Zionists in Istanbul or through their bureaucratic dealings with the Zionist movement in the forms of petitions or legal questions. Among this group there was a wide range of perceptions, ranging from positive to negative, with some exhibiting a great amount of mistrust towards the Zionist movement, while others took a sympathetic stance. However, what united all of these opinions among the first group is that they were based on practical and concrete reasoning.

The second main group opposed to Zionism was composed of an intellectual elite in Istanbul that based its opposition first and foremost on strong anti-Jewish sentiments that existed in the capital, surfacing after the 1908 Young Turk Revolution. For them, Zionism was part of a foreign conspiracy against the Ottoman state, controlled not only by Jewish factions, but also by the Freemasons, an organisation integrally related to the Young Turks' party, the Committee of Union and Progress. Ironically, the anti-Zionist faction's anti-Semitic stance was detrimental to the Palestinian cause since the Palestinian parliamentarians Said al-Husayni and Ruhi al-Khalidi, who were both part of the ruling CUP party possessing an overall positive stance on Jews, despite being staunchly anti-Zionist, pitted them against the anti-Semitic group of anti-Zionists. In other words, the Palestinians found themselves on the side of the first group of Ottoman state bureaucrats, which included also those who were sympathetic to the Zionist cause.

Just months after the 1908 revolution, a new openness towards Zionism was marked by the opening of a Zionist Office, under the auspices of the Anglo-Levantine Banking Company, making Istanbul 'the first city in the Islamic world to be endowed with a Zionist office'.[2] Leading the office was Dr Victor Jacobson, who made it the main address for official Zionist activity in the capital. Jacobson explained its role four years later in a 1912 speech to the Zionist Central Committee in Berlin:

> [T]he Zionist movement must abide by the principle it had hitherto followed [since establishing itself in Istanbul], namely, to enlighten public opinion and to convince political circles in Turkey that a land with such a sparse population, dependent for centuries mainly upon agriculture, could only develop economically through a powerful immigration, and that the Jews contributed the most suitable material for this purpose. They did not want to wrest a province from the Ottoman Empire; on the contrary, they wished to give it something of value.[3]

In his speech, Jacobson does not highlight his own role; yet he is often in the background and is tied to multiple events covered in the current work, in addition to serving as a resource for an array of independent actors coming from Palestine to Istanbul to test the limits of Zionism in the capital's public sphere. Nevertheless, and despite the government's new openness, it would become apparent very quickly to Jacobson that if Zionism did not transform into an autonomous movement and completely abandon all claims to an independent state in Palestine, then his ability to create real change for Zionism in the Ottoman Empire would remain well out of reach.

One of the first steps that the Zionists took under Jacobson was to launch and support a network of newspapers (happening over the course of a few years) to infiltrate the Ottoman cultural elite and to influence both government policy and the local Jewish population. In order to establish and supervise this network, the Zionist Organization dispatched Vladimir Jabotinsky, a young Russian political Zionist (who later would become the founder of Revisionist Zionism). The Zionist intervention into Istanbul's press was first marked with initial support given to the French daily *Courrier d'Orient*.[4] Shortly after, in the autumn of 1909, there was a falling out, between the newspaper's owner, Ebüzziya Tevfik, and the editor, Celal Nuri, seemingly over the question of the Zionist support, and ties were severed. Nuri, then, with Zionist support, started the pro-CUP newspaper *Le Jeune Turc* (incorporating the name of the revolution), bringing on the influential Turkish nationalist, Ahmad Agayeff, known by his much more famous name, Ahmet Ağaoğlu. While Zionism would never become a major focus of this paper, it supported Jewish immigration to the Empire, and the call for transforming Palestine into a centre for Jewish culture.[5] Even if in the end, it 'was unable to influence official policy towards Zionism',[6] it gained great respect among the Turkish educated elite and was often quoted in Parliament and among foreign dignitaries.[7]

The second objective of the newspapers was to persuade the local Jewish population to adopt Zionism as an ideology,[8] and to counter the anti-Zionist Jewish press, *El Tiempo*. For this, three main papers were established: *L'Aurore*, a French weekly; the Judeo-Spanish weekly *El Judeo*; and later in 1910, the Hebrew weekly *HaMevasser*.[9] During this period, in Istanbul alone there were over 50,000 Jews, and together with the Jewish population in Anatolia, Jews numbered over 116,000,[10] and while the number of active Zionists remained small, the goal was recruitment, with the simultaneous aim of creating a space where Zionism could exist and grow. One group of people the Zionist movement reached out to was the Jewish middle class, who were striving to gain power vis-à-vis their notable community. Further, they cemented ties with the local Jewish 'masses', which strengthened their stance against the prestigious anti-Zionist Alliance Universelle, which was the bastion of the Francophone Jewish society.[11] As a result of their anti-Alliance stance, the Zionists appealed to the supporters of the German Jewish school, the *Hilfsverein der Deutschen Juden*, the B'nai B'rith organisation and traditional Jewish factions.[12]

The Hebrew revolution was not limited to the borders of Palestine, but spread throughout the Ottoman Empire: in Istanbul, Izmir, Beirut, Damascus and Cairo. In Istanbul, the Zionist-supported Hebrew journal *HaMevasser* embodied the spirit of the Hebrew revival, for, according to Aryeh Shmuelevitz, it

> argued eloquently that Zionism was not politically minded and certainly not anti-Turkish . . . [and] considered itself nationalist on the cultural level, fighting staunchly for the Hebrew language; after all, it was published in Hebrew and had to justify itself to its readers. Hence it preached the revival of Hebrew in lieu of Judeo-Spanish.[13]

No less important was its stance on encouraging Jews to incorporate Turkish into their lives, focusing on covering events related to the Jewish community in the Ottoman Empire, the daily agenda of what was happening in the Empire and making connections between the two different worlds.[14] Nevertheless, with such a small portion of Jews in Istanbul speaking Hebrew, *HaMevasser* only had limited success and, in 1912, it was eventually shut down.

At this junction, it is particularly important to take into consideration the overall impact Zionism had on Istanbul's Jewish community. According to Esther Benbassa and Aron Rodrigue, in their work on Sephardic Jewry, Zionism's contribution to the historical development of the Istanbul community was the following:[15]

> Zionism not only introduced a certain national and political consciousness. Above all, it appeared to be a cure for the lethargy of a once flourishing community, now taken over by foreign Jewish philanthropic societies engaged in a relentless struggle to secure local predominance, and associated with imported identities. Zionism also came from abroad, but it was able to summon this community to assume its responsibilities and take itself in hand. The struggle between the Zionists and their opponents set up a real dynamic which, albeit conflictual, promoted the propagation of Zionism. This in some ways furthered the process of Westernization of those Jews who were in transition without cutting them off completely from their traditions. It led them to discover one of the extensions of Westernization that was also a Jewish identity.

The Zionist newspaper network created great suspicion among the Ottoman government and among some of Istanbul's politicians as well. A secret document sent to the Ministry of Interior from the Internal Security Offices dated November 1909 outlined the danger the Zionists presented in Istanbul and recommended that more attention be directed towards the Jewish community. Specifically they pointed to Nahum Sokolov's travels in Asia Minor, claiming his work was politically motivated and that he was trying to import Zionist ideology, especially targeting the local Jewish communities by setting up Zionist centres throughout the Empire.[16] The Ottoman official who wrote the document was certainly correct to take notice of Sokolov as he had only recently resigned from his post as the secretary general of the Zionist Organization. In this report, the head of general security, however, went further and set out to explain the political aims: 'Nahum Sokolov and two bureaucrats are coming to Istanbul in order to establish a center for the local [Jewish] community . . .' and the Zionists aimed to attract and persuade the local Jews with Zionist thought, and among their aims is to settle Jews in Palestine in order to 'work to achieve independence in their ancient homeland'.[17] This perhaps was not obvious since 'the political aims' undertaken by Mr Sokolov were 'purposely made obscure [as a result] of the way the language is used'. The document goes on to outline how they are collecting money from among the Jews of the Ottoman lands by passing out 'donation boxes', a practice common in Jewish communities throughout the world, where individual Jews donated 'a shekel' to the Jewish Yishuv, which was one of the dynamic attempts to incorporate support and loyalty among Jews worldwide.[18]

The last major point made by the head of internal security was that Zionists had set up a vibrant press which was based in different Ottoman cities such as Istanbul, Salonica and Izmir, and that 'Zionism had already began to occupy an important place in the realm of the press'.[19] Among the newspapers sympathetic to the Zionist cause was the German *Osmanischer Lloyd*, the French *La Turquie*,[20] and he mentioned that Istanbul's French newspapers *Courier D'Orient* and *L'Aurore*, and the Judeo-Spanish newspaper *El Judeo*, were directly funded by the Zionists.[21] This document is notable since it is one of the only cases where Zionism is discussed in such a frank and open manner. In fact, following the issuance of this investigation of Nahum Sokolov and his political activity within Ottoman borders, the issue of political Zionism in the Ottoman Empire (excluding Palestine) would be left to investigations and related to specific cases.

This investigation seemed to have sparked the Chief Rabbi, Haim Nahum, a staunch opponent of the Zionist movement, to call on the Jewish MPs to meet in order to discuss the damage that the Zionists were doing to their community, including its press. However, Nahum realised that the battle against Zionism was a lost one, and remarked that the newspaper network indeed had succeeded to persuade the community, and that Zionism was 'spreading like lightning', and that this was a result of propaganda 'being carried out in clubs and newspapers and with the greatest possible vigour'. According to him, it was only the editor of *El Tiempo*, David Fresco, who openly rejected Zionism and that this had turned against him, commenting that Fresco 'is attacked on all sides, here [in Istanbul] and in the provinces, insulted, publicly abused and his paper is even boycotted'.[22]

The Debate in Tasvir-i Efkar and the Debate of 1909

The settlement of Jews in the Ottoman Empire was the subject of an ongoing 1909 debate in Istanbul and was supported by influential Jews such as Moiz Kohen and Nissim Russo, both staunch supporters of the Committee of Union and Progress. These Ottoman loyalists, similar to the Jewish population in Palestine, believed that there was no contradiction between Ottomanism and Zionism. However, in stark contrast to the Jewish Yishuv, they believed that Zionism was not bound by borders, and that any mass migration of Jews to the Ottoman lands was within the realm of Zionism. In a letter to the editor of Salonica's influential Judeo-Spanish newspaper *La Epoca*, Kohen explained his type of Zionism, which was even held suspect by mainstream Zionists. Zionism, he wrote, was a movement 'of Jewish immigration into Turkey and preferably into Palestine, which holds a certain historical attraction for the Jews'. He continues:

> I worked out a special formula to serve as a basis for Ottoman Jews. According to this formula, approved by certain Zionist leaders, Zionism would be a movement of Jewish immigration into Turkey with a cultural centre in Palestine. We were always energetically opposed to the Basle Programme, but they assured us at the Hamburg Congress that this Programme would be modified and would no longer be understood as 'creating in Palestine a Jewish homeland guaranteed by public law'.[23]

However, in reaction to the congress refusing to modify the Basle Programme,[24] declaring it 'sacred and unimpeachable', Kohen broke all ties with the Zionist Organization, which led to accusations against him. According to Kohen:

> Consequently, according to the Zionists, I have never been a Zionist; [but] I have been, am and shall always be a Zionist, which means a partisan of a large Jewish immigration into Turkey; in my article . . . published in *Tasvir-i Efkar*, in *Zaman*, and in *Yeni Asir*, etc. I have always favoured, with great insistence, this immigration – from an Ottoman as well as from a Jewish point of view – since I am convinced that it may contribute very much to the progress

of the country and guarantee the security of thousands of our unfortunate co-religionists. I shall always continue publishing articles in the Turkish and Jewish press in favour of this immigration . . .[25]

Certainly, Moiz Kohen was not alone in his assessment that Zionism could be fulfilled within the framework of the Ottoman Empire. Significantly, there was a small number of Jews who were an integral part of the Ottoman political elite who did not see an autonomous Jewish homeland within the borders of the Ottoman state as contradictory. While the mass immigration of Jews to Palestine was against government policy, this was not the case for Jewish immigration to other regions such as Anatolia. In fact, Jewish immigration was often looked on positively by some of the high members of the CUP. An example of this was when Speaker of the Parliament Ahmet Rıza, one of the CUP founders, reported to Chief Rabbi Haim Nahum that as long as the Jews entered the country with capital, their presence could lead to the development of industry and agriculture.[26] Another high-ranking CUP member, Rıza Tevfik, also expressed his support of Zionism during a lecture on the Jewish question he held in Istanbul in the spring of 1908, where he was speaking at a meeting of the Society for Young Jews. In an answer to the question whether a good Ottoman could be a Zionist, the influential lawmaker replied:

> Certainly, I myself am a Zionist. Zionism is fundamentally nothing more than the expression of the solidarity which characterises the Jewish people. What is the aim of Zionism? A humanitarian one: co-religionists, where they can live as free men in the enjoyment of their rights. The methods of Zionism are exclusively peaceful. Palestine is your land more than it is ours; we only became rulers of the country many centuries later than you. A service would be rendered to our common fatherland by the undertaking of the colonisation of the uncultivated land, Palestine.[27]

Tevfik was no stranger to the Jewish community: as a child in Edirne he was educated at the place of his father's employment, the Alliance Israelite Universelle, where he also learned Ladino. This statement when placed in the context of his closeness to the Jewish community gains special importance as it is highly likely that he was expressing a stance that some Jews within the Empire were not only aware of, but also supported. True, over time Tevfik would tone down his support for the movement,[28] but it should be clear that from the start he did not support a Jewish independent state but was much closer to those Ottoman Jewish counterparts who understood Zionism as an integrationist movement, looking positively towards other initiatives supporting the migration of Jews to the Ottoman Empire at large.

The policy of allowing Jewish immigration throughout the Empire (save for Palestine) was in no way an innovation. The ousted Sultan Abdülhamid II (1876–1909) had allowed Jewish communities to sprout up throughout Anatolia during his reign. These communities were part of a greater plan of the Jewish Colonization Association (ICA) which had taken up Abdülhamid's offer to settle Jews in the heart of the Ottoman lands in areas which are today part of modern Turkey. For example, during the early part of the twentieth century, the ICA established no less than seven Jewish farming communities,[29] near the cities of Eskişehir (Mamure), Istanbul (Mesila Hadasha), Silivri (Fethiköy), Akhisar (Or Yehuda) and Balıkesir (Tekfur Çiftliği).[30] Among these settlements, Mamure seems to have been settled by immigrant Jews who were leaving areas in Romania once under Ottoman control, making them internal migrants. One 1904 article in *The Times* estimated that this Jewish farming settlement, together with another nearby settlement, was made up of once Ghetto-residing Jews, with about 100 families, who were supported by ICA.[31]

Or Yehuda, the most successful of these settlements, comprised 2,600 hectares and was situated on the railway line, 107 kilometres west of the port city of Izmir,[32] which on the train took about five hours.[33] This settlement, founded in 1899,[34] came to serve two purposes: first, to establish a self-sufficient farming community made of Russian Jewish immigrants, and, second, to house an agricultural school where farmers from ICA's other Near Eastern settlements could come and be trained in farming.[35] In 1912, there were forty-five 'poor Jewish students', who learned about agriculture and worked in its fruit orchards and tobacco and cotton fields, originating from Romania, Russia, Galicia, Palestine and Turkey. However, according to a 1912 report, the school was working at a financial loss, and there was already a Jewish farming community close by which was made up of sixty people.[36]

The Jewish Territorial Organization (JTO), established in 1905, and led by the influential Jewish writer Israel Zangwill, embarked on a comprehensive plan together with the ICA, for the settlement of millions of Jews in the Ottoman province of Mesopotamia, the region of present-day Iraq. In June 1909, just days before the Zionist congress was to be held in New York City, the *New York Times* covered the growing divide between the JTO and the Zionist movement. According to the *Times*, the proposal included securing a deal with the Ottomans to open the gates to Jewish migration to Mesopotamia, which they would irrigate and colonise in exchange for a sum of $40,000,000, eventually leading to a Jewish state.[37] However, just days later it was reported that the plan was repudiated at the congress, with the president of the Zionist Federation of America,

Dr Harry Friedenwald, stressing that the focus of the Zionists should remain solely on Palestine. However, while opposition to the plan was stated at the meeting, Friedenwald took a conciliatory stance, stating, 'we shall look with favor on the settlement of Jews in Mesopotamia or elsewhere in the Turkish Empire, but our own course of action is definite and unalterable.'[38]

It was this very plan that Moiz Kohen had adopted and lobbied for, engaging in a public debate in the newspaper *Tasvir-i Efkar* between him and its editor, Ebüziyya Tevfik, who had also been an opposition MP since 1908 as well as an experienced politician from the days of the former sultan, Abdülhamid II. In fact, Tevfik was already known by the Jewish community and was characterised as anti-Semitic ever since the publication of his inflammatory late nineteenth-century pamphlet entitled *Millet-i Israiliyye* (The Israeli [Jewish] People), where he declared Jews were one of most 'vile' and 'inferior' of peoples.[39] Moreover, Tevfik was one of the first Ottomans to put forth the claims of a Jewish–Freemason alliance which endangered the Ottoman state.[40] What needs to be stressed, however, is that his opposition cannot be simply disregarded as an individual's personal views, as he was one of the most prolific figures of the Young Ottoman period, working closely with the legendary Namık Kemal (the father of previously discussed Jerusalem governor, Ali Ekrem Bey), and succeeding to retaining his status during the Young Turk period until his death in 1913.[41]

In an article for *Tasvir-i Efkar*, Moiz Kohen laid out why he supported the mass immigration of Jews to Iraq.[42] In an attempt to educate the Muslim readership, Kohen argues that Jewish immigration did not pose a threat to the Empire, explaining the differences between the main European Jewish movements that supported Jewish migration from Russia. Interestingly, he points to three types of Jewish organisations: one supporting the settlement of Jews in Argentina, another, the 'Zionism which we are familiar with', supporting Jewish immigration to Palestine, then the organisation led by Israel Zangwill, the JTO, which promoted the settlement of Jewish refugees in Mesopotamia, and was the one he supported himself. According to Kohen, the benefits of this Jewish immigration were obvious and not worth enumerating; but it would be necessary to discuss the dangers they [the Jewish migrants] might pose to the state.

Kohen starts by addressing the greatest fear of Ebüziyya Tevfik: that the Ottoman state was essentially importing another ethnic problem such as 'Bulgarian independence, the Bosnian-Herzegovina Uprising [and] the events in Crete'. Clearly, Tevfik, as an intellectual whose notoriety was based in the Young Ottoman period and who had seen during his career the Ottoman state slowly lose its base in the Balkans, was correct in questioning what would happen if this large concentrated strip of Jewish migrants might turn on the state. However, Kohen was quick to refute this possibility, calling the Jews 'patriots of the state' asking if it could really be believed the Jews being transferred could ever challenge the Ottoman army.

Ebüziyya Tevfik was disappointed with Kohen's assurances and challenged him, stating that he too 'was confident that the Children of Israel [if they would challenge the state] would remain trembling and wretched in the face of an Ottoman attack'.[43] Nevertheless, Ebüziyya Tevfik said, an uprising would certainly take a toll on the Ottoman forces and it was unknown how far the state would need to go to suppress it. According to Tevfik, the other main problem of importing such a huge number of Jews was the imminent economic danger it posed to the state. This consideration on Tevfik's part demonstrates to what extent anti-Semitism was present in the capital, including a fear of Jewish economic hegemony. Moiz Kohen was quick to refute such claims and explained that the Jews of the Iraqi Strip would be limited to agriculture. Unsatisfied by this, Tevfik went further: 'Perhaps the greatest danger from among what we have discussed is material; [meaning] the outcomes and details of such an economic struggle which will spread like a great deluge . . .' He then went on to expand on such suspicions in detail:

> We are confident those Jews which will be transferred [to Iraq] will not work in agriculture but rather be those who watch their accounts carefully even as they appear to be simple and pure individuals, and they will bring disasters and calamity – such as the Plague of Locusts – [which] will spread over all the Ottoman lands . . . Perhaps now the Jews which wish to be transferred are not in the thousands, but in the hundreds of thousands, and even millions are being discussed. Now, if there are not thousands of Jewish farmers, what will hundreds of thousands of Jews be preoccupied with?[44]

What emerged from this debate was that the opposition to Jewish immigration derived greatly from a fear of Jews taking over the economy; a fear embedded in anti-Semitism, as Tevfik's words demonstrate. However, this polemic between two well-known journalists was still in its early stages, and two years later, in 1911, the debate on Ottoman Iraq would resurface. With so much attention being paid in Istanbul to such settlement, the anti-Jewish immigration camp would continue, to a great extent, to be oblivious to the steady immigration of Jews to Palestine.

Here it is necessary to tackle how the Zionist question turned into a debated topic in Istanbul. Also, it must be explained how a newly established anti-Semitism, which emerged in Istanbul, threatened Jewish mass immigration to the Empire. Following the Young Turk Revolution, conspiracy theories placing Jews, Dönme and Freemasons behind the revolution ran rampant throughout the Ottoman Empire.[45] These theories developed as a result of the prominent places Jews held within the CUP, even though their numbers in high places were insignificant. However, despite their small numbers, they rose in the ranks due to their ability to look beyond their communal interests, and to adopt issues that were of import to the overall Muslim majority. This fact is well documented in a short article by M. Şükrü Hanioğlu, who, examining a survey of the CUP's French supplement of their central organ *Meşveret*, concludes that the Jewish writer, Albert Fua, in comparison to his Armenian, Greek and Arab counterparts,[46] was much more interested in the general problems facing the Ottoman state. At the same time, he paid little attention to his own Jewish community, whereas the other minority representatives focused mostly on their own communities' problems.[47] Moreover, Albert Fua was praised by the majority of CUP members at the First Young Turk Congress, which was held in February 1902. Here, Fua, along with one other minority member, separated himself from the other seventeen non-Muslim members and voted with the forty-seven Muslim contingent against encouraging foreign intervention in order to restore the constitutional regime.[48]

By 1911, the conspiracy theories linking the Jews with the 1909 overthrow of Sultan Abdülhamid II began to shake the very foundations of the CUP government. Although this has been previously pointed out by scholars, I believe that it was much more widespread than earlier assessments have described it. One only need examine London's *The Times* to understand the breadth of this phenomenon. Elie Kedourie first documented these conspiracy theories in his article entitled 'Young Turks, Freemasons, and Jews', in which he based a great part of his research on a private and confidential letter written by Istanbul's British Ambassador Gerard Lowther, which was dispatched to his superior, Sir C. Hardinge in London, dated 29 May 1910.[49] According to Lowther, who relied heavily on information from his chief dragoman G. H. Fitzmaurice, Jewish Freemasons had infiltrated the Young Turks. At the head of this group was the Jewish deputy from Salonica, Emanuel Carasso.[50] Furthermore, Salonica's large Dönme population worked hand in hand with the Jews. According to Lowther, together these two groups made up the Salonica contingent that secretly took over the Young Turk movement, with many of its members oblivious of their dominant status. In addition to the internal threat of Freemasons, there was also an external one, as Carasso was collaborating with Jewish Freemasons in Italy, and because of the appointment of a Jewish ambassador by the United States (Oscar Strauss) and Italian consul-general (Primo Levi) in Salonica. Most significantly, Lowther accused Oscar Strauss of promoting the Jewish immigration scheme to Mesopotamia, which he understood to be an extension of Zionism. In fact, according to Lowther, the revolution itself was the work of Jews:

> Shortly after the revolution in July 1908, when the Committee established itself in Constantinople, it soon became known that many of its leading members were Freemasons. Carasso began to play a big role, including his successful capture of the Balkan Committee, and it was noted that Jews of all colours, native and foreign, were enthusiastic supporters of the new dispensation, till, as a Turk expressed it, every Hebrew seemed to become a potential spy of the occult Committee, and people began to remark that the movement was rather a Jewish than a Turkish revolution.[51]

Despite the presence of such conspiracy theories, Jacob Landau points out in his work that 'most, very probably all, allegations of freemasonic-Jewish or freemasonic-Zionist collaboration have been presented without any solid proof whatsoever'. Further, he argues that this was used more as a tactic to smear all the accused groups.[52] Still, the conspiracy theories continued to simmer and once again resurfaced in 1911, just a little over a month after the Haram al-Sharif incident and the much more extensive debate taking place in the Ottoman Parliament on Zionism. In March 1911, the opposition accused Minister of Finance Cavid Bey, a Dönme, of showing undue preference to Jewish capitalists and their agents, some of whom were suspected of favouring Zionism, which eventually hit the parliament floor. In a parliamentary session, Talat Bey set out to defend Cavid Bey, stating, 'proposals had been made to Cavid by the Jewish General Colonization Society, but were not accepted.' Talat also admitted despite Zionist activity, there had been no policy shift and that Jewish immigration to Palestine remained forbidden.[53]

The Ottomans' suspicion of Jewish resettlement in their lands in general, and Iraq in particular, was addressed by *The Times'* Istanbul correspondent, who reported that while gentiles might be sympathetic to the resettling of Jews 'to lands intimately connected by history and tradition with the fortunes of their race', most Turks and Arabs were suspicious of such schemes.[54] He goes on to explain that the

> Jews are among the most quick-witted and versatile of races, while a large proportion of the present inhabitants of Mesopotamia and the neighbouring countries, many of whom are still in the nomadic tribal stage, are so low in the economic or educational scale as to be quite unfit in their present condition to cope with the newcomers.

He goes on to mention that the Ottomans would also fear importing the new types of nationalism, socialism and crime that the Jews would bring with them.[55] For example, commenting on this (in an answer directed to Jewish parliamentarian Carasso Efendi) a Muslim deputy from Amasya stated that 'if you come in crowds, there'll be no room for us'.

With pressure growing on the CUP, influential Jews such as Moiz Kohen, and MP Carasso Efendi, began to distance themselves from the Zionist movement. For example, in an interview in the newspaper *Le Jeune Turc*, Carasso stressed his growing dismay with the Zionist movement, showing remorse for the Zionists not toning down their demands, and 'portraying [Zionism] in a way that causes suspicion'. For him, reaching this conclusion was a disappointment, since he had originally been under the impression that 'the movement had no other aim other than to find a shelter for persecuted Jews from other countries' and that Turkey had seemed like the perfect government to take them in.[56] The Zionist Organization's leader, Max Nordau, also explained that, despite the favourable statements directed towards Turkey, there was a growing hostility to the Zionist movement, which he attributed to rumours being spread by the anti-Zionist Jewish camp.[57]

As for Moiz Kohen, in his personal journal he addressed his growing dismay with opponents of Zionism and how the tension had reached unbearable levels by the spring of 1911. Kohen commented that 'the question of Zionism continues to worry me, one can clearly see that anti-Semitism has already started to take root in Turkey as a result of this stupid movement'.[58] In addition to Kohen's concerns with how Zionism was leading to the rise of anti-Jewish sentiments, he was also a devoted Freemason, and was preoccupied with the idea that other Freemasons would question his loyalty to them since he was constantly working for Jews, and had even joined the local B'nai B'rith organisation, making his fellow masons suspicious.[59] This led him to the conclusion that he was

> inclined to retire from the activities ministered until now for the exclusive interests of the Israelites, [for] as a real Mason I need to work for the good of humanity in general and not only for the Masonic lodges. We can also work for the good of the *patrie*, meaning for the good of all my citizens.[60]

And on his participation in B'nai B'rith he explained: 'this may serve to create a bad reputation for me in the eyes of the Turks who may consider me a Jewish nationalist while I am (actually) a fierce enemy of Jewish nationalism.'[61] This drive to work with all citizens led Kohen to meet with other non-Muslims, such as an Armenian priest, and ponder on the idea of writing a book on the difficulties faced by the different nationalities in the

Ottoman state. He was also involved in setting up a committee aimed at publishing works in Turkish for the national library.[62]

Kohen's April journal entries serve as a general metaphor for the situation the Jews were facing in Istanbul. Similar to the other non-Muslim groups that welcomed the CUP, new forces arose during the post-Young Turk Revolution period that highlighted the predicament of having to choose between communal loyalties and the state. Kohen's disillusionment with the Turkish Muslim population is key to understanding that Ottoman Jews, no matter how much they supported the state, still possessed divided loyalties, or at least appeared to be conflicted in the eyes of the majority. While Kohen stressed that he would continue his 'efforts dedicated to the good of the *patrie* and to the Ottoman nation',[63] he also declared that he was 'unjustly suspected by the Turks and Jews'.[64] And, concerning the Turkish Muslim population, he mentions with great disappointment that his 'opinion about the spirit of tolerance of the Turks has started to be shaken' as a result of the publications of the *Roumeli*, an influential Istanbul newspaper that was attacking Zionism.[65] In the following quote, he leaves unnamed the cited group that 'despises Jews'; however, it is possible from the context to speculate that he is speaking about the Turks in general:

> I observe that the '. . .' (a space purposely left blank) despise the Jews. It is hidden disregards which can suddenly burst. I persist in my idea that it is not a cause from which we [Jews] should distance ourselves; on the contrary this should push us to get closer and closer, because scorn and misunderstanding often come from the lack of knowing one another.[66]

While it is not possible to track the rise of anti-Semitism in Ottoman Istanbul, so far we can see that the dynamics behind anti-Zionism in Istanbul were radically different than in Palestine. And, in a twenty-four-page pamphlet in Turkish entitled *Siyonizm Tehlikeleri* (The Dangers of Zionism), which came to light in Istanbul in 1913, we see that once again that those Ottoman Muslims outspoken about 'the dangers of Zionism' were in essence anti-Semitic.[67] In fact, the pamphlet is basically a repetition of what we have seen above, reinforcing the claims that the driving force behind the CUP party were 'the Jews, the Zionists, and the Freemasons'.[68]

The Zionist Debate in the Ottoman Parliament

With Zionism increasingly becoming a subject of debate in the Sublime Porte, it is necessary to return to the previously discussed debate in the Ottoman Parliament, to highlight the growing rift between the anti-Zionist debate in Istanbul with the one in Palestine. In fact, this debate provides one of the most vivid examples of how Zionism was perceived in such radically different ways among different Ottoman parliamentarians, foreshadowing the tensions between the different ethnic and religious groups of the Empire in the years leading to its break-up. This is relevant to our topic since the ethnic tensions that plagued the parliamentary debate made discussing the issue of Zionism all the more difficult and led some of the non-Muslim members to question if Muslims criticising Zionism were not actually driven by a Turkish Muslim chauvinism. Furthermore, this debate illustrates that a great number of Ottoman parliamentarians did not have a clear grasp of the meaning of Zionism; thus, it is easy to speculate that if these people who were so connected to the political circles of Istanbul were not aware of Zionism, then certainly the greater population must have taken little interest in the movement.

Interestingly, this debate was initiated by the opposition in Parliament, the Decentralization Party, and as in the Lynch concession, which was discussed in Chapter 2, the opposition was able to capture the support of those Arabs belonging to the ruling CUP party.[69] Hasan Kayali argues that this debate was organised by the opposition in order to address the growing rift between the Arabs of the Empire and their hegemonic Turkish counterparts in Istanbul, a rift which had already begun to play out in the Arab press. This debate came after previous parliamentary discussions which underscored the Arabs' frustration surrounding their inferior status in the Empire, and brief accusations that the CUP was working with the Zionists.[70] In fact, my findings show that most MPs were unaware of Zionism and Jewish settlement, and to some extent uninterested. Kayali reaches a parallel conclusion in his statement that 'speeches of the Arab deputies did not create the desired alarm'.[71] I would add that, from what can be construed from the following, the opposition made a mistake in bringing this debate to the floor since neither the Palestinians, nor the opposition itself, benefited from the drawn-out deliberations.

Returning to the parliamentary debate, we see that while it did not convince the parliamentarians of an imminent Zionist threat, it succeeded in bringing to the surface the discontent that CUP members had with their state, and the real problems that would challenge the future of the Ottoman Empire. Foremost, the debate strengthens the argument that the Palestinians were acutely aware of Zionist history and the threat it posed. This truth arises within the words of their representative Ruhi al-Khalidi, who commented on the internal Jewish debate over whether the Jewish people were simply a religious group or a national one. Khalidi pointed out that in contrast to such Jews as Moshe Mendelssohn, the spiritual father of Reform Judaism, Theodor Herzl claimed that 'Judaism is a nation, a social group', and Khalidi claimed that 'for this reason the Jews need to create a nation and a state. But where will this state be formed? Perhaps in America, or perhaps in Africa; [no,] they finally decided that it would be in Jerusalem'. [72]

Khalidi emphatically stressed that he was not an anti-Semite but rather an anti-Zionist, and that many Ottoman Jews, mainly of Sephardic origin, were also against Zionism. To stress this point, he read two telegrams sent to him directly from Jewish groups within the Empire who stated their adamant objection to Zionism. However, it seems that some doubt was thrown on his words by one simple question posed by Jerusalem's other representative, Said al-Husayni, who asked whether any of those telegrams originated from their Jerusalem constituency; and the answer that neither did must have led unconvinced MPs to believe that Khalidi was dodging the question of what the Jews of Palestine actually supported. Certainly, if the Jewish community in Palestine as a whole had held strong reservations, then Khalidi's point would have been much more vigorous; however, as was demonstrated in the previous chapter, the Jews were united in Palestine around one pillar of Zionism in particular: that there was a genuine need to strengthen the Jewish hold over Palestine.

Khalidi claimed it was just a matter of time before the Jews became the majority in Jerusalem, commenting that they had already opened a bank with one billion marks[73] which served 70–80,000 customers in Palestine, perhaps even 90,000. This was especially serious in light of the fact that the number of Muslims also had diminished to only 8,000 or 9,000. In response to this, the representative from Diyarbakir expressed his scepticism by asking why, if there were so many Jews, were there no Jewish representatives from Jerusalem. Khalidi responded that this situation was possible in light of the fact that they would be able to send two or three representatives to Istanbul if they became Ottoman citizens.

Important for this work, Khalidi's assessment of the Jewish Yishuv stands as a stark revelation of a situation that has erroneously been attributed to the Jewish community during the British Mandate: the fact that they were completely autonomous, having minimal relations with the ruling state. The purpose of his words was to illuminate the fact that this situation was detrimental to the Ottoman state. According to Khalidi:

In addition to Jerusalem there are also colonies (*müstemlekat*). In the Land of Palestine, whether in [the district of] Jerusalem or in [in the district of] Akka, there are as many as twenty to twenty-five colonies (*müstamere*). It is quite strange that within these colonies there is no one from the government. They manage themselves; they have courts, they have an apparatus for settling their own affairs. There are absolutely no government representatives among them: no gendarme, no police, no administrative officials. And some of these are even towns of significant size. No one from the government can be found, they get by on their own!

These words prompted a question from one of the MPs about whether or not the Jews in Palestine were paying their taxes. Khalidi answered in the affirmative. This point cannot be underestimated, since the Jewish community was in fact paying a higher proportion of taxes than the Palestinians, relative to their population. This meant the government was to a certain extent dependent on the Yishuv for maintaining its finances, which must have empowered the Jewish community vis-à-vis the Palestinians. This phenomenon would continue during the British Mandate and has already been noted by other scholars as a factor in determining the Yishuv's disproportionate influence on British policy. But as we can see, it was already a factor during the late Ottoman period. Furthermore, for Ottoman officials, the fact that Jews were paying their taxes was a clear sign that they were loyal to the state and that they in return were entitled to protection.

Said al-Husayni, as Jerusalem's other representative, then took the stand and continued Khalidi's argument. He too reflected on the dire situation in Palestine, estimating that the Jewish community was multiplying at such a rate that in the district of Jerusalem it had reached 100,000 and possessed in excess of 100,000 dunams of land.[74] Husayni concluded by stating that 'Palestine cannot support more Jews than this, and in consequence, the Jews who want to immigrate should go to other regions of the Ottoman state's lands', emphasising that if all the Jews were to adopt Ottoman citizenship things might be different.

Husayni's views regarding Jewish immigration deserve special attention because of the sharp contrast they present to those expressed by more polarising figures such as Ebüziyya Tevfik. As we have already seen, Tevfik vehemently objected to all Jewish immigration, believing that they would bring with them corruption and mayhem. Said al-Husayni, on the other hand, expressed a generally positive view of the Jewish community in Palestine, even though he favoured a moratorium on further immigration there:

> The Jews are a hard-working, intelligent and economical nation. Above all, they are most progressive in agriculture, and in crafts. It is undeniable that in the Jerusalem district . . . both they and the local population have benefited from the scientific, agricultural and industrial offices, which they have created and established. For this reason, the Jews wanting to immigrate from other countries to the Ottoman land should be allowed to do so, but on condition that they accept Ottoman citizenship, and go to other districts (*vilayet*) outside

of Palestine, as I said before, the ones in Palestine have reached a sufficient number. [In fact] there is no danger to accept and register various [Jewish] immigrants according to the limit the district is able to receive. On the contrary, I call on the attention of the minister of interior to take notice of the above-mentioned positive effects [of Jewish migration].[75]

The fact that both Khalidi and Husayni presented a generally positive outlook of Jews needs to be explained here. In his summary of this debate, Neville Mandel questioned the sincerity of these statements. But in my opinion, these two MPs were genuinely concerned that they not be classified as anti-Semitic, both because Jews made up a large part of their constituency and because anti-Semitism was an ideology that clashed with their own cosmopolitan worldview. Both men were quite familiar with the Jewish community in Palestine; both of them periodically attended the Alliance Israélite Universelle; and both had a basic knowledge of Hebrew.[76] Furthermore, Khalidi was a Freemason, and as such, undoubtedly stood in contrast to outspoken, extreme anti-Zionists in Istanbul such as Ebüziyya Tevfik, who (as discussed in detail above) linked Freemasonry with Zionism as a threat to the stability of the Ottoman state. In this sense, we can conclude that the inflammatory anti-Semitic language inside and outside of Parliament actually hindered the Jerusalem MPs' attempts to halt Jewish migration to Palestine.

It is important to remember that the Jews in Parliament during this debate, along with the two Palestinian MPs, were members of the same party, the CUP. As a result, the two representatives from Jerusalem certainly realised how sensitive the subject of Jewish immigration could be, not only because of the presence of Jewish parliamentarians, but also because numerous ethnicities and religious groups were represented in their parliamentary grouping. However, despite these good intentions, Khalidi had opened a Pandora's box by introducing to the floor the question of Jewish immigration. Upon the response of the Jewish parliamentarian from Izmir, Nissim Mazliah, Parliament rapidly slipped into chaos.

Neville Mandel mentions nothing about the very serious reaction from Mazliah, stating that he did not want to take a stand on the Zionist issue, because he was a Jew. However, according to the Ottoman parliamentary report, the exact opposite occurred: Mazliah challenged Khalidi for even mentioning the Torah (*Tevrat*) during his speech, even though it was not discussed in any derogatory way. First, however, Mazliah stressed that he wished to clarify a few points concerning Zionism and stated that 'if Zionism is indeed harmful to the state (*hükümet*), then without question my loyalty lies with the state'. However, he took offense to Khalidi's references to the Torah (*Tevrat*), stating, what is the sin of the local and foreign Jews living in this region as a result of such things being written in the Torah? If he wishes, let him burn the Torah. Let's have the Torah burnt for the state! I suppose Ruhi Bey is a Muslim, I am also a believer. In order to be a believer, the Torah's *ahkam* (legal provisions) were superseded following the dignified and honourable revealing of the Glorious Quran; this is my belief.

Khalidi was quick to defend himself, explaining that this was only done to 'exemplify the foundation of Zionism'. Angrily, Mazliah answered back that 'you have gone so far in your presentation as to speak of things which no one in the government has ever heard of before . . . by claiming the existence of an Israeli government (*hukümet-i israiliyye*) in Ottoman lands'. With shouts of discontent arising from the floor, Ebüziyya Tevfik stepped in, exclaiming that the formation of a Jewish government 'is the secret goal. Undoubtedly you are also aware of this!' In closing, Mazliah reiterated the need to fully investigate the matter but concluded confidently that 'I am obliged to present to this session that Ottoman Jews are very devoted to the state, and I believe they will be found as patriotic lovers of their nation (*hammiyetli vatanperverler*)'. And, in relation to the foreign Jews, 'we firmly believe that the Jews look upon the Ottoman state with the best intentions (*rahat yüzü görmüşler*)'. Finally, echoing Ruhi al-Khalidi's earlier statement, Mazliah concluded that

the oppression and hostility that the European Jews have experienced . . . humanity cannot bear. I believe that this intelligent nation will live here in comfort and will not betray it. [In fact,] this nation will be better served and no one will be able to find a friend better than the Jews.

What is remarkable about this statement is how similar it is to Moiz Kohen's previously discussed article. This should not be surprising. As we saw in the Introduction, Mazliah supported cultural Zionism, which included the spread of Hebrew among Ottoman Jews throughout the Empire and believed that the Ottomans lands were ideal for the foreign Jews to make their home, as there was almost no anti-Semitism. A strong defendant of Jewish issues, Mazliah was a staunch CUP supporter who was known for his previous work with them as a lawyer. He also prided himself on the fact that he managed to capture the vote of many Muslims, in addition to Izmir's Jewish constituency, which was divided among 25,000 Jews.[77] Back in 1909, he explained this to the Zionist newspaper *HaOlam*:

The settlement of Jews is desirable in a number of aspects. Is it not clear that the settlement of people who admire work, are educated and who possess modern labour can strengthen the financial state, and culture of a land lacking people, culture and capital. As a Jew, I would like that Jews concentrate more and more in this Land, where there is almost no anti-Semitism. The concentration of Jews will stimulate our development in all places (throughout the Empire); I am not saying that the Jews should solely concentrate their presence in *Eretz Israel*; there are many landscapes in the Asian part of Turkey (especially in Asia Minor) where Jews could successfully establish Jewish farming communities.[78]

Following Nissim Mazliah, the floor was turned over to an Armenian MP, Vartkes Efendi, who expressed that fear of Zionism was nothing short of Muslim chauvinism. In my opinion, this is one of the more fascinating explanations of how a non-Muslim Ottoman perceived Jewish immigration to Palestine and its possible implications for the status of non-Muslims in the Empire. By first tackling the Jewish question, this Armenian parliamentarian provides a chilling prophecy of what the Armenian people might endure in the Ottoman state:

Gentleman, why is Russia driving the Jews out? Perhaps over there they [the Jews] want to establish a kingdom (*padişahlık*) as well? Why in Austria, Germany and England are they rising against the Jews? Perhaps over there, also is another Land of Palestine? Over which they [perhaps] want to establish a kingdom? The Ottoman state has never attacked the Jews [so] why should they begin now? (Calls of: 'This is wrong!') Please, this is not wrong! When we say [such] things [about Jews] here, if the primitive people outside see a Jew next to them, they will say this is a traitor! How is this so? They said this first about the Armenians! I am saying the people shouldn't take a lesson from these words and find an excuse to act against them [the Jews]. Once upon a time when people complained to the government about the activities of the Armenian nationalists (Ermeni Komitecileri) the Armenians would say in response 'what can we do? This nationalist idea (*komitelerin fikri*) has been spread as propaganda throughout the Armenian population, we cannot stop it, it circulates by itself'. Now, aren't we faced with exactly the same situation? (Calls of: 'this is different!') It is the same! Gentlemen, I am speaking as an Armenian. I am afraid that what has happened to me will happen to the Jews. (Calls of: 'That is the problem!') And I say this from an Ottoman perspective; not an Armenian one, or a Jewish one. [Simply] the Jews are in the Land of Palestine, and the Armenians, in the mountains of Anatolia. They are so far apart from one another that I have no reason to do them any special favours.[79]

In response to Khalidi, Vartkes continued saying that he did not attribute such bad characteristics to the Jerusalem representatives. Finishing his point, however, he revealed his fear that the violence against Jews could even spill over and reach the Armenians: 'if tomorrow in the Land of Palestine, or anywhere else, a riot should occur, they will behead more

Armenians than anyone else!' This inflamed one of the Muslim MPs, who blurted out 'wrong, wrong! The Turks are not that savage!' To which Vartkes replied, 'I saw the person who beheaded my father. You did not see this! Please, I know whether it was a savage act or not.' In response, the Muslim yelled that that event was during the period of Abdülhamid, at which point Vartkes quickly returned to the main topic, Zionism. Finally, before moving on to the question of the current violence directed at the Armenians, Vartkes reiterated that he wanted the government to assess the situation in Palestine, in order to understand the whole picture. Following this, Vartkes continued his talk, focusing completely on Armenian matters.

The parliamentary debate continued and, following a discussion of the Armenians, new tensions were aired concerning discrimination against the Greek population in the public sector.[80] Only after this debate, and other related ones, did the issue of Zionism once again reach the floor, which in turn lead to a bigger issue for the Ottomans: the growing Arab question. Leading the discussion was the parliamentarian representing the district of Syria (*Sham*), Shukri al-Asali. The role of Asali was especially important since northern Palestine was under his jurisdiction, and, unlike the Jerusalem parliamentarians, he was not Palestinian.

Asali was in some senses the most effective speaker, focusing concretely on how Zionists were able to achieve dominance. The first interesting point he touched on, which has not been addressed in detail so far in this work, is that some Jews actually did adopt Ottoman citizenship, but retained their former citizenship as well – a choice that proved helpful if they ran into legal issues, where they simply used their former passports, and denied the existence of their new ones. Like Khalidi, he also stressed that the Jewish community in Palestine was completely autonomous, not even using Ottoman courts or other services. Asali's points also support the earlier statement of the *mukhtar*s (addressed in Chapter 2). According to Asali, Jews were slowly taking over villages and regions to such an extent that they were administrating them on their own: 'three quarters of the district of Tiberias, half of the district of Safad . . . half of Haifa, above all Jaffa (the district) has totally been filled with Jews, and such is the case with Jerusalem,' he commented, adding that this was possible since 'they have in their homes *martin*s and other such illegal weapons'.[81] Following this, a Greek parliamentarian questioned him on his remarks about Tiberias, pointing out that there were also local [Ottoman] Jews in Tiberias. To this, Asali explained that this was true for the city but not for the villages, which were completely filled with foreigners. Continuing about the proliferation of weapons, he stated the following:

At first when they arrived, they employed local guards, at that time they were not brave; but slowly, they became brave and their bureaucrats (*memurlar*) started to smuggle hundreds of weapons, and passed out *martin*s. I know this very well. Following this, they began to employ their own guards, and it is has reached such a stage that this year . . . they have come from their villages to the village of Yemha, where they raided the village's property (*eşyasını gaspedip gitmişlerdi*).

He went on to explain that they met secretly without letting either Muslims or Christians into their clubs, and there they sang their national anthem, and on holidays, they raised their Zionist flag in place of the Ottoman flag. He further went on to explain the effectiveness of the Zionist postal service. However, his words did not seem to capture the interest of Parliament, so he then started to address what practical steps could be taken to protect Palestine from the Zionists, reporting the previously discussed case of Salah al-Din al-Ayyubi's fortress being sold to Zionists. At that point, he was cut short by Ibrahim Efendi, who steered the debate back to the Jews.[82] What is interesting, and something we saw in the case of the Haram al-Sharif incident, is that by including only the debates where they explicitly mention Zionism, past scholars have overlooked some important information concerning Palestine in the parliamentary report, thus missing the whole picture. What we see in the continuation of this debate is that through the discussion of Zionism, the extent to which the Ottoman state was divided over so many ethnic questions made Zionism irrelevant for many Ottomans, or it was perceived as just another ethnic/religious conflict.

Ibrahim Efendi challenged Asali on a number of points – providing us with a unique perspective on how other Ottomans perceived the Jewish community as a whole, which would have implications for how they perceived the Jewish Yishuv in Palestine. First he was quick to point out that the Jewish question was not at all new in Parliament, having previously been debated fifteen times.[83] He further stated, similarly to what Ebüziyya Tevfik mentioned in his article, that he did not see the Jewish community (in Palestine) as a serious threat since the Ottoman army numbered over 'one million soldiers and [an army] that costs us more than 18 million lira'. He continued, '100,000 Jews (including their wives and children) came to Jerusalem, and they are not going to conquer Iraq and Syria,' debunking the idea that the Jews were interested in founding a state not only in Palestine, but also in Syria and Iraq.

Ibrahim Efendi continued, stating that Jews who were not Ottoman citizens should not be seen as a threat, pointing out that foreigners were found throughout the Empire and that both Beirut's commerce and Salonica's trade were in the hands of foreigners. Moreover, 'foreigners have not revolted, they have worked for years, for centuries [here], they have studied in the commerce schools, they have taught in these schools . . . Let us open our eyes, we too want to advance our country, we also want to be human . . .' Following his recognition that foreign citizens had played a positive role in the development of the Empire, he moved the discussion on to a consideration of the state budget.

As if this talk had not gone far enough, the last group to raise concerns about their future in the Empire were the Arabs, led by Khalid al-Barazi Efendi, from Syria. Perhaps realising what a controversy this might cause, Barazi first demanded that he be allowed to have 'freedom of speech' (*hurriyet-i kelam*), threatening that if anyone cut him short he would simply leave. Thus beginning, Barazi first stated that 'if someone from another race (*anasır*) will be suspicious of the loyalty of the Arab people, I would totally reject (*kemal-i şiddetle red*) and disapprove of this with all my being'.[84] He continued by stressing the importance the Arabs placed on Islam and that in the end 'this state is an Islamic one', and that anyone that questions the law (*hak*) and justice of the sultan (*emir ül-müminin*) is in essence a rebel.[85] Focusing on the inequalities between the Arabs and Turks, he reminded the chamber that this discussion had been previously addressed by Shukri al-Asali, and noted that there were no Arabs among the ministries, and that there were no Arab governors, and that Arabs only made up 1 per cent of the high positions in the bureaucracy. According to Barazi, the Arabs lagged behind the other ethnic groups seriously in terms of their knowledge of Turkish; yet Arabic had special status since it was the holy language of the Quran. He stressed that he did not wish only Arabs to fill the government positions in their regions, but demanded that the Ottoman administration at least learn Arabic, and went so far as to point out that even the British send to their colonies (Egypt, Indian and Sudan) bureaucrats that know the local language – an assertion which one MP disputed. The debate continued, reaching no real conclusion, and shifted to the Ottoman state's problems in Yemen. Following this, the discussion returned to the Haram al-Sharif incident.

This very long parliamentary debate exhibits the problems the Ottoman state was facing just three years before the start of World War I. Most importantly, it shines light on what a chaotic state Parliament fell into once they began discussing Zionism. In this multi-ethnic and -religious atmosphere, we find that there was not one singular perception of Zionism, and that the Palestinian and Syrian representatives were losing an uphill battle, which was hindered by the fact that they were from different parties, with the Palestinians coming from the ruling party, and most the other

Arab MPs coming from the opposition. From this report, it is evident that Zionism, for many MPs, especially the non-Muslims, was seen through their own reality, as a question of the future status of non-Muslims, and to some extent, the non-Turkish, elements of the Empire. In other words, in the parliamentary debate, Zionism and Jewish immigration were treated more as a 'Jewish question', and the Palestinian population was never taken into consideration. In fact, the interconnectedness of the debate on Zionism with the other purging questions of ethnic-national religious groups (Armenian and Greek), and that of the demands of the ethnic Arab constituency, must have sent a strong message to the Jews of the Empire that a heavy price could come with the support of a cultural Zionism, and that is their own presence in the Empire could come under question. It is in this atmosphere that we saw the sudden switch among Ottoman Jewish politicians, such as Carasso and Kohen, who realised this very dangerous trend. Within this context, the parliament debate also serves as a worrying sign of what would occur to the Ottoman non-Muslims, especially the Armenians, during World War I.

*A Zionist Society (*Siyonist Cemiyeti*) in Istanbul*

Just as Jerusalem's governor was praising the Jewish community, Palestinian complaints were growing and boiling over by the spring of 1914, and, as we saw in Chapter 2, the Zionist movement was celebrating a victory in Istanbul as well. For the first time, in March 1914, the Ottoman government had approved the opening of an official Zionist Office, which opened under the Hebrew name *Histadrut Siyonist Otmanit* (Ottoman Zionist Union; in Turkish, Osmanlı Siyonist Cemiyeti), and was situated in the Beyoğlu neighbourhood of Istanbul, just off the main Grand Rue de Pera (today's Istiklal Caddesi).[86] The government approval, which also allowed the organisation to open branches throughout the Empire and not just in Istanbul, was based on its platform, which included the following points:[87]

1. The name of the organisation is: Ottoman Zionist Union (Osmanlı Siyonist Cemiyeti).
2. The aim of the organisation is to: facilitate Jewish migration and their nationalisation within Ottoman lands; to ensure the well-being of Jews in Palestine and those Jews who are immigrating there; to propagate the Hebrew language, teach this history of Hebrew (people), to progress their national life and to establish the essence of being an Ottoman, and to improve the state of their welfare.

3. To reach this goal, the organisation will hold classes and conferences run by its members and has permission to issue newsletters in accordance with the law.
4. It is forbidden for the organisation to deal with political issues in its meetings.
5. The organisation will work with other organisations who have mutual goals and will set up branches throughout the Ottoman lands.

The Hebrew press in Palestine and Europe applauded this move by Istanbul, among them Warsaw's *HaTzfira*, and Jerusalem's *HaHerut* and Jaffa's *Ha-Poel Ha-Tsair*, which stated: the Ottoman government recognises that 'Zionism is a movement that aspires to improve [the] economic, financial and industrial state of the Turkish state'.[88] Quoting one of its members, the newspaper went on,

> In the first days following the declaration of the constitution (of the Young Turk Revolution), the Ottoman government did not look positively at the aspirations and aims of the Zionist movement. Now, after examination and inspection the government has come to a clear conclusion: the Zionist movement has no hidden agenda, and that not only does it not pose any danger to the development and strengthening of the Ottoman state, but rather it strengthens and empowers its . . . Zionists want to strengthen a sense of love for their new homeland in the hearts of the hundreds of immigrants residing in Palestine.[89]

The author adds that

> from among all the foreign elements that are coming to Turkey, the Jew is the most energetic, peaceful, and full of love for it. He is not the cause of the recent political conflicts. The Jew who is coming to settle in *Eretz Israel* has only one aspiration and that is to live out his nationalist aspirations in the home of his forefathers, to develop his language, culture and literature, and to work the land and live in peace under the accommodating Ottoman skies.[90]

What perhaps the Ottoman government did not know was that this office was an official branch of the Zionist Organization. A Zionist activist in Istanbul confirmed this, stating, 'with the opening of this office we are marking the beginning of Zionism in Turkey (of course not taking into account *Eretz Israel*) . . .' And, that 'it will be central in spreading Zionist thought among the local Sephardic community'. He also admits that Zionists 'had vested interests in Istanbul [in the past] but that until now they remained only minor and disorganised and that in place of bringing people together, they actually caused divisions in the community'.[91]

Just months after the opening of the Zionist Society, Nahum Sokolov returned to Istanbul to meet a limited group of Zionists, mostly university students from Palestine and Russia, and shared his support for the Zionist students in Istanbul and the opening up of new relations between the two groups of Zionists. There, he spoke about how the Yishuv and commented on the wonders of the 'Hebrew *Eretzisraeli* young boy, the symbol that captures a natural and vibrant people'.[92] Some people in the audience raised the point that young Jews in Istanbul did not show great interest in Zionism. Sokolov did not comment, but he must have timed his trip to Istanbul that week because there was the annual meeting of the B'nai B'rith organisation, which, even if it was not officially a Zionist organisation per se, appears to have had quite a number of Zionists among its members, who arrived from cities as far away as Cairo, Beirut, Damascus and some apparently coming from Palestine itself.[93] Importantly, the Chief Rabbi, Haim Nahum Efendi, was a guest of honour as well. While many scholars point out that Zionists made up only a small part of Istanbul's Jewish community, it seems that there was a clear surge in activity there in 1914; in July, just a month later, the Maccabi clubs in Istanbul, representing some 700–800 members, and known centres of Zionist activities, held a central meeting of the Istanbul branches in Pera. At this meeting about 50 people took part, coming from the neighbourhoods of Kuzguncuk, Hasköy, Balat, Ortaköy and Haydarpaşa.[94]

However, in no time at all the Zionist Union was closed by the Ottomans, which seems to have been the work of a low-level bureaucrat suspicious of this Ottoman Jewish society, since the investigation originated in the offices of the local Beyoğlu authorities. This fact is important because it meant the investigation was not a result of state policy or a greater investigation into Istanbul's local Jewish community. Thus this account shares a striking resemblance with the case of the oranges in Budapest, which was discussed in the Introduction, with both of them showing how far lower-level administrative officials were able to influence Ottoman policy. After discussing the issue with the Ministry of the Interior, in which the assistant governor of Istanbul stated that even as political activities could not be found in the society's name and programme, the fact that they were dealing with Jewish immigration and nationalisation exhibited that they were dealing with both 'internal and external politics'. In a separate memo, we learn that the society was found to be illegal due to its nationalist aims (*gaye-i milliye*), and that the name of the society was found to be in violation of the law since it was related to 'nationalism and race'. The government also found that the 'establishment and nationalisation of migrant Jews in Palestine was not only against the benefit of the Sublime Porte, it was [simply] forbidden. For this reason, the establishment of the above-mentioned society is not permitted'.[95] However, within the Ottoman file, there is no information that it was actually shut down; nor do we find any mention of it being closed in the Hebrew press.

Despite this, the Jews registering were Ottoman citizens and the fact that their loyalty to the Ottoman state was in question must have been a blow to the Ottoman Jews opening the doors of the organisation, because this challenged their dual Jewish and Ottoman identities. Despite the fact that their encouragement of foreign Jews adopting Ottoman citizenship was found to be 'against the benefit of the Ottoman state', this lack of support for an Ottoman citizenship drive is important as it is the direct opposite of the policy in Palestine, where the local Ottoman authorities, the Jewish Yishuv and the Palestinians all supported the Ottomanisation of Jews. Simply put, the closing of the society's doors should be seen as having little to do with what was actually happening in Palestine, but had much more to do with internal politics in Istanbul.

While the situation in Palestine and in government reports is cut and dried, it is difficult to pinpoint the exact source of the anti-Zionist movement in Istanbul. Where it is obviously related to anti-CUP factions, it seems that this explanation is too easy. This question demands further research to check how widespread these currents were before the Young Turk period. Perhaps, as the Zionists were now spreading their ideology as the result of their new-found freedoms, so their opponents were free to spread their anti-Semitic ideology, which would not have been possible during the reign of Abdülhamid II. In spite of this, it is clear that the Jews of the Ottoman Empire and subsequently in the Turkish Republic would never have such political clout as they did in Istanbul during 1908–11. In fact, later Jewish immigration to the Empire would be subjected to great scrutiny. This lack of tolerance exhibited towards the Jews would not only be directed towards them, but also to other non-Muslim and non-Turkic subjects of the Empire, and later of the Turkish state. In this sense, the current work can help us understand the status of other non-Muslims in the Empire.

However, in retrospect, whether the Zionist Union was opened or closed would not have made a huge difference. This case once again confirmed the government's lack of understanding – or its indifference – of who the Zionists were, and what were there aims. True, one could argue that once again the government had succeeded in blocking the Zionists from using Istanbul as a major base, and that despite many attempts, Istanbul never became a major base for political Zionist activity. However, with World War I just around the corner these debates would no longer be relevant as London would replace Istanbul as the capital where Zionist leaders would lobby for support.

In this chapter, I have discussed a number of characteristics of Zionism in the Young Turk period. However, with the growing opposition in Palestine, Zionism being debated in Parliament and the rise of anti-Jewish sentiment, it is clear that by 1911, the goals of Zionism, or a Jewish autonomous region within the Empire, would be impossible. Parallel to this, the Jews of the Ottoman state, like the other non-Muslim communities, would soon need to reassess their future and their role in a society which was becoming less tolerant towards them. Certainly the Jewish community in Istanbul could never have realised what dramatic changes they would undergo in the newly founded Turkish state; nevertheless, it was clear that their status would be challenged. Furthermore, Jewish immigration to regions outside of Palestine that were still within the Empire also would become a thing of the past.

At the same time, the future first leaders of Israel seemed to have misjudged the coming end of the Empire and instead supported the Ottoman state right up to its last days. However, some Zionists, such as Vladimir Jabotinsky, understood that their future would lie in the hands of the British. The Ottoman state bureaucracy seems not to have perceived the Zionist immigration as a major threat, but rather had to take into consideration the demands of the Arab population – the 'indigenous population' – which was becoming increasingly impatient. The Palestinians were losing faith in the Ottoman state at a crucial time, and this in turn led them to reassess their identity, or to strengthen underlying identities such as the Palestinian one. Yet it is significant that even as this identity formed more and more in opposition to the Zionists, the anti-Zionism in Istanbul surfaced for different reasons, and the Palestinians' needs were a distant second consideration. For Istanbul anti-Zionists, Zionism, along with Masonism, was out to destroy the Ottoman state. Perhaps, by taking such an active interest in changing the perceptions of Zionism in Istanbul, and by seizing on the Young Turk Revolution as an opportunity, some Zionists actually missed an opportunity to demonstrate that for many Zionists there was no contradiction between Zionism and Ottomanism.

Notes

1. A section of this chapter has been published in the following article: Fishman, 'Understanding the 1911 Ottoman Parliament Debate on Zionism in Light of the Emergence of a "Jewish Question"', in *Late Ottoman Palestine*, pp. 103–23.
2. Benbassa, 'Zionism in the Ottoman Empire at the End of the 19th Century and the Beginning of the 20th Century', *Studies in Zionism*, pp. 127–40.

3. *The Jewish Chronicle*, 6 September 1912.
4. As Yaron Ben Naeh correctly notes, ironically *Courrier d'Orient* was owned by Ebüzziya Tevfik, who, as we see in this book, was known for his anti-Semitism and also owned *Tasvir-i Efkar*; see Ben Naeh, 'The Zionist Struggle as Reflected in the Jewish Press in Istanbul in the Aftermath of the Young Turk Revolution', in *Late Ottoman Palestine*, p. 247.
5. Ben Naeh, 'The Zionist Struggle', p. 247.
6. Ibid.
7. Friedman, *Germany, Turkey, and Zionism*, p. 149.
8. Jabotinsky, *Igrot*, p. 112.
9. Friedman, *Germany, Turkey, and Zionism*, p. 149; Schechtman, *Rebel and Statesman*, p. 155. The newspaper *Courrier d'Orient* was established in April 1909. *L'Aurore* was established in 1908 following the Young Turk Revolution, and was the only Jewish journal published in French. See Groc and Çağlar, *La Presse Francaise de Turquie de 1795 à nos Jours*, pp. 68, 87. *HaMevasser* was published between December 1909–December 1911; for more information on *HaMevasser*, see: Jacob Landau, '*Comments on the Jewish Press* in Istanbul: The Hebrew Weekly *HaMevasser* (1909–1911)', in *Jews, Arabs, Turks*, pp. 89–96.
10. Landau, *Tekinalp*, p. 338.
11. Benbassa and Rodrigue, *Sephardi Jewry*, p. 124. Jacob Landau also is in agreement that recruitment of local Jews by the Zionist movement concentrated on the middle and lower classes; Landau, *Tekinalp*, p. 347.
12. Benbassa and Rodrigue, *Sephardi Jewry*, p. 124.
13. Shmuelevitz, 'Comments on the Jewish Press in Istanbul: The Hebrew Weekly *HaMevasser* (1909–1911)', p. 95.
14. Landau, *Tekinalp*, p. 367.
15. Benbassa and Rodrigue, *Sephardi Jewry*, p. 124.
16. DH.MUI 1327.L.29, 27–1/66; 13 November 1909.
17. Ibid.
18. Ibid.
19. Ibid.
20. *La Turquie* was established in 1906, two years before the Young Turk Revolution. It was briefly suspended in October 1911 and briefly was published under the title *Constitution*, and, *Liberté*. See Groc and Çağlar, *La Presse Francaise de Turquie de 1795 à nos Jours*, p. 181.
21. DH.MUI 1327.L.29, 27–1/66; 13 November 1909.
22. Nahum, *Correspondences*, pp. 160–1.
23. Kohen, 'An Explanation', *La Epoca*, 20 December 1910, quoted in Landau, *Tekinalp*, p. 55 (translation on p. 271).
24. The Basle Programme was adopted at the first Zionist Organization's conference, which was the charter of the organisation and clearly stated that Jewish settlement would be directed to Palestine. For more on the programme, see Laqueur, *The History of Zionism*, pp. 105–6.

25. Kohen, 'An Explanation', p. 55.
26. Sonyel, *Minorities and the Destruction of the Ottoman Empire*, pp. 318–19.
27. *The Times*, 12 March 1909.
28. Mandel, *The Arabs and Zionism before World War I*, p. 75.
29. The ICA was a philanthropic organisation founded by Baron Maurice de Hirsch in 1891 with the sole purpose of relocating Jews who lived in countries where they were persecuted or suffered bad economic conditions. Thus, most of its energies were spent relocating Russian Jews to the Americas and Palestine. However, not being Zionists ICA also worked with Jewish farmers in Russia to aid them in their work.
30. For more on the Jewish settlements during this period, see Bora, 'Alliance Israelite Universelle'in Osmanlı Yahudi Cemaatini, Tarım Sektöründe Kalkındırma Çalışmaları ve İzmir Yakınlarında Kurulan Bir Çiftlik Okul: Or Yehuda', *Çagdaş Türkiye Tarihi Araştırmaları Dergisi*, pp. 387–400.
31. *The Times*, 31 December 1904, p. 2.
32. Norman, *An Outstretched Arm*, pp. 106–7. While a comparison between these settlements and those in Palestine does not lie within the scope of this book, it is long overdue; not only because they both were under Ottoman governance, but also because they supported self-sustenance and the introduction of Hebrew. Such a comparison might well break down the perception of the 'uniqueness' of the Jewish Yishuv in Palestine during its first years. See Esin, '19. Yüzyılın Sonunda Osmanlı İmparatorluğu'nda Kurulan Musevi İskan Birliği (JCA) Çiftlikleri', *Toplumsal Tarih*, pp. 22–33.
33. *Ha-Zman*, 4 September 1912, p. 3.
34. Ibid.
35. Norman, *An Outstretched Arm*, pp. 106–7.
36. *Ha-Zman*, 4 September 1912, p. 2.
37. *New York Times*, 7 June 1909, p. 7.
38. Ibid., 13 June 1909, p. 5.
39. Ebüzziya Tevfik, *Millet-i İsrailiyye*.
40. Lewis, *The Emergence of Modern Turkey*, p. 208.
41. For more on Ebüziyya Tevfik see Gür, *Ebüzziya Tevfik*.
42. *Tasvir-i Efkar*, 16 November 1909, p. 2.
43. Ibid.
44. Ibid.
45. For more on the history of the role the Freemasons played in the development of the Committee of Union and Progress, see Hanioğlu, 'Notes on the Young Turks and the Freemasons', *Middle Eastern Studies*, pp. 186–94; Landau, *Exploring Ottoman and Turkish History*. Landau dedicates a whole chapter to Muslim opposition to Freemasonry: chapter 1, pp. 3–20.
46. The newspaper employed five writers, each from different ethnic and religious backgrounds. The editor was Ahmet Rıza, one of the most influential Young Turk leaders in Europe, and later in the CUP.

47. Hanioğlu, 'Jews in the Young Turk Movement', in *The Jews of the Ottoman Empire*, p. 520.
48. Ibid., pp. 520–1. A comparison between Jewish politics of the Ottoman period and that of the modern Turkish period would help us understand the reasons behind this. This is due to the fact that despite some very tense moments between Turkish Muslims and Jews, members of the Jewish community had been among the staunchest supporters of the late Ottoman state and the Turkish Republic.
49. Kedourie, 'Young Turks, Freemasons and Jews', *Middle Eastern Studies*, pp. 89–104; Sonyel, *Minorities and the Destruction of the Ottoman Empire*, p. 320.
50. Hanioğlu, 'Jews in the Young Turk Movement', p. 523.
51. Kedourie, 'Young Turks, Freemasons and Jews', pp. 94–5.
52. Landau, *Exploring Ottoman and Turkish History*, p. 18.
53. *The Times*, 3 March 1911, p. 5.
54. Ibid., 14 April 1911, p. 3.
55. Ibid. This is not to say that there were any members of the CUP that did not support this plan. *The Times* correspondent briefly mentions that since the Jewish immigrants 'would take kindly to agricultural pursuits in their new home and supply the want labour, which must otherwise be the greatest bar to the early realisation of any schemes for Mesopotamian development, they dream also of the creation, in one of the Arab centres, of a force which will in some degree be a counterpoise to the numerical superiority of the Arabs'.
56. *HaOr (HaTzvi)*, 30 March 1911, p. 3.
57. *The Times*, 14 August 1911.
58. Kohen, Unpublished diaries, entry 12 March 1911.
59. The B'nai B'rith during this period was in the midst of establishing its first lodge in the Ottoman state. For a history of the B'nai B'rith in the Ottoman Empire, see Bali, 'Bir Yahudi Dayanışma ve Yardımlaşma Kurumu', *Müteferrika*, pp. 41–60.
60. Kohen, Unpublished diaries, entry 12 March 1911. The unpublished diaries are now included in a three-part series on Moiz Kohen and his writings (in Turkish). See Bali, *Bir Günah Keçisi: Munis Tekinalp.*
61. Ibid., entry 29 March 1911.
62. Ibid., entry 3 April 1911, and 5 April 1911.
63. Ibid., entry 6 April 1911.
64. Ibid., entry 9 April 1911.
65. Ibid., entry 10 April 1911.
66. Ibid., entry 16 April 1911.
67. Muhsin, *Siyonizm Tehlikeleri*. In fact, the anti-Semitic literature widespread in Turkey today is almost an exact copy of what is found in this pamphlet.
68. Hanioğlu, 'Notes on the Young Turks and the Freemasons', p. 519.
69. Kayali, *Arabs and Young Turks*, pp. 101–2.
70. Ibid.

71. Ibid., p, 104.
72. Parliament report, 3 May 1327 (1911), p. 556.
73. Khalidi's estimate seems like a gross exaggeration. However, it needs to be stated that the Zionist Organization periodically strengthened the notion that they possessed enormous amounts of capital, as we see when Theodor Herzl sometimes stressed this. According to Khalidi, this bank was Chase Bank. However, as is well known in Zionist history, the bank that was opened to facilitate Jewish immigration was the Anglo-Palestine Bank. See Parliament report, 3 May 1327 (1911), p. 556.
74. Parliament report, p. 557.
75. Ibid.
76. Khalidi, *Palestinian Identity*, pp. 69, 77.
77. According to Feroz Ahmad, Mazliah's district had 25,002 Jews out of a population of 627,850; in order to be elected he needed 25,000 male eligible voters; Ahmad, *The Young Turks and the Ottoman Nationalities*, p. 103.
78. *HaOlam*, 3 March 1909, pp. 13–14.
79. Parliament report, p. 566.
80. Ibid.
81. Ibid., p. 572.
82. Ibid., p. 574.
83. Ibid.
84. Ibid., p. 575.
85. Ibid.
86. DH.ID 1332.R.27, 126/58; 24 March 1914; the report was also featured in Warsaw's Hebrew newspaper *HaTzifra*, 27 March 1914.
87. In addition to the file found in the Ottoman archive, the newspaper *HaHerut* also published the platform; *HaHerut*, 26 April 1914, p. 2.
88. *HaPoel HaTzair*, 20 March 1914, p. 9.
89. Ibid, p. 10.
90. Ibid.
91. *HaTzfira*, 24 June 1914, p. 2.
92. Ibid.
93. Ibid.; *HaHerut*, 9 June 1914, p. 2.
94. *HaTzifra*, 23 July 1914; *HaHerut*, 26 June 1914.
95. DH.ID 1332.R.27, 126/58; 24 March 1914.

Conclusion

Tracing the roots of the Palestinian–Israeli conflict is a daunting task as nationalist narratives have obscured real historical origins. This book has sought to offer a new interpretation of the first years of the conflict and presents a new context in which to understand it by going back to the late Ottoman era. This starting point is crucial to understanding how the conflict later developed into a full-fledged clash between two national movements during the British Mandate and the subsequent 1947–8 war. This book has clearly shown that the Jewish population in Ottoman Palestine was able to become a dominant force even before the Balfour Declaration, something that was accomplished within the Ottoman system.

For Palestinians, going back to the Ottoman era offers a new look at how Palestinian resistance formed around civic protest. As citizens of the Ottoman state, Palestinians voiced their opposition to Zionist settlement through petitions, newspapers and within the Ottoman Parliament. Their inability to stop Jewish migration fed into a frustration that led to a broader resentment against European dominance. Despite the multitude of Palestinian voices – from village leaders to the urban elite – calling on the Ottoman government to take measures to staunch the flow of Jewish settlers, their words often fell on deaf ears.

What is clear is that during the years leading up to World War I, Palestinians, Christian or Muslim, began to imagine themselves as a modern political community, with new bonds created as the urban elite adopted the cause of the Palestinian peasant. The essence of being Palestinian, or *Palestinianism*, was not an ethnic or separatist nationalist identity; rather it was a local identity, which developed within the context of a larger Arab identity. With the lack of a government response to the burning questions about the threat of Zionism to them, this local identity and patriotism transformed Palestinians into a viable political community, and they emerged as a united people, taking concrete steps to protect their homeland from an imminent threat. The basis of this new identity emerged not solely around the desire to put a halt to the Jewish immigration, but by attempting to strengthen claims to the land itself. Certainly, the term *Palestinianism* will be important for later periods as well in order to highlight the markers that help shape a modern sense of Palestinian identity that has remained resilient for over a century, despite the fact that they have yet to achieve statehood.

For the Jewish community, the 1908 Young Turk Revolution provided the chance to create an autonomous homeland in Palestine; however, this would not be possible through separation from the Ottoman system, but rather by integration into it. Throughout the Empire, new understandings of Zionism as a cultural movement emerged, providing a platform of legitimacy that had been impossible to achieve during the rule of the ousted Sultan Abdülhamid II. While many Jews in Istanbul and other cities in the Ottoman lands remained sceptical of the aims of the Zionist movement, the Jews in Palestine were well on their way to merging into a national community. Both Arabs and Jews in Palestine were on the brink of transforming a local identity into a national one.

While recent studies have highlighted ties between Palestine's urban residents and the Jewish population via Ottomanism, this current work has shown how, among the Jewish community in Palestine, the ideas of equality ushered in with the Young Turk Revolution were not based on creating a new notion of citizenship and brotherhood among Jews and Palestinians, but rather the recognition of their national demands vis-à-vis Istanbul. In fact, this was common among other non-Muslim communities, such as the Armenians, who believed the freedoms of the revolution would lead to cultural autonomy. Therefore, even if in some of Palestine's urban arenas there were relations between Jews and Palestinians, the Jewish community, whether Ashkenazi or Sephardic, locals or immigrants, never included Palestinians within the conceptual boundaries of their envisioned homeland; rather it created a clear separate boundary between the two communities, in what I call the 'Renegotiating of the Millet system', which ironically created new divisions within a new political system that was aimed at equality.

By going back to the Ottoman period, we also see that important trends were set in motion even before the First World War, which continued to characterise Jewish and Palestinian relations during and after the British Mandate. Already during the Ottoman era, the Palestinians engaged in a fixed pattern of protest against Jewish migration that produced few results; with time, frustration transformed this resistance from a civic protest towards violent action, with Palestine finally erupting in the 1936 revolt. The phenomenon of a growing landless peasant class, frequently identified as a key factor in the revolt, originates in the Ottoman period as we saw in Chapter 2. In the north, following the Fula land sale, peasants were left landless, while in the southern region with the Daran Petition, the peasants leaving the land sparked a hierarchical breakdown between the *mukhtar*s and the peasants. Finally, the potential sale of the Baysan Çiftlik, located in the Jordan River valley, led to calls among Palestinians to jointly purchase lands in order to create a national ownership similar to the Jewish National Fund; not surprisingly, this call emerged once again in the 1930s and the years immediately following World War II.

While the Palestinians often exaggerated the numbers of Jews arriving in the midst of Ottoman indifference, their demands on the Ottoman government were well within reason. As under the later British Mandate, the Palestinians made clear that the migration had to be stopped but, as demonstrated in the Jerusalem Petition, the Jews who had arrived would be able to stay, stating 'in the event that it is not possible to reduce this number, we request that significant and rational measures be taken by the government in order to keep it at this number'. Even in the Ottoman Parliament, Jerusalem MP Said al-Husayni praised how Jewish migration could have positive results in other regions of the Ottoman lands.

The case of the two universities in Jerusalem, one Arab and one Jewish, provides us with one of the most salient examples of how the Palestinians and Jews did not envision the other as part of the social (and political) polity of the land. The universities were undoubtedly a step to strengthen each one's hold over what they both saw as their spiritual homeland. This would not only have cultural repercussions but also political. While many of the Zionists were outwardly promoting a pro-Ottoman stance, it is clear from the documents found in the British archives concerning the Jewish university that the Zionist movement had a keen eye on the future in general, and specifically, already before the outbreak of World War I, on the potential role Britain would play in Palestine. This has been overlooked by previous works and demonstrates that the Palestinians were indeed justified in their fear that they were at risk of losing Palestine to a European power.

Following the 1908 Young Turk Revolution, Istanbul became a centre for Zionist activities; while this work only looks briefly at the steps the Berlin-based Zionist Organization was taking to convince the Ottoman government, the Jewish immigrants to Palestine seized the moment and started to make their way to the Ottoman capital to pursue the Zionist cause. With new understandings of Zionism emerging as a movement promoting a Hebrew culture, Zionist members of the Yishuv saw this moment as a chance to push for an autonomous homeland under the Ottoman state. These activities would provide an important experience once the British took control of Palestine; the centre to which they appealed then changed from Istanbul to London.

One member of the Hebrew Students' Union, Moshe Sharett, provides an interesting link between the late Ottoman period, the British Mandate and the new Israeli state. After cutting short his law studies in Istanbul due to the Balkan Wars, he was recruited into the Ottoman army during the war as a translator, and he remained a solider until even after the British issued the Balfour Declaration. However, following the war, Sharett made his way back to Istanbul to pick up his transcripts, and continued his studies in London, which now was the new centre of Zionist activity. Later, following the founding of Israel, he would serve as its first foreign minister, and second prime minister. Similarly, Gad Frumkin, who was also active in Istanbul, actually finishing his degree there, would become the only appointed Jewish judge in the British court system of Palestine, and later a Supreme Court judge in the newly founded Jewish state.

This book demonstrates the many complexities involved in trying to frame Zionism and the debates surrounding it. Zionism took on many forms; for Ottoman MP Nissim Mazliah, it did not contradict his loyalty to the Ottoman state, but rather was the promotion of Hebrew culture; for Karmi Eisenberg, it was serving in the Ottoman army and fighting for the land where he was born. He also, according to his brother-in-law Gad Frumkin, could well have been the first to imagine a population exchange between Jews and Arabs decades before the Palestinian Nakba; for David Ben-Gurion, who studied law in Istanbul, and organised the Zionist student union, Istanbul was where he had a chance to enter politics; however, this was cut short due to the breakout of the war. For the Chief Rabbi Haim Nahum and Albert Antebi, their anti-Zionism in no way meant they were against Jewish migration to Palestine; rather they were against an attempt at creating an independent state in Palestine (much different from how anti-Zionism is defined today). Further, despite their verbal opposition, it is clear that the majority of Sephardic Jews in Palestine had clearly adopted Zionism as a cultural and national movement.

Due to the rise of anti-Semitism in the Ottoman state, the Palestinians' claims against Jewish migration were often misconstrued as not just against the population influx, but rather derived from an overall anti-Semitic stance. This is far from the truth. For example, Ottoman authorities suspended the newspaper *Filastin* because Jews claimed it was anti-Semitic, even though its position was far more nuanced. The editors opposed the unchecked Jewish migration, but never allowed writers to engage in anti-Semitic rhetoric. Further, while some Ottoman figures spread anti-Semitic sentiments, blaming Zionists and Freemasons for the overthrow of Abdülhamid II, the real issue concerning Palestinians – the migration of Jews to the land – often was removed from the Istanbul debate, which proved detrimental to their cause. The debate over Zionism in Istanbul seemingly had more to do with a growing Jewish question there, which would re-emerge in the post-1923 modern Turkish state.

In short, the late Ottoman era set the stage for the conflict that has lasted for over a century, and is an essential component in developing an understanding of how the two communities were set on a collision course. Following the 1908 Young Turk Revolution, both communities set out to 'claim the homeland', and Palestinians found themselves in a position of protesting a growing Jewish hegemonic political power. This trend would continue following the 1917 Balfour Declaration, the British occupation and Mandate, and subsequently until today.

Bibliography

Primary Sources

ARCHIVAL SOURCES

Başbakanlık Osmanlı Arşivi (BOA), Istanbul, Turkey
Bâb-ı Âlî Evrak Odası (BEO)
Dahiliye Nezareti, Emniyet-i Umumiye Müdüriyeti (DH.EUM)
Dahiliye Nezareti Emniyet-i Umumiye Müdüriyeti (DH.EUM.4.Şb)
Dahiliye Nezâreti Kalem-i Mahsus Müdüriyeti (DH.KMS)
Dahiliye Nezareti İdare-i Umumiye (DH.ID)
Dahiliye Nezâreti Mektubî Kalemi (DH.MKT)
Dahiliye Nezareti, Muhaberât-ı Umumiye İdaresi (DH.MUI)
Dahiliye Nezâreti Şifre Kalemi (DH.ŞFR)
Dahiliye Nezâreti Siyasî Kısım (DH.SYS)
Dahiliye Nezareti Umûr-ı Mahalliye-i Vilayât Müdüriyeti Belgeleri (DH.UMVM)
Dahiliye Nezareti İdâre-i Umumiye (DH.IUM)
Meclis-i Vükela (MV)
Public Record Office, British National Archives (PRO)

OFFICIALLY PUBLISHED GOVERNMENT PAPERS

Meclis-i Mebusan Zabıt Cerideleri (MMZC), Istanbul: 1908–20, 36 volumes

NEWSPAPERS

Al-Quds, Jerusalem
Filastin, Jaffa
Ha-Herut, Jerusalem
Ha-Olam, Berlin
Ha-Poel HaTsair, Jaffa

Ha-Tzvi, Jerusalem
Ha-Zfira, Warsaw
Ha-Zman, St Petersburg/Vilna
Moriah, Jerusalem
New York Times, New York
Tanin, Istanbul
Tasvir-i Efkar, Istanbul
The Jewish Chronicle, London
The Times, London

Other Primary Sources

UNPUBLISHED

Captain Montague B. Parker, Report on Progress of F. J. M. P. V. Syndicate
Moiz Kohen's Diaries, Rıfat Bali's private archives, Istanbul

PUBLISHED

Ben-Gurion, D. and Y. Ben-Tzvi, 'Excerpt of a Letter to Djemal Pasha, 5 March
    1915', in I. Friedman (ed.), *The Rise of Israel: Germany, Turkey, and Zionism
    1914–1918* (New York: Garland Publishing, 1987), pp. 122–3.
Ben-Tsvi, Y., *Zikronot VaReshumot (Essays and Reminiscences)* (Jerusalem:
    Sion, 1967).
Blyth, Estelle, *When We Lived in Jerusalem* (London: John Murray, 1927).
Dalman, Gustaf, 'The Search for the Temple Treasure at Jerusalem', *Palestine
    Exploration Fund Quarterly Statement*, January 1912, 44(1), pp. 35–39.
Frumkin, Gad, *Derekh Shofet Be'Yerushalayim* (Tel Aviv: Dvir, 1954).
Herzl, Theodor, *The Jewish State*, translated by Harry Zohn (New York: Herzl
    Press, 1970).
Jabotinsky, Ze'ev (Vladimir), *Igrot* [Letters], edited by Daniel Carpi and Moshe
    Halevi (Jerusalem: Mossad Bialik, 1992).
Nahum, Haim, *Correspondences*, edited by Esther Benbassa and translated from
    the French by Miriam Kochman (Tuscaloosa: University of Alabama Press,
    1995).
Muhsin, A., *Siyonizm Tehlikeleri* (Istanbul: Osmanlı Şirketi Matbaası, 1911).
Ruppin, Arthur, *The Jews of To-Day*, translated by Margery Bentwich and
    introduced by Joseph Jacobs, Litt.D. (New York: Henry Holt and Company,
    1913).
Ruppin, Arthur, *Syria: An Economic Survey* (New York: The Provisional Zionist
    Committee, 1918).
Ruppin, Arthur, 'A General Colonization Policy', in *Three Decades of Palestine:
    Speeches and Papers on the Upbuilding of the Jewish National Home* (Westport:
    Greenwood Press, 1936).

Ruppin, Arthur, *Building Israel: Selected Essays 1907–1935* (New York: Schocken Books, 1949).

Ruppin, Arthur, Arthur Ruppin's report cited and translated in: Charles Issawi, *The Economic History of the Middle East, 1800–1914* (Chicago: University of Chicago Press, 1966).

Sharett, Moshe, *Mikhtavim mehaTsva haOthmani* [Letters from the Ottoman Army], edited by Yaacov Sharett (Tel Aviv: HaAmutah leMoshe Sharett, 1998).

Shochat, Israel, 'Slihot VaDerekh', in Y. Ben-Tsvi (ed.), *Sefer HaShomer (The Book of Shomer)* (Tel Aviv: Davir Co., 1957).

Al-Tabba', 'Uthman Mustafa, *Ithaf wa-A'izzah fi Tarikh Ghazzah* (Gaza: Maktabat al-Yazaji, 1999).

Temimi, Mehmet Refik, *Wilayat Bayrut* (Beirut: Matbaa al-Aqbal, 1987).

Tevfik, Ebüzziya, *Millet-i İsrailiyye* (Istanbul: Kitabhane-i Ebüzziya, 1888).

Thon, O., 'The Zionist Programme and Practical Work in Palestine', in Israel Cohen (ed.), *Zionist Work in Palestine* (London: T. Fisher Unwin, 1911), pp. 13–20.

Vincent, Hugues, *Underground Jerusalem: Discoveries on the Hill of the Ophel (1909–1911)* (London: Horace Cox, 1911).

Volney, Constantin-Francois, *Travels through Syria and Egypt, in the Years 1783, 1784, and 1785: Containing the Present Natural and Political State of Those Countries, Their Productions, Arts, Manufactures, and Commerce: With Observations on the Manners, Customs, and Government of the Turks and Arabs* (London: G. Robinson, 1805).

Yaari, A., *Zikhronot Eretz-Isra'el* [Memoirs of the Land of Israel] (Jerusalem: Dafus Yerushaliyim, 1947).

Yellin, David, 'The Renaissance of the Hebrew Language in Palestine', in Israel Cohen (ed.), *Zionist Work in Palestine* (London: T. Fisher Unwin, 1911), pp. 143–6.

Other Sources by Title

Bali, Rıfat (ed.), *A Bibliography of Books, Theses and Articles Published in Turkey Concerning Judaism 1923–2003* (Istanbul: Turkuaz Publishing House, 2005).

Eliav, Mordechai (ed.), *Britain and the Holy Land 1838–1914: Selected Documents from the British Consulate in Jerusalem* (Jerusalem: Yad Izhak Ben-Zvi and The Magnes Press, 1997).

Kuneralp, Sinan (ed.), *Son Dönem Osmanlı Erkan ve Ricali (1839–1922) Prosopografik Rehber [Ottoman Officers and High Officials: Prosopographic Guide]* (Istanbul: ISIS Press, 1999).

Uygur, Ziya (ed.), *Osmanlı Arşiv Belgelerinde Filistin Sorunu Ve Siyonizm [Documents Pertaining to the Palestine Question and Zionism in the Ottoman Archives]* (Istanbul: Bayrak Maatbası, 1998).

Reference Sources

Duman, Hasan, *Osmanlı-Türk Süreli Yayınları ve Gazeteleri* (Ottoman-Turkish Serials and Newspapers), vols 1–2 (Ankara: Enformasyon ve Dokümantasyon Hizmetleri Vakfı, 2000).

Tunaya, Tarik Zafer, *Türkiyede Siyasal Partiler, İkinci Meşrutiyet Dönemi* (Political Parties in Turkey, The Second Constitutional Period), vol. 1 (Istanbul: İletişim, 1998).

Secondary Sources

Abou-El-Haj, Rifaat Ali, 'The Social Uses of the Past: Recent Arab Historiography of Ottoman Rule', *IJMES*, 1982, 14, pp. 185–201.

Abu-Manneh, Butrus, 'The Rise of the Sanjak of Jerusalem in the Late 19th Century', in G. Ben Dor (ed.), *The Palestinians and the Middle East Conflict* (Tel Aviv, 1978), pp. 21–32.

Ahmad, Feroz, *The Young Turks: The Committee of Union and Progress, 1908–1914* (Oxford: Oxford University Press, 1969).

Ahmad, Feroz, 'Unionist Relations with the Greek, Armenian, and Jewish Communities of the Ottoman Empire', in B. Braude and B. Lewish (eds), *Christian and Jews in the Ottoman Empire, 1908–1914* (New York: Holmes and Meier Publishing, 1982), pp. 287–324.

Ahmad, Feroz, *The Young Turks and the Ottoman Nationalities: Armenians, Greeks, Albanians, Jews, and Arabs, 1908–1918* (Salt Lake City, UT: University of Utah Press, 2014).

Ajay, Nicholas Z., Jr, 'Political Intrigue and Suppression in Lebanon During WWI', *IJMES*, 1974, 5, pp. 140–60.

Alroey, Gur, *An Unpromising Land: Jewish Migration to Palestine in the Early Twentieth Century* (Stanford: Stanford University Press, 2014).

Al-Salim, Farid, *Palestine and the Decline of the Ottoman Empire: Modernization and the Path to Palestine Statehood* (London: I. B. Tauris, 2015).

Anderson, Benedict, *Imagined Communities: Reflections on the Origin and Spread of Nationalism*, 2nd edn (London: Verso, 2006).

Antonius, George, 'Syria and the French Mandate', *Royal Institute of Internal Affairs*, July-August 1934, 13(4), pp. 523–39.

Antonius, George, *The Arab Awakening* (London: Hamish Hamilton, 1938).

Asali, K. J. (ed.), *Jerusalem in History* (Brooklyn: Olive Branch Press, 1990).

Auld, Sylvia and Robert Hillenbrand (eds), *Ottoman Jerusalem: The Living City* (London: Altajir World of Islam Trust, 2000).

Ayalon, Ami, *The Press in the Middle East* (New York: Oxford University Press, 1995).

Ayalon, Ami, *Reading Palestine: Printing and Literacy, 1900–1948* (Austin: University of Texas, 2004).

Baer, Marc, 'The Double Bind of Race and Religion: The Conversion of the

Dönme to Turkish Secular Nationalism', *Society for Comparative Study of Society and History,* 2004, pp. 682–708.

Bali, Rıfat N., 'Bir Yahudi Dayanışma ve Yardımlaşma Kurumu: B'nai B'rith XI. Bölge Büyük Locası Tarihçesi ve Yayın Organı HaMenora Dergisi [A Jewish Support and Assistance Foundation: The History of B'nai Brith's 16 Division Grand Lodge and Its Organ of Publication HaMenora]', *Müteferrika,* Spring-Summer 1996 (8–9), pp. 41–60.

Bali, Rıfat N., *Cumhuriyet Yıllarında Türkiye Yahudileri: Bir Türkleştirme Serüveni 1923–1945* (Istanbul: İletişim, 2000).

Bali, Rıfat N., *Bir Günah Keçisi: Munis Tekinalp* (Istanbul: Libra, 2012).

Benbassa, Esther, 'Zionism in the Ottoman Empire at the End of the 19th Century and the Beginning of the 20th Century', *Studies in* Zionism, 1990, 11(2), pp. 127–40.

Benbassa, Esther, 'Associational Strategies in Ottoman Jewish Society in the Nineteenth and Twentieth Centuries', in A. Levy (ed.), *The Jews of the Ottoman Empire* (Princeton: Darwin Press, 1994), pp. 457–84.

Benbassa, Esther and Aron Rodrigue, *Sephardi Jewry: A History of the Judeo-Spanish Community, 14th-20th Centuries* (Berkeley: University of California Press, 2000).

Ben-Bassat, Yuval, *Petitioning the Sultan: Protests and Justice in late Ottoman Palestine, 1865–1908* (London: I. B. Tauris, 2013).

Ben Naeh, Yaron, 'The Zionist Struggle as Reflected in the Jewish Press in Istanbul in the Aftermath of the Young Turk Revolution, 1908–1918', in Yuval Ben-Bassat and Eyal Ginio (eds), *Late Ottoman Palestine: The Period of the Young Turk Rule* (New York: I. B. Tauris, 2011), pp. 241–58.

Ben-Tzvi, Yitzhak, *Sefer haShomer* [The Shomer Book] (Tel Aviv: Davir Co., 1957).

Ben-Tzvi, Yitzhak, *Zikhronot veResumot* [Essays and Reminisciences] (Jerusalem: Tziyyon, 1967).

Beška, Emanuel, 'Responses of Prominent Arabs towards Zionist Aspirations and Colonization Prior to 1908', *Asian and African Studies,* 2007, 16(1), pp. 22–44.

Beška, Emanuel, 'Shukri al-Asali, An Extraordinary Anti-Zionist Activist', *Asian and African Studies,* 2010, 19(2), pp. 237–54.

Beška, Emanuel, 'Political Opposition to Zionism in Palestine and Greater Syria: 1910–1911 as a Turning Point', *Jerusalem Quarterly,* 2014 (59), pp. 54–67.

Biger, Gideon, *The Boundaries of Modern Palestine, 1840–1947* (London: Routledge Curzon, 2004).

Bora, H. Siren, 'Alliance Israelite Universelle'in Osmanlı Yahudi Cemaatini, Tarım Sektöründe Kalkındırma Çalışmaları ve İzmir Yakınlarında Kurulan Bir Çiftlik Okul: Or Yehuda', *Çagdaş Türkiye Tarihi Araştırmaları Dergisi,* 1993, 1(3), pp. 387–400.

Brubaker, Rogers and Frederick Cooper, 'Beyond "Identity"', *Theory and Society,* 2000, 29(1), pp. 1–47, <http://www.jstor.org/stable/3108478> (last accessed 6 June 2019).

Budeiri, Musa, 'The Palestinians: Tensions between Nationalist and Religious Identities', in James Jankowski and Israel Gershoni (eds), *Rethinking Nationalism in the Arab Middle East* (New York: Columbia University Press, 1997), pp. 191–206.

Buheiry, Marwan (ed.), *Intellectual Life in the Arab East, 1890–1939* (Beirut: American University of Beirut, 1981).

Büssow, Johann, *Hamidian Palestine: Politics and Society in the District of Jerusalem 1872–1908* (Leiden: Brill, 2011).

Campos, Michelle U., 'A "Shared Homeland" and Its Boundaries: Empire, Citizenship and the Origins of Sectarianism in Late Ottoman Palestine, 1908–13' (PhD dissertation: Stanford University, 2003).

Campos, Michelle U., 'Between "Beloved Ottomania" and "The Land of Israel": The Struggle over Ottomanism and Zionism among Palestine's Sephardi Jews, 1908–13', *IJMES*, 2005, 37, pp. 461–83.

Campos, Michelle U., *Ottoman Brothers: Muslims, Christians, and Jews in Early Twentieth-Century Palestine* (Stanford: Stanford University Press, 2011).

Chazan, Meir, 'The Murder of Moshe Barsky: Transformation in Ethos, Pathos, and Myth', *Israel Affairs*, June 2006, 12(2), pp. 284–306.

Cleveland, William L., *The Making of an Arab Nationalist: Ottomanism and Arabism in the Life and Thought of Sati' al-Husri* (Princeton: Princeton University Press, 1971).

Cleveland, William L., *Islam against the West*: *Shakib Arslan and the Campaign for Islamic Nationalism* (Austin: University of Texas Press, 1985).

Cleveland, William L., *A History of the Modern Middle East* (Boulder, CO: Westview Press, 2016).

Cohen, Julia Phillips, *Becoming Ottomans: Sephardi Jews and Imperial Citizenship in the Modern Era* (New York: Oxford University Press, 2014).

Cohen, Julia Phillips and Sarah Abrevaya Stein (eds), *Sephardi Lives: A Documentary History, 1700–1950* (Stanford: Stanford University Press, 2014).

Cohen, Mark R., 'The "Golden Age" of Jewish-Muslim Relations: Myth and Reality', in Abdelwahab Meddeb and Benjamin Stora (eds), *A History of Jewish-Muslim Relations: From the Origins to the Present Day* (Princeton: Princeton University Press, 2013), pp. 28–38.

Commins, David, 'Religious Reformers and Arabists in Damascus, 1885–1914', *IJMES*, 1986, 18, pp. 405–25.

Commins, David, *Islamic Reform: Politics and Change in Late Ottoman Syria* (New York: Oxford University Press, 1990).

Dawn, C. Ernest, *From Ottomanism to Arabism: Essays on the Origins of Arab Nationalism* (Urbana: University of Illinois Press, 1973).

Deringil, Selim, *The Well Protected Domains: Ideology and the Legitimation of Power in the Ottoman Empire, 1876–1909* (New York: I. B. Tauris, 1998).

Deringil, Selim, 'Jewish Immigration to the Ottoman Empire at the Time of the First Zionist Congresses: A Comment', in Minna Rozen (ed.), *The Last*

Bibliography

Ottoman Century and Beyond: The Jews in Turkey and the Balkans, 1808–1945 (Tel Aviv: Tel Aviv University, 2002), pp. 141–9.

Der Matossian, Bedross, *Shattered Dreams of Revolution: From Liberty to Violence in the Late Ottoman Empire* (Stanford: Stanford University Press, 2014).

Divine, Donna Robinson, *Politics and Society in Ottoman Palestine* (Boulder: Lynne Reinner, 1994).

Dolbee, Samuel and Shay Hazkani, 'Impossible Is Not Ottoman: Menasha Meirovitch, 'Isa Al-'Isa, and Imperial Citizenship in Palestine', *IJMES*, May 2015, 47(2), pp. 241–62.

Doumani, Beshara, 'Rediscovering Ottoman Palestine: Writing Palestinians into History', *Journal of Palestine Studies*, Winter 1992, 21(2), pp. 5–28.

Doumani, Beshara, *Rediscovering Palestine: The Merchants and Peasants of Jabal Nablus, 1700–1900* (Berkeley: University of California Press, 1995).

Eldem, Edhem, 'Istanbul as a Cosmopolitan City: Myths and Realities', in Ato Quayson and Girish Daswani (eds), *A Companion to Diaspora and Transnationalism* (Malden: Blackwell Publishing Ltd, 2013), pp. 212–30.

Eldem, Edhem, '(A Quest for) the Bourgeoisie of Istanbul: Identities, Roles and Conflicts', in Ulrike Freitag and Nora Lafi (eds), *Urban Governance Under the Ottomans: Between Cosmopolitanism and Conflict* (New York: Routledge, 2014), pp. 159–87.

Eroğlu, Ahmet Hikmet, *Osmanlı Devletinde Yahudiler* [The Jews in the Ottoman State] (Ankara: Alperen Basın Yayın ve Tan. TİC. LTD. ŞTİ, 2000).

Escovitz, Joseph H., 'He Was the Muhammad 'Abduh of Syria: A Study of Tahir al-Jazari and His Influence', *IJMES* 1986, 18, pp. 293–310.

Esin, Taylan, '19. Yüzyılın Sonunda Osmanlı İmparatorluğu'nda Kurulan Musevi İskan Birliği (JCA) Çiftlikleri', *Toplumsal Tarih*, Eylül 2014, 249, pp. 22–33.

Even-Zohar, Itamar, 'The Emergence of a Native Hebrew Culture in Palestine: 1882–1948', *Studies in Zionism*, October 1981, 2(2), pp. 167–84.

Fahmy, Ziad, *Ordinary Egyptians: Creating the Modern Nation through Popular Culture* (Stanford: Stanford University Press, 2011).

Farhi, David, 'Documents on the Attitude of the Ottoman Government towards the Jewish Settlement in Palestine after the Revolution of the Young Turks (1908–1909)', in M. Maoz (ed.), *Studies on Palestinians During the Ottoman Period* (Jerusalem: Magnes Press, 1975), pp. 192–3.

Fishman, Louis, 'The Haram al-Sharif Incident: Palestinian Notables versus the Ottoman Administration', *Journal of Palestine Studies*, Spring 2005, 34(3), pp. 6–22.

Fishman, Louis, 'Understanding the 1911 Ottoman Parliament Debate on Zionism in Light of the Emergence of a "Jewish Question"', in Yuval Ben-Bassat and Eyal Ginio (eds), *Late Ottoman Palestine: The Period of the Young Turk Rule* (New York: I. B. Tauris, 2011), pp. 103–23.

Fishman, Louis, 'The Limitations of Citadinité in Late Ottoman Jerusalem', in Vincent Lemire and Angelos Dalachanis (eds), *Ordinary Jerusalem 1840–*

1940: Opening New Archives, Revisiting a Global City (Boston: Brill, 2018), pp. 510–31.

Freas, Erik Eliav, 'Ottoman Reform, Islam, and Palestine's Peasantry', *Arab Studies Journal*, 2010, 18(1), pp. 196–231.

Friedman, Isaiah, *Germany, Turkey, and Zionism, 1897–1918* (Oxford: Clarendon Press, 1977).

Gellner, Ernest, *Nations and Nationalism* (Ithaca: Cornell University Press, 1983).

Gelvin, James, *Divided Loyalties: Nationalism and Mass Politics in Syria at the Close of Empire* (Berkeley, University of California Press, 1998).

Gelvin, James, *The Modern Middle East: A History* (New York: Oxford University Press, 2005).

Gerber, Haim, 'Zionism, Orientalism, and the Palestinians', *Journal of Palestine Studies*, Fall 2003, 3(1), pp. 23–41.

Gerber, Haim, *Remembering and Imagining Palestine: Identity and Nationalism from the Crusades to the Present* (Basingstoke: Palgrave Macmillan, 2008).

Gilbar, Gad G., *The Question of Palestine 1914–1918: A Study of British-Jewish-Arab Relations* (London: Routledge and Kegan Paul, 1973).

Gilbar, Gad G. (ed.), *Ottoman Palestine 1800–1914: Studies in Economic and Social History* (Leiden: Brill, 1990).

Goldstein, Yaakov, חבורת הרועים [The Fraternity of the Shepherds] (Tel Aviv: Ministry of Defence, 1993).

Groc, Gerard and Ibrahim Çağlar, *La Presse Francaise de Turquie de 1795 à nos Jours: Histoire et Catalogue* (Istanbul: Isis, 1985).

Gribetz, Jonathan Marc, *Defining Neighbors: Religion, Race, and the Early Zionist-Arab Encounter* (Princeton: Princeton University Press, 2016).

Güleryuz, Naim, *Türk Yahudi Tarihi* (Istanbul: Gözlem, 1993).

Gür, Alim, *Ebüziyya Tevfik: Hayatı; Dil, Edebiyat, Basın, Yayın, ve Matbaacılığa Katkıları* (Ankara: Kültür ve Turizm Bakanlığı Yayınları, 1998).

Haddad, Mahmoud, 'Iraq Before World War I', in Rashid Khalidi, Lisa Anderson and Reeva S. Simon (eds), *The Origins of Arab Nationalism* (New York: Columbia University Press, 1991), pp. 120–50.

Haddad, William W. and William Ochsenwald (eds), *Nationalism in a Non-National State: The Dissolution of the Ottoman Empire* (Columbus: Ohio University Press, 1977).

Hakim, Carol, *Origins of the Lebanese National Idea* (Berkeley: University of California Press, 2013).

Hallaq, Hassan Ali, *Mawqif al-Dawlah al-'Uthmaniyah min al-Harakah al-Suh-yuniyah, 1897–1909* [The Ottoman State's Position on the Zionist Movement] (Beirut: Jami'at Bayrut al-'Arabiyah, 1978).

Halperin, Liora R., *Babel in Zion: Jews, Nationalism, and Language Diversity in Palestine, 1920–1948* (New Haven: Yale University Press, 2014).

Halperin, Liora R., 'A Murder in the Grove: Conceptions of Justice in an Early Zionist Colony', *Journal of Social History*, 2015, 49(2), pp. 427–51.

Hanioğlu, M. Şükrü, 'Notes on the Young Turks and the Freemasons', *Middle Eastern Studies,* April 1989, 25(2), pp. 186–94.

Hanioğlu, M. Şükrü, 'Jews in the Young Turk Movement', in Avigdor Levy (ed.), *The Jews of the Ottoman Empire* (Princeton: Darwin Press, 1994), pp. 519–26.

Hanioğlu, M. Şükrü, *The Young Turks in Opposition* (New York: Oxford University Press, 1995).

Hanioğlu, M. Şükrü, *A Brief History of the Late Ottoman Empire* (Princeton: Princeton University Press, 2008).

Hourani, Albert, 'Ottoman Reform and the Politics of Notables', in W. R. Polk and R. L. Chambers (eds), *Beginnings of Modernization in the Middle East: The Nineteenth Century* (Chicago: The University of Chicago Press, 1968), pp. 41–68.

Hourani, Albert, *Arabic Thought in the Liberal Age 1798–1939*, 12th edn (Cambridge: Cambridge University Press, 1983).

Issawi, Charles, *The Economic History of the Middle East 1800–1914: A Book of Readings* (Chicago: University of Chicago Press, 1966).

Itzkowitz, Norman, *Ottoman Empire and Islamic Traditions* (Chicago: University of Chicago Press, 1972).

Jacobson, Abigail, 'Sephardim, Ashkenazim, and the "Arab Question" in Pre-First World War Palestine: A Reading of Three Zionist Newspapers', *Middle Eastern Studies*, April 2003, 39(2), pp. 105–30.

Jacobson, Abigail, 'From Empire to Empire: Jerusalem in the Transition between Ottoman and British Rule, 1912–1920' (PhD dissertation: The University of Chicago, 2006).

Jacobson, Abigail, *From Empire to Empire: Jerusalem between Ottoman and British Rule* (Syracuse: Syracuse University Press, 2011).

Kaiser, Hilmar, 'The Ottoman Government and Zionist Movement during the First Months of World War I', in M. Talha Cicek (ed.), *Syria in World War I: Politics, Economy, and Society* (London: Routledge, 2015), pp. 107–29.

Kansu, Aykut, *The Revolution of 1908 in Turkey* (Leiden: Brill, 1997).

Kark, Ruth, *Jaffa: A City in Evolution, 1799–1917* (Jerusalem: Yad Izhak Ben-Zvi Press, 1990).

Kark, Ruth and Seth J. Frantzman, 'Bedouin, Abdul Hamid II, British Land Settlement, and Zionism: The Baysan Valley and Sub-District 1831–1948', *Israel Studies*, Summer 2010, 15(2), pp. 49–79.

Karpat, Kemal H., 'The Ottoman Emigration to America, 1860–1914', *IJMES*, May 1985, 17(2), pp. 175–209.

Karpat, Kemal H., 'Jewish Population Movements in the Ottoman Empire, 1862–1914', in Avigdor Levy (ed.), *The Jews of the Ottoman Empire* (Princeton: Darwin Press, 1994), pp. 399–422.

Kayali, Hasan, 'Jewish Representation in the Ottoman Parliament', in Avigdor Levy (ed.), *The Jews of the Ottoman Empire* (Princeton: Darwin Press, 1994), pp. 507–17.

Kayali, Hasan, 'Elections and the Electoral Process in the Ottoman Empire, 1876–1919', *IJMES*, 1995, 27(3), pp. 265–86.

Kayali, Hasan, *Arabs and Young Turks: Ottomanism, Arabism, and Islamism in the Ottoman Empire, 1908–1918* (Berkeley: University of California Press, 1997).

Kedourie, Elie, *England and the Middle East: The Destruction of the Ottoman Empire, 1914–1921* (London: Bowes & Bowes, 1956).

Kedourie, Elie, 'Young Turks, Freemasons and Jews', *Middle Eastern Studies*, January 1971, 7(1), pp. 89–104.

Kedourie, Elie, *England and the Middle East: The Destruction of the Ottoman Empire, 1914–1921* (London: Mansell publishing, 1987).

Kenyon, Kathleen, *Digging Up Jerusalem* (New York: Praeger Publishers, 1974).

Khalidi, Rashid, *British Policy towards Syria and Palestine 1906–1914: A Study of the Antecedents of the Hussein-McMahon Correspondence, the Sykes-Picot Agreement and the Balfour Declaration* (London: Ithaca Press, 1980).

Khalidi, Rashid, ''Abd al-Ghani al-Uraisi and *al-Mufid*: The Press and Arab Nationalim before 1914', in M. Buheiry (ed.), *Intellectual Life in the Arab East, 1890–1939* (Beirut: American University Press, 1984), pp. 38–61.

Khalidi, Rashid, 'The 1912 Election Campaign in the Cities of *Bilad al-Sham*', *IJMES*, 1984, 16, pp. 461–74.

Khalidi, Rashid, 'The Economic Partition of the Arab Provinces of the Ottoman Empire before the First World War', *Review*, Spring 1988, 11(2), pp. 251–64.

Khalidi, Rashid, 'The Formation of Palestinian Identity: The Critical Years, 1917–1923', in James Jankowski and Israel Gershoni (eds), *Rethinking Nationalism in the Arab Middle East* (New York: Columbia University Press, 1997), pp. 171–90.

Khalidi, Rashid, *Palestinian Identity: The Construction of Modern National Consciousness* (New York: Columbia University Press, 1998).

Khalidi, Rashid, *The Iron Cage: The Story of the Palestinian Struggle for Statehood* (Boston: Beacon Press, 2006).

Khalidi, Rashid, L. Anderson, R. Simon and M. Muslih (eds), *The Origins of Arab Nationalism* (New York: Columbia University Press, 1991).

Khoury, Philip, *Syria and the French Mandate: The Politics of Arab Nationalism, 1920–1945* (Princeton: Princeton University Press, 1987).

Kılıçdağı, Ohannes, 'The Bourgeois Transformation and Ottomanism among Anatolian Armenians after the 1908 Revolution' (MA thesis: Boğazici University, 2005).

Kimmerling, Baruch and Joel Migdal, *Palestinians: The Making of a People* (New York: Free Press, 1993).

Klein, Menachem, *Lives in Common: Arabs and Jews in Jerusalem, Jaffa, and Hebron* (Oxford: Oxford University Press, 2014).

Kollat, Israel, 'The Idea of the Hebrew University in the Jewish National Movement', in Shaul Katz and Michael Heyd (eds), *The History of the Hebrew*

University of Jerusalem: Origins and Beginnings (Jerusalem: The Magnes Press, 1997), pp. 3–74.

Krämer, Gudrun, *A History of Palestine: From the Ottoman Conquest to the Founding of the State of Israel*, translated by Graham Harman (Princeton: Princeton University Press, 2011).

Kushner, David, *The Rise of Turkish Nationalism 1876–1908* (London: Frank Cass, 1977).

Kushner, David (ed.), *Palestine in the Late Ottoman Period: Political Social and Economic Transformation* (Jerusalem: Yad Izhak Ben Tzvi, 1986).

Kushner, David, 'The Ottoman Governors of Palestine, 1864–1914', *Middle Eastern Studies*, 1987, 23(3), pp. 274–90, <www.jstor.org/stable/4283185> (last accessed 6 June 2019).

Kushner, David, *Moshel Hayyiti be-Yerushalayim: Ha'ir ve haMaahoz be'einav shel Ali Ekrem Bey* [A Governor in Jerusalem: the City and District according to Ali Ekrem Bey] [Ali Ekrem Bey's letters translated to Hebrew] (Jerusalem: Yad Izhak Ben-Zvi, 1995).

Kushner, David, 'Ali Ekrem Bey, Governor of Jerusalem, 1906–1908', *IJMES*, 1996, 28, pp. 349–62.

Kushner, David, *To be Governor of Jerusalem: The City and District during the Time of Ali Ekrem Bey, 1906–1908*, translated by David Kushner (Istanbul: The ISIS Press, 2005).

Kushner, David, 'The Administering of the Districts of Eretz Israel according to the Ottoman Year Books 1864–1914' (Hebrew), *Katedra*, 1997, 88, pp. 57–72.

Landau, David, 'Walter Henrich Juvelius, Information Based on Finnish Sources', in pamphlet *In Search of the Temple Treasures, The Story of the Parker Expedition 1909–1911* (Hebrew) (Jerusalem: Yad Izhak Ben-Zvi, 1996).

Landau, Jacob M., *Tekinalp, Turkish Patriot 1883–1961* (Leiden: Nederlands Historisch-Archaeologisch Instituut, 1984).

Landau, Jacob M., '*Comments on the Jewish Press* in Istanbul: The Hebrew Weekly *HaMevasser* (1909–1911)', in Jacob M. Landau, *Jews, Arabs, Turks: Selected Essays* (Jerusalem: Magnes Press, 1993), pp. 89–96.

Landau, Jacob M., *Exploring Ottoman and Turkish History* (London: Hurst & Company, 2004).

Laqueur, Walter, *The History of Zionism* (London: Tauris Parke Paperbacks, 2003).

Lemire, Vincent and Angelos Dalachanis (eds), *Ordinary Jerusalem 1840–1940: Opening New Archives, Revisiting a Global City* (Boston: Brill, 2018).

Levy, Avigdor (ed.), *The Jews of the Ottoman Empire* (Princeton: Darwin Press, 1994).

Levy, Avigdor (ed.), *Jews, Turks, and Ottomans: A Shared History, Fifteenth through the Twentieth Centuries* (Syracuse: Syracuse University Press, 2002).

Lewis, Bernard, *The Emergence of Modern Turkey* (London: Oxford University Press, 1961).

Lockman, Zachary, 'Imagining the Working Class: Culture, Nationalism, and

Class Formation in Egypt, 1899–1914', *Poetics Today*, Summer 1994, 15(2), pp. 157–90.

Lockman, Zachary, *Comrades and Enemies: Arab and Jewish Workers in Palestine, 1906–1948* (Berkley: University of California Press, 1996).

Lowry, Heath, 'The Young Triumverate, Ambassador Henry Morgenthau, and the future of Palestine, December 1913–January 1916', in Minna Rozen (ed.), *The Last Ottoman Century and Beyond: The Jews in Turkey and the Balkans, 1808–1945* (Tel Aviv: Tel Aviv University, 2002), pp. 151–64.

Makdisi, Ussama, 'Ottoman Orientalism', *The American Historical Review*, June 2002, 107(3), pp. 768–96.

Mandel, Neville, J., *The Arabs and Zionism before World War I* (Berkeley: University of California Press, 1976).

Manna', 'Adel, *A'lam Filastin fi awakhir al-'ahd al-'uthmani 1800–1918* [The Notables of Palestine at the End of the Ottoman Period], revised edn (Beirut: Institute for Palestine Studies, 1994).

Maoz, Moshe, *Ottoman Reform in Syria and Palestine* (Oxford: Clarendon Press, 1968).

Maoz, Moshe (ed.), *Studies on Palestine during the Ottoman Period* (Jerusalem: Magnes Press, 1975).

Mardin, Şerif, *The Genesis of Young Ottoman Thought* (Princeton: Princeton University Press, 1962).

Mazza, Roberto, *Jerusalem: From the Ottomans to the British* (New York: I. B. Tauris, 2009).

Mazza, Roberto, 'Missing Voices in Rediscovering Late Ottoman and Early Jerusalem', *Jerusalem Quarterly*, Spring 2013, 53, pp. 61–71.

McCarthy, Justin, *The Population of Palestine: Population Statistics of the late Ottoman Period and the Mandate* (New York: Columbia University Press, 1990).

Migdal, Joel S., *Boundaries and Belonging: States and Societies in the Struggle to Shape Identities and Local Practices* (New York: Cambridge University Press, 2004).

Mints, M., 'Ha-Shomer ve Rai'on ha-Hitnadvut ba-Tzva ha-"Othmani" [The Shomer and the Idea of Volunteering in the Ottoman Army]', in P. Ginosar (ed.), *Iyunim ba-Tkumat Yisra'el* [Studies on the Establishment of Israel] (Jerusalem: Daf Nui, 1991).

Morris, Benny, *Righteous Victims: A History of the Zionist-Arab Conflict, 1881–1999* (New York: Alfred A. Knopf, 1999).

Muslih, Muhammad Y., *The Origins of Palestinian Nationalism* (New York: Columbia University Press, 1988).

Muslih, Muhammad Y., 'The Rise of Local Nationalism in the Arab East', in Rashid Khalidi, Lisa Anderson and Reeva S. Simon (eds), *The Origins of Arab Nationalism* (New York: Columbia University Press, 1991), pp. 167–86.

Nobuyoshi, Fujinami, 'Patriarchal Crisis of 1910 and Constitutional Logic', *Journal of Modern Greek Studies*, May 2009, 27(1), pp. 1–30.

Norman, Theodore, *An Outstretched Arm: A History of the Jewish Colonization Association* (London: Routledge and Kegan Paul, 1985).

Öke, Mim Kemal, *Osmanlı İmparatorluğu, Siyonizm ve Filistin Sorunu (1880–1914)* (İstanbul: Doşuş Matbaası, 1982).

Öke, Mim Kemal, 'The Ottoman Empire, Zionism, and the Question of Palestine (1880–1908)', *IJMES*, August 1982, 14(3), pp. 329–41.

Ortaylı, İlber, 'Ottomanism and Zionism during the Second Constitutional Period, 1908–1915', in Avigdor Levy (ed.), *The Jews of the Ottoman Empire* (Princeton: Darwin Press, 1994), pp. 527–38.

Ortaylı, İlber, 'Ottoman Jewry and the Turkish Language', in Minna Rozen (ed.), *The Last Ottoman Century and Beyond: The Jews in Turkey and the Balkans, 1808–1945* (Tel Aviv: Tel Aviv University, 2002), pp. 129–39.

Parfitt, Tudor, *The Jews in Palestine: 1800–1882* (Suffolk: Boydell Press, 1987).

Parfitt, Tudor and Yulia Egorova (eds), *Jews, Muslim, and Mass Media* (London: Routledge Curzon, 2004).

Penslar, Derek J., 'Zionism, Colonialism and Postcolonialism', *Journal of Israeli History*, 20(2–3), pp. 84–98.

Porath, Yehoshua, *The Emergence of the Palestinian-Arab National Movement, 1918–1929* (London: Frank Cass, 1974).

Ramsaur, Ernest Edmonson, Jr, *The Young Turks: Prelude to the Revolution of 1908* (Princeton: Princeton University Press, 1957).

Reilly, James, 'The Peasantry of Late Ottoman Palestine', *Journal of Palestine Studies*, Summer 1981, 10(4), pp. 82–97.

Richter, Daniel K., *Facing East from Indian Country: A Native History of Early America* (Cambridge: Harvard University Press, 2001).

Rodrigue, Aron, *French Jews, Turkish Jews: The Alliance Israelite Universelle and the Politics of Jewish Schooling in Turkey 1860–1925* (Bloomington: Indiana University Press, 1990).

Rodrigue, Aron (ed.), *Ottoman and Turkish Jewry: Community and Leadership* (Bloomington: Indiana University Turkish Studies, 1992).

Rogan, Eugene, *Frontiers of the State in the Late Ottoman Empire: Transjordan* (Cambridge: Cambridge University Press, 1999).

Rozen, Minna (ed.), *The Last Ottoman Century and Beyond: The Jews in Turkey and the Balkans, 1808–1945* (Tel Aviv: Tel Aviv University Press, 2002).

Sachar, Howard M., *A History of Israel: From the Rise of Zionism to Our Time* (New York: Alfred A. Knopf, 1976).

Sa'di, Ahmad H., 'Modernization as an Explanatory Discourse of Zionist-Palestinian Relations', *British Journal of Middle Eastern Studies*, May 1997, 24(1), pp. 25–48.

Saposnik, Arieh B., *Becoming Hebrew: The Creation of a Jewish National Culture in Ottoman Palestine* (New York: Oxford University Press, 2008).

Schechtman, Joseph B., *Rebel and Statesman: The Vladimir Jabotinsky Story* (New York: T. Yoseloff, 1956).

Scholch, Alexander, *Palestine in Transformation 1856–1882: Studies in Social,*

Economic and Political Development (Washington, DC: Institute for Palestine Studies, 1993).

Seikaly, Samir, 'Damascene Intellectual Life in the Opening Years of the 20th Century: Muhammad Kurd 'Ali and al-Muqtabas', in M. Buheiry (ed.), *Intellectual Life in the Arab East, 1890–1939* (Beirut: American University Press, 1984), pp. 125–53.

Shafir, Gershon, *Land, Labor and the Origins of the Israeli-Palestinian Conflict, 1882–1914* (Berkeley: University of California Press, 1996).

Shalev-Khalifa, Nirit, 'In Search of the Temple Treasures, The Story of the Parker Expedition 1909–1911' (Hebrew), in pamphlet bearing the same name as article (Jerusalem: Yad Izhak Ben Tsvi, 1996).

Shapira, Anita, *Land and Power: The Zionist Resort to Force, 1881–1948* (Stanford: Stanford University Press, 1999).

Shapira, Anita, *Ben-Gurion: Father of Modern Israel* (New Haven: Yale University Press, 2014).

Shapira, Anita, *Israel: A History* (London: Weidenfeld & Nicolson, 2015).

Shapira, Anita and Derek J. Penslar (eds), *Israeli Historical Revisionism: From Left to Right* (London: Frank Cass, 2003).

Shaw, Stanford J. and Ezel Kural Shaw, *History of the Ottoman Empire and Modern Turkey: Volume II: Reform, Revolution, and Republic: The Rise of Modern Turkey, 1808–1975* (Cambridge: Cambridge University Press, 1977).

Shepherd, Naomi, *The Zealous Intruders: The Western Rediscovery of Palestine* (San Francisco: Harper & Row, 1988).

Shilo, Gideon, 'Shi'ur be-Ziyonut-Hidat He'almuto shel "Hawajeh Ibry"', *Kathedra*, 1990, 58.

Sicker, Martin, *Reshaping Palestine: From Muhammad Ali to the British Mandate, 1831–1922* (Westport: Praeger, 1999).

Silverman, Neil, *Digging for God and Country: Exploration, Archeology, and the Secret Struggle for the Holy Land 1799–1917* (New York: Alfred A. Knopf, 1982).

Singer, Amy, *Palestinian Peasants and Ottoman Officials: Rural Administration around Sixteenth-Century Jerusalem* (Cambridge: Cambridge University Press, 1994).

Singer, Amy and Amnon Cohen (eds), 'Aspects of Ottoman History', papers from CIEPO IX, Jerusalem, Scripta Hierosyolymitana, vol. 35 (Jerusalem: Magnes Press, 1994).

Sonyel, Salahi R., *Minorities and the Destruction of the Ottoman Empire 1280–1923* (Ankara: Turkish Historical Society Printing House, 1993).

Spagnolo, J. (ed.), *Problems of the Middle East in Historical Perspective: Essays in Honor of Albert Hourani* (Reading: Ithaca Press, 1992).

Stein, Sarah Abrevaya, *Making Jews Modern: The Yiddish and Ladino Press in the Russian and Ottoman Empires* (Bloomington: Indiana University Press, 2003).

Stein, Sarah Abrevaya, 'The Permeable Boundaries of Ottoman Jewry', in Joel S.

Bibliography

Migdal (ed.), *Boundaries and Belonging: Sates and Societies in the Struggle to Shape Identities and Local Identities* (Cambridge: Cambridge University Press, 2008), pp. 49–70.

Strohmeier, Martin, 'Al-Kulliyah al-Salahiyya, A Late Ottoman University in Jerusalem', in Sylvia Auld and Robert Hillenbrand (eds), *Ottoman Jerusalem: The Living City, 1517–1917* (London: Altajir World of Islam Trust, 2000), pp. 57–62.

Swedenburg, Ted, 'The Role of the Palestinian Peasantry in the Great Revolt (1936–1939)', in Edmund Burke, III, and Ira M. Lapidus (eds), *Islam, Politics, and Social Movements* (Berkeley: University of California Press, 1988), pp. 169–203.

Tamari, Salim, *The Emergence of the Arab Movements* (London: Frank Cass, 1993).

Tamari, Salim, 'Jerusalem's Ottoman Modernity: The Times and Lives of Wasif Jawhariyyeh', *Jerusalem Quarterly*, Summer 2000 (9), pp. 5–27.

Tamari, Salim, 'Ishaq al-Shami and the Predicament of the Arab Jew in Palestine', *Jerusalem Quarterly File*, 2004, 21, pp. 10–26.

Tauber, Eliezer, *The Arab Movements in World War I* (London: Frank Cass, 1993).

Teveth, Shabtai, *Kin'at David (David Ben-Gurion's Biography)* (Tel Aviv: Shocken, 1977).

Tibawi, A. L., *Anglo-Arab Relations and the Question of Palestine, 1914–1921* (London: Luzac, 1978).

Tufan, Naim M., *Rise of the Young Turks: Politics, the Military, and Ottoman Collapses* (London: I. B. Tauris, 2000).

Tunaya, Tarık Zafer, *Türkiye'de Siyasal Partiler: Cilt 1, Ikinci Meşrutiyet Dönemi* (Istanbul: İletişim Yayınları, 1998).

Vester, Spafford Bertha, *Our Jerusalem: An American Family in the Holy City, 1881–1949* (Garden City: Doubleday, 1950).

Wallach, Yair, 'Rethinking the Yishuv: Late-Ottoman Palestine's Jewish Communities Revisited', *Journal of Modern Jewish Studies*, 2017, 16(2), pp. 275–94.

Yazbak, Mahmoud, 'Nablusi Ulama in the Late Ottoman Period, 1864–1914', *IJMES*, 1997, 29, pp. 71–91.

Yazbak, Mahmoud, *Haifa in the Late Ottoman Period, 1864–1914: A Muslim Town in Transition* (Leiden: Brill, 1998).

Zeevi, Dror, *An Ottoman Century: The District of Jerusalem in the 1600s* (Albany: The State University of New York Press, 1996).

Zeine, Z. N., *Arab–Turkish Relations and the Emergence of Arab Nationalism* (Beirut: Khayat, 1958).

Zürcher, Eric, *Turkey: A Modern History* (New York: I. B. Tauris, 1993).

Index

Index

Damascus, 16–17, 34, 37, 73, 86, 125, 132, 150, 164, 175, 197

Egypt/Egyptians, 32–5, 37, 40, 45, 49, 69–70, 77, 80, 84, 87–8, 91–2, 96, 113–14, 122–4, 142–3, 157, 168n
Eisenberg, Aaron, 162
Eisenberg, Karmi, 134, 161–162, 165–166, 171n, 207
El Tiempo (newspaper), 18, 66, 174
Elmaliah, Avraham, 8, 142

fellah (fallah/fallahin), 8, 69, 74, 79, 80, 86, 108, 109
Filastin (Arabic newspaper), 13–14, 22, 25, 58, 65, 66, 70, 81–2, 84, 89–90, 92, 98n, 111–12, 120–1, 125, 148, 151, 204, 207
Freemasons, 173, 180, 182–3, 185, 189, 201n, 208
Frumkin, Gad, 160, 162–3, 165–6, 207
Fula (land sale), 71–5, 81–3, 86, 115, 206

Gaza, 33, 36, 37, 71, 77–8, 81–2, 102, 113–15, 130n, 147
Greeks, 7, 9, 19, 56, 58, 134, 163

HaAhdut (Hebrew newspaper), 23
HaHerut (Hebrew newspaper), 23, 75, 84, 88, 91–3, 95, 109, 112, 129, 134, 139–49, 151, 196, 170n, 203n
Haifa, 16, 22, 36, 40, 49, 65, 73, 75, 81, 84, 116, 123, 146–7, 150, 169n, 192
HaMevasser (Hebrew newspaper), 174–5, 200n
HaPoel HaTzair (Hebrew newspaper), 23
Haram al-Sharif (the Temple Mount, Arabic entry), 24–5, 33, 83, 89, 102–26, 193–4
HaTzfira (Hebrew newspaper), 109, 196
HaTzvi (Hebrew newspaper) 23, 75, 111, 129, 134, 165, 171n
Hebron, 37, 40, 77, 111
Herzl, Theodore, 17, 19, 21, 42, 44, 46, 136, 187, 203n

Ibry, Benjamin, 153–6
Iraq, 17, 32, 123, 124, 166, 179–81, 183, 193
Istanbul, 1, 3–6, 9–10, 17–18, 23–6, 34–5, 40, 43–4, 46, 48–9, 52–5, 57–9, 65–6, 68, 71–5, 78–9, 80, 82–3, 87–9, 105–6, 108–16, 118–19, 123, 125,

136, 141–3, 150, 151, 157–9, 160–2, 165–6, 172–9, 181–3, 185–7, 189, 195–9, 205, 207–8

Jabotinsky, Vladimir, 174, 199
Jacobson, Victor (Zionist Representative), 160–1, 173–4
Jaffa, 2, 4, 6–7, 9, 22, 36, 37, 40, 48, 49, 52–3, 55, 65, 70–1, 77, 78, 80–1, 84, 107–8, 111–13, 120, 122, 142, 147, 156, 192, 196
Jewish Colonization Association (ICA), 179, 201n
Jewish immigration, 17, 19, 21, 33, 40, 43–50, 52, 56, 61n, 67–8, 76–8, 80–1, 83, 86, 87–90, 92, 115, 122, 136, 151, 155, 157, 173–4, 177–81, 183, 188–9, 191, 195, 197–9, 203n, 205
First Aliyah, 19, 36, 42–5, 49, 135
Second Aliyah, 19, 42, 46, 49, 135, 141, 157

Karniel, Nahman, 134, 166n–167n
Kohen, Moiz, 177, 178, 180–1, 184–5, 190, 195

Ladino, 17, 138–9, 145, 178, 180
Lebanon/Lebanese 5, 15, 23, 35, 43, 67, 73, 76, 84
Lowther, Gerard (British Ambassador), 110, 182–3

Malul, Nissim, 141–3, 168n
Mazliah, Nissim (member of parliament), 7, 18, 172, 189–91, 207
Mecid Bey 2, 80, 91–2, 102
Mehmed V (Sultan), 7
Millet system, renegotiating, 10, 57, 143
Moria (Hebrew newspaper), 23, 49, 65–6, 84, 108–9, 129, 130n
Moyal, Esther, 142–3
Moyal, Shimon, 141–3

Nablus, 31, 35–7, 43, 81, 102, 111–13, 117, 122–4
Nazareth, 37, 72
Nahum, Haim (Chief Rabbi), 18, 59, 66, 151, 165, 176, 178, 196–7, 207

oranges, 1–2, 24, 36, 80, 197
Ottoman State (Devlet-i Osmaniyye), 5, 18–19, 21, 26–7, 31, 47, 58, 59, 66–8, 71, 74, 77, 82, 96, 102, 107, 115, 117,

Ottoman State (*cont.*)
121, 136–7, 140, 152, 157–8, 172–3,
178, 180–2, 185, 187–91, 193–4, 196,
198–9, 202n, 204, 207–8
Ottoman army recruitment 73, 134, 138,
160–2, 164–5, 167n, 171n, 207
Ottoman Ministry of Interior, 1–6,
73, 80, 82–3, 87, 90, 110–11, 113,
115–20, 151–2, 160, 169n, 175, 189,
197
Ottoman Parliament, 6–8, 10, 23, 26,
31, 54–5, 58–9, 62n, 73, 81, 86, 92–3,
96, 100n, 106, 111–13, 116–20, 125,
158, 172, 174, 178, 183–6, 189, 191,
192–5, 199, 203n, 204, 206
Ottomanism, 6, 10, 15, 19, 23, 26, 55,
57–8, 135, 165, 177, 199, 205

Palestine Exploration Fund, 103, 107, 120,
155
Palestinian emigration, 50–1, 76–8, 87–8,
95–6, 99n, 113
Palestinianism, 15, 16, 25, 29n, 56, 58, 67,
70, 97n, 205
Parker, Montague (captain), 103–8, 116,
118–20
Petah Tikvah, 1–4

Ramlah, 37, 120
Rehovot, 78, 162
Ruppin, Arthur (Zionist representative),
50, 77, 99n, 139, 145, 167n
Russia/Russians, 3, 17, 34–6, 41–9, 52–4,
56, 69, 87, 90, 134, 144–5, 148, 153,
156–7, 161–2, 167n, 174, 179–80,
191, 197, 201n

Sakakini, Khalil, 58, 92, 95, 132
Saladin (and *Salah al-Din*), 33, 73, 75,
84–5, 114–15, 121, 125–6, 132, 139,
140, 193
Salonica, 10, 17, 48, 139, 160, 165, 167n,
176–7, 182–3, 193
Sawt al-'Uthmaniyya (Arabic newspaper),
23
Sharett, Moshe, 138, 157, 165, 207
Shochat, Israel, 158, 160–1

Sokolov, Nahum, 176, 196–7
Southern Syria (Syria al-Janubiyya),
12–14
Strauss, Oscar (US Ambassador), 183
Syria/Syrians 3, 5, 12–16, 21, 23, 25, 32,
34, 35, 51, 54, 56, 59, 65–8, 71–2,
75–7, 84–6, 88, 96, 122–3, 138,
140–1, 146, 152, 166, 168n, 192–4

Talat Bey (Minister of Interior), 151, 160,
183
Tanin (Turkish newspaper), 106, 108, 113
Tanzimat (Ottoman reforms), 5–6, 54
Tel Aviv, 80, 91, 100n
Tevfik, Ebüzziya (member of parliament),
174, 180–1, 188, 189, 190, 193
Tasvir-i Efkar (Turkish newspaper), 180–1

Union of Ottoman Hebrew Students
(Istanbul), 136, 158–9, 207

Vartkes Bey (Armenian member of
Ottoman parliament), 19, 191–2

World War I, 3–5, 8, 12–13, 15–22, 31,
42, 43, 50, 55–6, 58, 65–8, 77, 88,
122, 124–5, 132, 134, 138, 142, 161,
165, 194–5, 198, 204, 205, 206

Yishuv, 17, 20–1, 41–2, 44, 52–3, 91,
101n, 134–7, 140–50, 153, 157, 162,
165, 169n, 172, 176–7, 187–8, 193,
197–8, 207
Young Turk Revolution, 3, 6, 8, 10, 17–18,
20–6, 45, 49, 51–60, 72, 95, 105, 116,
134–7, 143, 173, 182, 185, 196, 199,
205, 206

Zangwill, Israel, 179–80
Zionism, 12, 17–19, 21, 23, 25–6, 32,
41–3, 49, 51, 58, 66–8, 71, 75, 88–94,
96, 114–15, 118–19, 135–7, 142, 151,
155–7, 162, 165, 172–8, 180, 183–7,
189–99, 205–8
Zionist Organization, 17, 42, 46, 136–7,
154, 160–1, 173–4, 176–7, 184, 200n,
203n, 206

CPSIA information can be obtained
at www.ICGtesting.com
Printed in the USA
JSHW041433180321
12663JS00005B/287

9 781474 454001